Praise for *Finding True North*

"With a flow of lovely language and imagery of lush pines, full moons, and clear Adirondack lakes and skies, *Finding True North* is a testament to the unique spirit of preservation, regeneration, and place."
— *Foreword Reviews*

"The book is a gift linking past and present."
— *Adirondack Daily Enterprise*

"It's a fun read that combines memoir with the fascinating history of this remote part of the Adirondacks. It includes numerous photographs of the hard work that went into bringing this beautiful place back to life."
— Albany *Times Union*

"Gifted storyteller Fran Yardley has harnessed her many voices to the printed page in this remarkable memoir. Yardley interweaves her firsthand experience hinged to historic documentation with her imagination as she reveals the lives and ways of those who went before and coexisted with her and Jay Yardley at Bartlett Carry. *Finding True North* is a must-read love story about Adirondack place and people."

— Caroline M. Welsh, Director Emerita,
Adirondack Museum

"In *Finding True North*, Fran Yardley has produced an immediate and necessary addition to the body of Adirondack literature and history. Long in the making, it is beautifully written, authoritative, and moving."

— Christopher Shaw, author of *Sacred Monkey River: A Canoe Trip with the Gods* and former editor of *Adirondack Life*

"Author and master storyteller Fran Yardley tells of the early history of the aquatic Adirondack crossroads known as Bartlett Carry, the later history of the place as a club for families eager to swap conventional orbits outside the mountains for the natural world within, and the reinvention of the place by the author and her visionary late husband, Jay. The stories that flow together here touch the heart and bring the reader to tears and laughter. For lovers of the Adirondacks and particularly for those keen on understanding how the past shapes the present and the future, this is a must read."

— Ed Kanze, author of *Adirondack: Life and Wildlife in the Wild, Wild East*

Finding True North

Finding True North

A History of One Small Corner of the Adirondacks

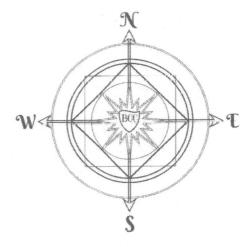

Fran Yardley

excelsior editions

AN IMPRINT OF STATE UNIVERSITY OF NEW YORK PRESS

Cover: iStockphoto by Getty Images; Adirondack Milky Way Reflection/Night/Lake/ Adirondack State Park/New York State/Analogdude.

Published by State University of New York Press, Albany

Excelsior Editions is an imprint of State University of New York Press

For information, contact State University of New York Press, Albany, NY
www.sunypress.edu

Library of Congress Cataloging-in-Publication Data

Names: Yardley, Fran, 1944– author.
Title: Finding true North : a history of one small corner of the Adirondacks / Fran Yardley.
Other titles: History of one small corner of the Adirondacks
Description: Albany, New York : State University of New York Press, [2018] | Series: Excelsior editions | Includes bibliographical references and index.
Identifiers: LCCN 2017038442 | ISBN 9781438470528 (paperback : alk. paper) | ISBN 9781438470535 (ebook)
Subjects: LCSH: Saranac Lake Region (N.Y.)—Biography. | Yardley, Fran, 1944– | Bartlett Carry Club. | Saranac Club. | Yardley, Jay, 1940–1984. | Married women— New York (State)—New York—Biography. | Mountain resorts—New York (State)— Adirondack Mountains—History. | Mountain life—New York (State)—Adirondack Mountains. | Saranac Lake Region (N.Y.)—Social life and customs. | Saranac Lake Region (N.Y.)—History.
Classification: LCC F129.S26 Y37 2018 | DDC 974.7/5—dc23
LC record available at https://lccn.loc.gov/2017038442

10 9 8 7 6 5 4 3 2

For Jay Yardley and his family who first came to the Adirondacks
For Virgil and Caroline Bartlett
For Robert Dun Douglass
And for the place in our hearts we each know as home

Contents

A place that ever was lived in is like a fire that never goes out.

—Eudora Welty, 1944

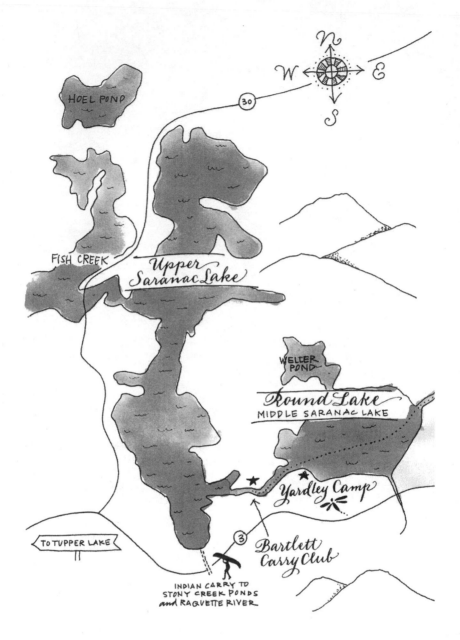

Map 1. Upper, Middle and Lower Saranac Lakes, by Gail Brill.

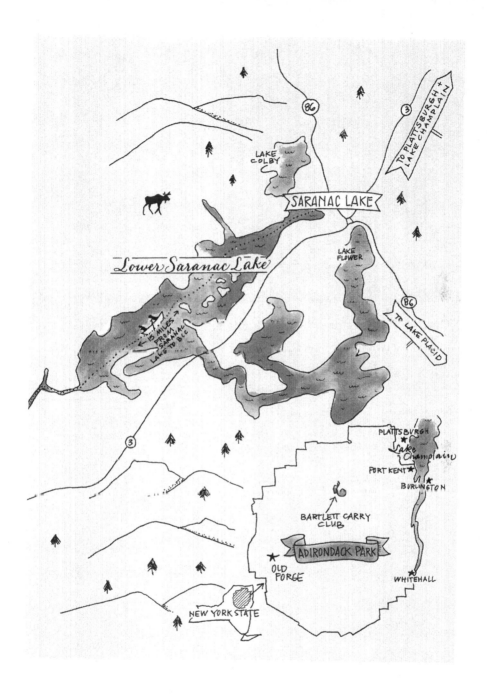

Chapter 1

Into the Wilderness

I

Boom. I bolt out of sleep into thick dark. *What was that?* I burrow into the warmth of two wool blankets and a comforter. *What was that sound?* Did a tree fall on our cabin? What else could it be? Maybe the corner of our tiny bedroom has broken off in the cold and is laying in a splintered heap in three feet of February snow. After a childhood in Buffalo, New York, I should be used to snow. But here it's been snowing for three days. On the first day, snow settled like a fluffy down coverlet on our roof. On the second day, snow coiled on tree branches like fat lazy snakes. By the third day, I felt completely cut off from the outer world.

And now, the sound of this boom has shaken me awake. Whatever it was, my husband, lying next to me, is still fast asleep. He doesn't seem concerned, so maybe I don't need to be either. I cannot be a wimp. I have to figure this out myself. Meanwhile, I fully expect to feel snowflakes land any minute and melt on my face.

I should get up, turn on the light, see what has happened. I begin to emerge from the covers and pause. *Damn, we don't have electricity*. Even after four months in this wilderness, I forget sometimes. Curling into a tight ball, I conserve the little warmth inside me. No hope of more sleep. Thinking, thinking. Why did I follow Jay Yardley here in the first place? I do love this man. I was intrigued by the idea of the adventure when I said "Yes I will marry you, Yes I will follow you anywhere." He was passionate, certain this was the right thing to do. And now our cabin is collapsing in the middle of the night and we probably won't be able to get out for days and days. *Why* is he still sleeping and here I am, eyes wide in the crystal black.

The cold and the dark send me to places deep inside that ask questions I don't allow in the daylight. *Really?* That part of me asks. *Am I up for this?* Even in daylight the situation is overwhelming. I can't stop thinking of the tour Jay took me on after we got here. I had to make him repeat how much land we have. One thousand acres. Bordering two lakes. I can't wrap my mind around what that means. One thousand acres of wilderness, trees, lakes, and rivers. I'm sure I'd get lost out there and never find my way home. There are some thirty-seven cabins and boathouses including an abandoned historic 1800s summer resort and a rustic summer camp—all in Jay's family for four generations. And a crumbling dam. And now we are responsible for it all.

The dark magnifies everything. How in god's name are we going to deal with thirty-seven buildings? Most are real houses, not cabins, some with five or six bedrooms. They have names like Maple and Birch and Fir. Jay has a vision, he is so sure of himself, but I cannot conceive of how we will possibly do all this. I'm willing to follow his lead, but I have to admit, in the middle of the tour, it took everything I had to not just stop and say I can't do this, I don't know how to do this.

At least I can now usually wash the glass chimneys for our kerosene lamps without smudging or breaking them so we can have light. And I was determined to figure out how to crank the gas generator to pump lake water up to a thousand-gallon tank on the hill above us. Without that water gravity feeding to our cabin through pipes buried below the frost line, we can't brush our teeth or flush the toilet. But no one warned me the roof would crack in the middle of the night. No one warned me how lonely it could be.

Our closest neighbors live a mile away, and we don't know them well. I have no one to talk to but Jay, and he is off working most of the day. We are eleven miles from any town. Who would want to live that far from anything? Just yesterday, on the walk down our half-mile driveway, for a moment I thought I saw my sister standing in the woods. I'd give anything to see her. Or anyone. I'm not used to having no one around at all. When Jay comes home for lunch after working with one building or another, I greet him at the door, lunch ready on the table. I don't want to miss a second of time with him, even if we often eat in silence. Jay is usually preoccupied with a bulldozer that broke down or a chainsaw that needs sharpening.

As I lie here, I think if I could keep the names of the cabins straight, repeat their names over and over, maybe I could go back to sleep. Maple, Birch, Fir, what are the others? . . . Maple, Birch . . . Finally, the warmth under my blankets soothes my racing mind. The scary questions, the doubts, and the bare-bones truth recede for at least a while, and eventually I go back to sleep.

A few hours later, daylight shines through our intact window, not streaming in from a gaping hole in the ceiling. Out the window, the clear blue sky looks brittle, as if I could break off a thin piece and crunch it exploding in a blue phosphorescence in my mouth. No snow covers our bed.

"What was that sound in the night?" I ask Jay.

"Ah! That's the ice on the lake cracking. It does that when it's really cold."

Okay, question answered. But the monologue of the night hangs in the cavern of my mind. *Do I really want to be here?* I'm twenty-four years old, married only a year and a half, living far from friends and family, homesick for the puppy pile of my four siblings and the neighborhood kids who gravitated to our apple orchard for kick-the-can. I never had to deal with long, silent days; dark, cold nights; getting lost on one thousand acres; or, for that matter, booming ice. I wonder if I can do this.

II

I remember vividly how it all began. It was fifty years ago, the fall of 1965, my senior year at the University of Colorado. The moment I walked into Creative Writing 304, I noticed the tall guy with jet-black hair in a

Norwegian ski sweater. At six feet tall myself, I still had to look several inches up at him. I could stand straight and tall next to this man without reliving the awkwardness of seventh grade dancing school where I towered over every boy. The direct, intent, honest look from under his dark brows transfixed me. As if he could see exactly what I was all about. I wanted to know what he was thinking, what those eyes had seen, where he'd been.

Our first assignment was to write about something that meant a great deal to us. In class, Mr. Warner said, "Jay, let's hear yours."

Jay opened his folder. I have kept this folder, so I can still read his unique, half-cursive, half-print scrawl.

The mist had risen to the height of the mountains beyond the lake. Josh walked down the long winding dirt road. His nostrils closed slightly as he allowed the smell of the balsam fir to gather in his head. It was that Adirondack smell.

When I heard this, I sat up straighter, leaned forward. I knew that smell of balsam. His character, Josh, was returning home after three years in the service.

The family had always lived there through hunting, fishing, and sugaring seasons. Some had walked down that road and kept on going just as Josh had once done. Some came back to be buried with the rest near the river.

Place. The setup for this story had such a strong sense of place. I wanted to go there.

That same day in class, I read a story based on *my* place—my grandmother's island, two hundred miles north of the border in Ontario, Canada—the first place I felt connected to, where my bare feet knew every root, where each early morning my warm skin knew the shock of cool lake water, where my days were filled with parents, sisters and brothers, cousins, aunts, uncles, and would-be boyfriends. The "old guard" faction—mainly my cousin Jerry and me, outfitted in blue jeans and moccasins—wanted to retain old ways and traditions, honor the natural setting, no phone or TV. We didn't even want electricity. Our enemy was my "conniving aunt" with tight dresses, high-heeled, fluffy-toed, sling-back shoes, frizzy Clairol-black, done-up hair, who wanted cocktail parties and the newest appliances.

After class, Jay asked me out to dinner. Over a T-bone steak and baked potatoes at Fred's Steak House, we talked about tradition and the essential timelessness of land. I told him about my childhood summers on Eagle Island. He told me of his summers in the Adirondack mountains in northern New York and his long family history there, of his fascination with a place up a river, a place called the Bartlett Carry Club.

"The Bartlett Carry Club?" I asked. "Interesting name. Why is it called that?"

"It's an old summer resort going back to the 1800s, not used any more, falling into ruins. It's called Bartlett Carry because it's a canoe carry between Middle and Upper Saranac Lakes. My great-grandfather was the first in our family to go there, in the 1800s. I spent a lot of summers there. Someday I'm going back. I want to take over the family property, restore all those abandoned houses, revive the Bartlett Carry Club. I know there are people who want to be in the woods by a lake, but comfortable, in a place where they can touch down, relax. This is the perfect place. I've been all over the world, but I've never seen anywhere as beautiful." He ran long fingers through his black hair. "I have a movie I could show you."

A turning point in my life, although I didn't know it then. As I think about it now, many years later, that moment comes right back.

I sat on a straight back chair waiting for the show to begin. The clicking whir of the 8mm projector broke the silence. Jay had invited me to his small mountain cabin outside Boulder, Colorado, to see this movie. The only light shot from the projector onto the dusty kitchen wall.

Then, instead of specks on the wall, a grainy black-and-white movie emerged. I leaned forward. Jay said "Okay, this is the beginning of the road going in to our family 'camp,' our summer home, on Middle Saranac Lake. The old name is Round Lake. I like that better." I sat stock-still, engrossed in the slow-motion travel up a narrow dirt road, past white pines and maples, fern-covered rocks, and moss on either side.

I knew trees, ferns, and rocks like these on Eagle Island. Woods to run free in, canoes to tip over, twenty-two at the dining-room table, everyone talking at once. In the peace of Jay's cabin, I dove into the images flickering on the wall. The eye of the camera escorted me around one sun-dappled bend after another. I wanted to watch forever.

Jay turned my world upside down. Before meeting him, I had planned to apply to the University of Michigan for a Master's degree in children's theater. Suddenly, I only wanted to be with him, do whatever he did, tell him my stories, and listen to his. He told me that at age seventeen, days after graduating from high school, he abandoned any obligation he had felt to conform to his parents' upper-class lifestyle and philosophy. He didn't even apply to college. He grabbed his backpack and forty dollars and hitchhiked across the country. He worked for meals and a place to rest his head. A year later, at eighteen, he joined the Marine Corps and then a Special Forces Recon Unit in Viet Nam. After a bayonet in the back and stateside recovery, he spent the rest of his military service working for the U.S. government in Poland, Russia, and Spain. He even delivered a briefcase chained to his wrist to President Kennedy. Only after an honorable discharge from the Marine Corps did he go to college. By that time, he had been to thirty-six countries and lived and worked in several of them.

I had grown up throwing snowballs in suburban Buffalo, surrounded by brothers and sisters, horses, dogs, cats, and the occasional rabbit; product of Miss Porter's girl's prep school, in New England. I was done with parties where I towered above everyone in the room and looked like Alice in Wonderland after she ate the wrong mushroom. I had loved acting on stage, from my kindergarten debut as Ceres, Roman goddess of agriculture, to a theater major in college. I had only traveled to Canada, and that was for family vacation. No wonder he fascinated me.

When Jay proposed marriage, a honeymoon to Alaska, and adventure, I accepted willingly to be his partner in all of it. Not just as a tagalong. Not just—*Okay, if you really want to do this.* Instead—*Yay! Let's hit the road and see what's up there!* A real adventure. The broader world intrigued me. I was curious to discover, especially after hearing Jay's stories of all the places he'd been and worked and lived. Alaska was a good beginning. Time to say goodbye to the culture I had grown up in where the man went to work and the woman stayed home to do the housekeeping. Time to claim the part of me that was adventuresome and willing to experiment. I had already started by moving into a small log cabin in the mountains outside Boulder which confirmed that traditional suburban life wasn't for me. Time for the next step.

A little over a year later, on May 12, 1967, in my parents' home, Jay and I exchanged rings and vows, including Kahlil Gibran . . . "When love beckons to you, follow him, though his ways are hard and steep."[1] . . . "Sing and dance together and be joyous, but let each of you be alone, even as the strings of a lute are alone though they quiver with the same music."[2]

Fran and Jay married May 12, 1967.

Family and friends threw rice and waved farewell. We hopped in our homemade camper and drove down the driveway, across Canada, and up the unpaved AlCan Highway to Alaska in search of a place to live. Jay was twenty-six, I was twenty-two. We rumbled north 1,519 miles from Dawson Creek, British Columbia, to Fairbanks, Alaska. Dall and Bighorn sheep perched on craggy rocks; moose grazed in bogs. After two months of driving on every Alaskan road, we had covered only a small fraction of the state. We hiked miles into the wilderness, skied on a summer snow field, and explored in our rubber raft. Finally, we decided it was just too remote to be our new home.

On to Plans B, C, and D: opening a craft shop in Park City, Utah; teaching at a small pre-high boarding school; working for the Bureau of Indian Affairs. After those fell through, Plan E stuck. Jay would be a field representative for CARE-Medico in their mission to serve individuals and families in the poorest communities throughout the world. CARE assigned us to Tunisia. I had to consult an atlas to find out where that was.

In February 1968, we landed in the completely foreign time/culture/climate zone of North Africa. Jay's job was to verify with schools across Tunisia that they had received CARE supplies. Each day he headed out with Ferjani, his Tunisian driver. Meanwhile, I put on the obligatory mid-length skirt to wear in public, tucked a straw basket under one freckled arm, and walked to the market for eggs, bread, chicken, veggies. All the way there, I rehearsed how to say *Good Morning!* in Arabic and *La bes? La bes. How are you? I am fine.* I tried not to notice staring dark-haired, short women, their sefsaris covering everything but their faces, and men in hooded jebbas, all astonished by this fair stranger a head taller than most of them.

After months, the Tunisian CARE boss announced he was going to file away Jay's detailed reports suggesting black-market maneuvers, because they did not mesh with the pristine record of his office. That decision did not mesh with Jay's integrity.

One August afternoon, in the cool of our Tunisian house, protected from the searing North African sun, Jay leaned forward.

"What do you think?" he said. "We could go back, move up to the Adirondacks."

The recent death of Jay's grandmother, Harriet Jenkins Yardley, meant the family estate, begun by Jay's great-grandfather, would now be broken up. This estate included his treasured place in the mountains.

"We could live at the family camp. I could do everything I've been talking about at the Bartlett Carry Club. Right now those buildings are being subleased for medical student housing by a hospital called Will Rogers, but that doesn't have to continue. I want to renovate them so families can come like they used to—connect with nature, with wilderness. That's what really matters." He paused.

"I'd have to figure it out with Pop. What do you think?" I had no idea of the magnitude of his plan, but he was compelling. I would not miss my constant scratchy throat from trying to speak guttural Arabic or the homesick feeling residing in my belly. We were both ready to leave North Africa.

"Okay!" I said. Time for the next chapter in our lives.

III

Our feet touched homeland soil for the first time in a year. I immediately settled into the familiar sound of English enveloping me. We visited my family in Buffalo, and, as I hugged my mom, my shoulders finally relaxed. Then we visited Jay's family in Darien, Connecticut. Jay stiffened as we entered the chandeliered front hall. Before dinner, he took a deep breath and sought out his father. I wanted to be there too, even as a bystander. The butler passed drinks. His dad sat on an overstuffed chintz chair. Ice crackled against crystal. Jay did not sit. After a few polite exchanges, he jumped in.

"Pop, I don't want any money as inheritance. I've saved from working overseas. There's something I do want. Up north. The family land in the Adirondacks. We want to live there. Full time." His father's face showed nothing. He said nothing.

"I want to own the land and restore the Bartlett Carry Club and even the family camp."

Jay paused, took a breath.

His whole life had led up to this moment. As a kid, he had to conform, play tennis at country clubs in perfect whites, polish his manners, and charm his parents' friends. He had never felt comfortable with any of it. He had no intention of putting on a suit, commuting by train, working in an office. From the moment he left home at seventeen, he had been looking for a place to make his own mark. Now he had come full circle, back to the home of his ancestors, willing to face his father. I liked the idea of being back on home turf and moving to the Adirondacks. So I held my breath, too.

Jay looked hard at his dad. "I know Mom doesn't care about being up there much, but it would mean you couldn't come for hunting season anymore." My heart thumped—What was his father thinking? Was he crushed to hear his son didn't want him there? Was he secretly glad to relinquish responsibility for this land?

His face still showed no emotion. It rarely did. He raised his glass and took a sip. "Well, I think this is something we can talk about."

For whatever reason, he soon agreed. The transfer of land took place and with that extraordinary gift and with Jay's savings and mine, we made the leap. Thus began our adventure into the wilderness.

IV

We arrive on October 25, 1968. Now, as we drive up that road so familiar to me from the movie, I'm not watching a black-and-white slow motion picture on a Colorado kitchen wall. Instead, I am immersed in burnt umber, dark green, faded red and orange. Jay has informed me our cabin will not have electricity.

"But hey!" he cheerfully adds. "At least part of the cabin has a basement, so I think we might be warm in winter." I do notice that by the time we turn off the main road, we have traveled eleven miles from the last sign of civilization.

We drive around another bend—more trees, moss, ferns. *How long is this road?*

"Oh wow, I recognize this from your movie!" I say this as much to brighten my spirits as anything.

"Okay, this road goes into the family camp. It's about a half mile. It ends at Middle Saranac Lake."

"But what about the Bartlett Carry Club?"

"Back at that last curve off the main road, you go right about a half mile on the gravel road and then across the river. We'll go see it soon."

I am completely confused, but I hear the excitement in his voice.

Finally the end of the dirt road, an opening in the trees, and there, perched on a hill looking out at a lake, squats a small brown cabin.

"Well, here we are," says Jay. "This is the Guide House. It's called that because it's sort of winterized so the caretaker for the family camp lives here. Guess that's us now."

We climb out of the Land Rover. I look over at Jay and lock eyes with him. We both inhale and catch the unmistakable scent of balsam. I latch on to the familiar smell. Down the hill are many cabins, each sided with spruce bark.

"Look at that. How many buildings are there?"

"Oh, a bunch. But this is nothing compared to the Club. Wait 'til you see that."

How long has this all been here? Who built it? When? Why here? What for? How? Light glints off water.

"And this is . . . which lake?"

"Round Lake was its name in the past. Most people call it Middle Saranac Lake now. I like calling it Round Lake and, once we have guests, I think we should refer to it that old-fashioned way."

I agree. I like honoring the old ways whenever we can.

Jay points out to the lake.

"See Ship Island out there? The little one? Great picnic spot. And if you got in a boat and followed the shoreline to the left, you'd come to the river, go a half mile up that and you'd be at the Bartlett Carry Club."

Great. Now I'm even more confused.

Late fall sun lies low in the sky. Jay says "Come on! I'll give you a quick tour of the family camp. There are about ten buildings. That's the Maid's Cabin over there."

"*Maid's* Cabin?"

"Oh yeah, you wouldn't believe the life back when Gramp and Granny Yardley came. Granny had a personal maid named Molly. And others too who did cooking and cleaning. They even had a chauffeur."

Jay's voice takes on a low tone, a note I've heard before when he's talked about his family. Not only did his Granny have a maid and chauffeur, his parents did, too. As a kid, he had played often with Eddie, the chauffeur's son. Jay would have much preferred living over the garage as Eddie did and not having a formal dinner every evening, served by the deferential butler.

"And this," says Jay as he walks down the hill, "is the icehouse and woodshed."

"Icehouse?" I can relate to this. "We have one of those on Eagle Island."

"They cut huge blocks of ice every winter and stored them here with sawdust. Before they had electricity, the ice kept everything cool."

I think about our having no electricity. Will we have to lug huge heavy blocks of ice up the hill to our cabin?

"How will *we* keep stuff cold?"

"We have a gas refrigerator."

"Ah." My shoulders relax.

"I slept in this cabin and my sister in that one." He points to two small one-room cabins.

"And David stayed in the cabin right next to the Guide House." David Rawle was Jay's best friend growing up and came here for part of every summer.

"Where'd you go to the bathroom?"

"Over here." He points to the biggest house in the enclave. "This one's called Windsor. Built later than the rest, in the 1930s, it has an indoor bathroom." We are now walking on raised wooden walkways connecting the small cabins.

"Why all these separate cabins?"

"A lot of Adirondack camps do this. Fire is a big deal with so many wooden structures, and the nearest fire department is eleven miles away. If there's a fire in one cabin, it hopefully means it won't spread to the others, so everything might not be lost. Something to consider when you're heating with wood and using kerosene lamps."

Jay has walked on.

Sleeping Cabins at family camp on Middle Saranac Lake, ca. 1960.

"Just a few more. Here's the kitchen cabin and right next door is the dining room cabin."

"Huh." I say. "How did they keep food warm getting from one to the other?"

Jay has opened the dining room cabin door. "You've got to see the inside." We walk in, enveloped in warm, late-afternoon light reflecting off wood-paneled walls. Twigs and white birch bark decorate the table and sideboards. An enormous wooden bowl sits on the table. Water laps against the shore just down the hill.

I have questions, but before I can ask, Jay heads out the door and says "And one more—my grandparents' cabin—well, it used to be. They haven't come for a long time. Gramp died a little over ten years ago, and you know Granny Yardley died this summer."

"Gramp is Farnham Yardley, right?" I say, trying to get the family history straight.

"Yup."

"And Granny Yardley is Harriet Jenkins Yardley."

"Right. They stayed here in the first cabin my great-grandfather built." Jay sees me searching for the name. "Alfred Blunt Jenkins, Harriet's father, the one who came in the late 1800s."

I pause at the door. "Look at this." A tarnished brass four-inch-long dragonfly is fastened at eye level. It looks about as out-of-place as I feel right now. Do dragonflies even live here? I make an attempt at humor. "It looks like it might have gotten lost and ended up on this door."

"Oh, right," Jay says. "The door knocker. We should save that."

I love this cabin. It reminds me of the one my mom and dad stay in on Eagle Island. Cozy living room with light reflecting off wooden wain-scoted walls; a fireplace, a small bedroom, even a bathroom. I especially love the covered porch with several rustic chairs, including a rocking chair, a perfect spot to sit and watch light play on water.

Jay breaks in on my musings. "And then there are the boathouses and docks, but let's save those. We'd better get back uphill and unpack the Rover before it gets dark."

One morning a few days later, Jay scrapes the last of his scrambled eggs and bacon from his plate and says, "Okay! I think we're settled in enough. Let's conduct a reconnaissance mission to the Bartlett Carry Club

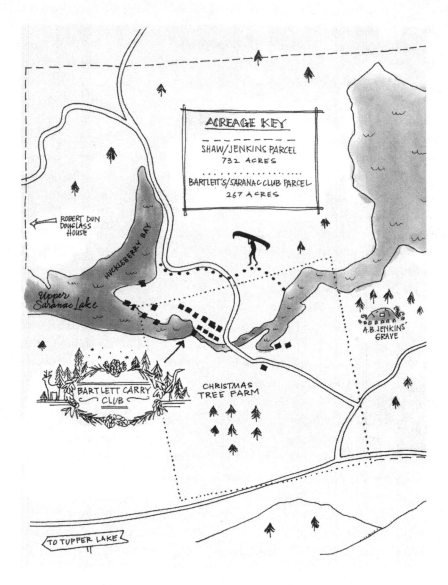

Map 2. Bartlett Carry Club and Yardley Camp 1968, by Gail Brill.

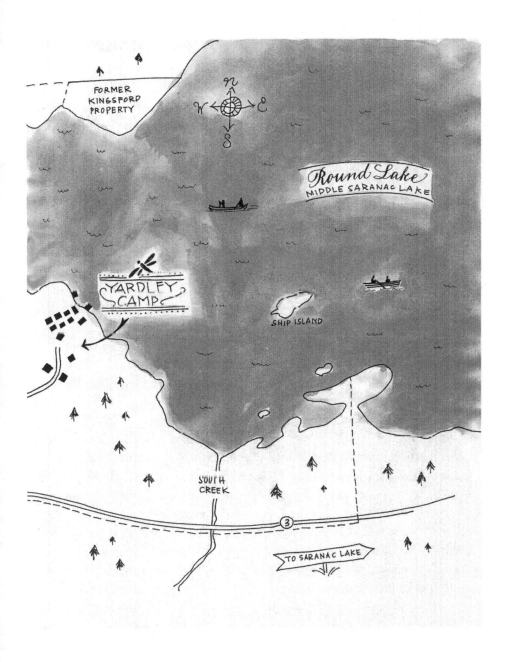

and take stock of what we have to do." We need to get going. Winter will come soon, sooner even than we know.

As I scrub plates, Jay sticks his pipe in the corner of his mouth and spreads a map on his large desk.

"Okay, take a look at this. Here we are on Round Lake."

"You mean Middle Saranac Lake?" I am still confused.

"Yup. Same thing. Round Lake . . ."

He puts a large dot on a point that juts out into a smallish lake.

"And this is our property line around the one thousand acres." Jay runs his finger around the edge of a patchwork of boundary lines.

"Why are there two pieces?"

"It's a combination of the 267 acres Virgil Bartlett had at the beginning, and the 732 acres Gramp bought in 1903."

"How big is Round Lake anyway?" I ask.

"About two or three miles long, one mile wide." Jay begins to draw an imaginary line.

"We can get to the Club by boat, too. We could canoe from here, around this point to the Saranac River, then go about a half mile 'til the rapids start. That's where Virgil Bartlett first came." Virgil Bartlett. His name keeps coming up.

I lean in over the map to see where Jay is pointing.

"Okay, here's how Virgil Bartlett used to get here. He took a boat from the village of Saranac Lake, six miles across Lower Saranac, through Round Lake—Middle Saranac—and then up this river until they had to stop because of the rapids. That's why there's a canoe carry to go overland to Upper Saranac Lake. I'm sure Native Americans used this, but it wasn't 'til Virgil Bartlett came that it was called Bartlett Carry. And that's where we're going today because this is where the Bartlett Carry Club is."

"Are we paddling or going by road?"

"Let's take the Land Rover."

That's fine with me on this chilly early November morning. We drive down the familiar half-mile dirt road lined with hemlocks and pines, turn right on the gravel town road.

After another half mile of driving, I ask, "This is still the property?"

"Yup. And it goes on for several more miles after this."

Miles? Wow.

Jay slows down.

"See the barn?"

I can't miss it. The weathered, three-story structure has solidly staked its claim along a big stretch on the left side of the road.

"It's huge! How old is it?"

"I think about 1898, and it looks in pretty good shape. Might be a good place to store stuff like furniture and boats 'til we figure out where we want everything."

I flash back to crawling with my sisters through our barn hayloft hunting for newborn kittens. I turn to Jay. "Hey, maybe someday, we can have some animals in there."

Just across from the barn stands a two-story frame house where one of our two employees, Al Tyrol, lives with his wife and two teenage sons. Before we arrived, Al was caretaker for both the Club and the family camp for fifteen years. He seems to be having trouble adjusting to our arrival. Before, his job was easy, no one looking over his shoulder, rarely anyone coming to camp. Now, each morning at eight, Jay has a list of jobs for him.

We rumble over a wooden bridge. I roll down the window. The sound of rapids rushes in with chill November air. Just on the other side of the bridge, we pause, look to our right at an overgrown field, yellowing grasses, an abandoned tennis court. Jay leans forward, looks beyond me out the window. "Remember the picture we found of the old Sportsmen's Home?"

I do remember. Within days of arriving, we discovered several wooden crates filled with old photographs, documents, and maps that go back over 100 years; among them, sepia photographs of Virgil Bartlett and his wife, Caroline, and fragile black-and-white photos of several ramshackle wooden buildings on the shore of a river.

"This is where Virgil Bartlett built his Sportsmen's Home, right in this field."

Jay gets out. I open my door. The shoosh of rapids fills my ears. I try to imagine this field with the old wooden buildings I saw in the photo. Virgil and Caroline must have heard this same rushing water. I take a minute to inhale familiar late fall smells—dried grasses, earth, and cool air. A silvery vee of geese undulates southward in the pale November sky.

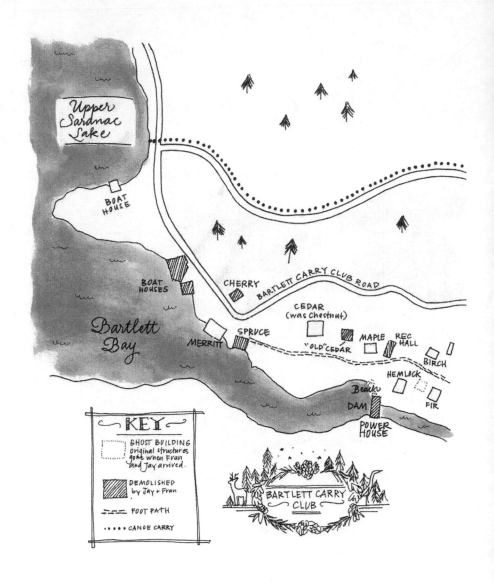

Map 3. Bartlett Carry Club detail, by Gail Brill.

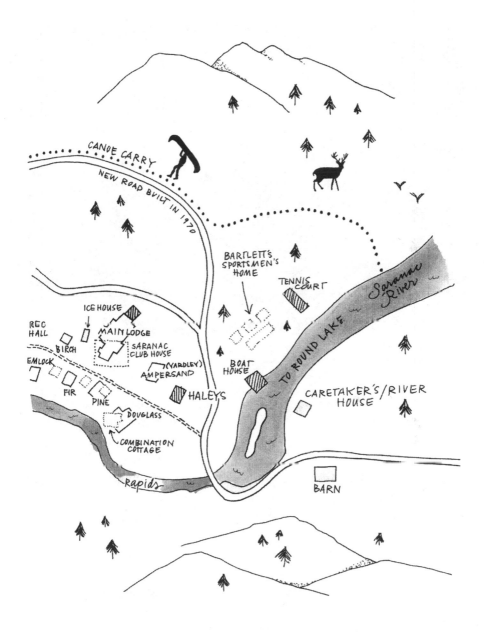

CANOE CARRY

NEW ROAD BUILT IN 1970

BARTLETT'S
SPORTSMEN'S
HOME

TENNIS
COURT

Saranac
River

ICE HOUSE

REC
HALL

MAIN LODGE

BIRCH

SARANAC
CLUB HOUSE

EMLOCK

(YARDLEY)
AMPERSAND

BOAT
HOUSE

TO ROUND LAKE

FIR

PINE

HALEYS

CARETAKER'S/RIVER
HOUSE

DOUGLASS

COMBINATION
COTTAGE

Rapids

BARN

Main Lodge pre-1970.

"What did they do here? What was the Sportsmen's Home?"

"A place for people to stay in the woods, to hunt and fish. A little like what we're going to do."

I turn around, look up the hill and point to two houses. "Were those part of what Bartlett built? They look a lot newer than the picture we saw."

Jay laughs. "Nope. That's part of the present day Bartlett Carry Club, such as it still is. That one on the right is Yardley Cottage, the one Granny Yardley built in the 1920s."

"Wait! Your grandmother?"

"Right. Harriet Jenkins Yardley."

"Why did she need a house here when she had the family summer camp down on Middle Saranac?"

"That's something I never figured out." Jay shrugs. "Maybe she just needed to get away from everything."

A mile down the road?

"And the one on the left is called Douglass. Built about the same time for the Douglass family."

"Wow, it's huge."

"Yeah." says Jay.

"I wonder how many bedrooms there are."

"Let's keep going. We still have a lot to look at."

As we drive up the hill, Jay sees me lean forward and crane my neck to look up at the roof of an enormous building on the left. "That's the Main Lodge. Built in the 1920s, too." Three stories loom above us. Jagged glass hangs from windows on the top floor. Shingles lay loose on the ground.

"Okay, I know I keep saying this, but wow. What was this for?"

"It has a kitchen and dining room. Everyone at the Club ate here."

I can't help it. I say this out loud. "Just how long will it take to renovate all this? Can we *do* this?"

Jay's voice is so low, I almost don't hear him.

"We'll see."

Just beyond that huge structure sits a smaller building, completely dwarfed by its neighbor.

"That's the Club icehouse."

Jay drives past a small house on the left and parks the Rover. I've lost track of how many buildings I've seen. I get out, lean way back and look up—sheer straight pine trees surround us, strain to pierce the sky. Scent of green envelops me. That and a sound—a roaring, but not like the rapids going under the bridge. Louder, more urgent.

We walk on golden pine needles down to a small bay. Mirror-calm water reveals a twin world of upside-down trees fringing the shore. Across the bay, more houses! Do those belong to the Club too? Just how far does this property go? I don't dare ask.

I can still hear that roaring sound. I follow my ears to the left, across a stretch of marshy grasses. Aha! The dam. I've been hearing a lot about this dam since we arrived. The water, calm in the bay, cascades over the edge, crashes with abandon and thunderous noise on boulders ten to fifteen feet below. I stand mesmerized by the spray and insistent drumming water.

Even though we've only been here about a week, Jay has already had an unsettling talk with the New York State Conservation Department [now the Department of Environmental Conservation] about this dam. They informed him of the need for serious repairs and that, as owners, we must do this at our expense. They claim if we don't repair the dam and it breaks, water will flood Route 3 on the downstream side, the Upper Saranac Lake water level

Bartlett Dam 1969 taken from Power House; Spruce in background.

will lower somewhere between five to eleven feet, and we will be responsible for damages. Jay figures the required repairs might amount to about $150,000. Our budget does not have a line for this item. We care about this dam because it provides our only electricity for the enormous amount of work we want to accomplish at the Club. Most people have alternating current (AC), but our dam is only able to provide direct current (DC).

Jay yells over the roar of pounding water, points to a building perched on the edge of the dam. "That's the power house!"

Even though Jay has already explained to me how we get electricity, I'm still trying to grasp the concept. We stand on the shore of Bartlett Bay at the southern end of Upper Saranac Lake. The power house sits here, housing a generator. Jay explains again.

"See? The current picks up in this narrow bay because this is where Upper Saranac Lake flows into the Saranac River. It flows right through this spillway."

He points to a six-foot opening where water rushes through a metal grate holding back leaves, branches, beaver-chewed sticks, and other debris.

"From here, the water goes into that concrete chamber and then through an eighteen-to-twenty-inch metal pipe to the turbine below. Understand?"

I nod, pretending I do. Jay tells me Al Tyrol has to clean the grate once a day to keep the cubic-feet-of-water-per-second output at maximum potential. The DC electricity also feeds Al's house, and the strength of the electric voltage he receives lies in direct proportion to the efficacy of the power house operation, so he pays close attention.

"See those wires?" Jay points up. Wires indeed loop from one pole to another, extending from the power house to one building, and then to another and another. "They power all the houses at the Club and down a mile to Al's house."

"Not too attractive." I say.

"Yeah, we're going to get rid of them and the poles and bring in AC electricity and bury the lines."

"But where will that electricity come from?"

"Under the lake, across about three miles, and then down the river."

"Aha." My shoulders tense. *Can we really do this? How?*

The power house seems like a solid structure—a good thing since it sits smack in the middle of the dam. We walk carefully across a narrow cement walkway to a room filled with huge machinery. It is even louder inside with reverberations from both the generator and roaring water. The floor shakes from the water power pounding underneath us. The tremor surges through my body.

Jay gestures, and we leave to continue our tour. We pass a long, narrow, unappealing building with two chipped-cement shuffleboard courts running the length of an exterior wall and three smaller houses.

"The Rec Hall," says Jay. "They built this in the 1930s so they'd have a place for kids to go."

Jay moves on to three smaller houses.

"Are we going inside any of these?" My feet scuff the dirt as they drag. Jay stops.

"I'm pretty sure these each have two bedrooms, a living room, and a bathroom. And chimneys, so they each have a fireplace. But we'll never finish if we go in all of them now."

"Okay." I point at the huge building up the hill. "What about that?"

"Yeah. Let's go see the Main Lodge."

We climb the hill and approach the opposite side of that huge building I saw as we drove up the road. It still looks enormous. In the lock of the old door, Jay tries one after another of the ancient looking keys hanging from his belt.

"You've got to be careful with these old keys so you don't break them." He works a four-inch-long pewter skeleton key in and around with patient deliberation. It finally clicks, and Jay opens the door. We enter what looks like a front lobby. Musty air, much cooler than outside. The space feels empty, lonely, as if many hot summers and cold winters have come and gone with no one placing a jacket on the brass hooks of two free-standing, ten-foot-long wooden coat racks, no one reaching into one of the cubby holes on the back wall for mail. A large, black safe presides over the back corner.

"A safe? Huh, what do you suppose is in there?"

"Don't worry," says Jay. "We'll find out—if we can figure out how to unlock it."

Our footsteps echo as we walk into a room about half the size of a basketball court with tall rafters, wainscoted paneling, floor-to-ceiling windows, and a grand, grey stone fireplace. Bat droppings cover the hearth, the nose-curling odor rising up. Fraying cushions sag on wicker couches and chairs.

Two sets of floor-to-ceiling French doors lead to an even bigger room with about twelve round wooden tables and a few rectangular tables—the dining room. I walk past another large stone fireplace to a picture window.

"What a view! That's Ampersand Mountain, isn't it?"

Jay has disappeared through swinging double doors. I follow him into another cavernous, cold room—the kitchen. Ragged cobwebs drape dusty floor-to-ceiling windows like long-neglected curtains. A smell of stale grease and more bat droppings, enormous industrial sinks, heavy old rubber mats on the floor, and pots—at least fifteen to twenty tarnished copper and brass pots. The smallest could boil pasta for a group of thirty to forty people. I try to lift one. I have to grab the long handle with my right hand and the shorter rounded handle on the other side with my left. How heavy would this be filled with hot soup? Even bigger pots, about fifteen inches tall, fifteen inches circumference, crouch under long metal counters. Other smaller ones hang on hooks.

"We're not going to run a restaurant, are we?"

"Nope. I want to put kitchens in each lodge, and they can cook for themselves."

Phew. "Great! What do we do with these huge pots?"

Jay pauses. "Maybe put kindling in them since the lodges all have fireplaces."

Chipped white china plates and dozens of small copper trays look like they have been waiting for years on dusty shelves.

"Huh," I say. "There's no way we have enough china for nine houses, and it's not in good enough shape anyway. And where's the silverware?"

I move down to the end of the shelves.

"Look at these!"

At least ten old metal flat irons, rusted with age, queue up, ready to heat on the stove so they can press starched aprons and shirts on wash day.

Jay says, "Maybe you can paint over the rust and use them for doorstops."

After we tour the whole kitchen, all we've found for our soon-to-be-renovated houses are blackened pots, small copper trays, and rusty flat irons.

Out the back door, we step down to the icehouse. Jay yanks the foot-thick door open.

"This one's bigger than the icehouse at camp. They got blocks of ice out of Upper Saranac Lake."

I'm grateful for the small gas refrigerator back at our little cabin. I pause, a hollow in my stomach, my eyes and brain blurry.

"How many more to go?"

Jay looks a bit fatigued himself.

"Okay, let's just walk down to the far end and at least say we've looked at them all."

During the next hour, we walk by at least six more houses plus a few boathouses. How will I ever make sense of it all? The biggest house at the far end has eight bedrooms, seven bathrooms, and an enormous living room with a large stone fireplace. They didn't do fireplaces in a small way. The house stands partially on land, partially on a rock jutting out into the bay. Four other houses stand nearby, some with only one bedroom, some with three or four. Some of them seem only just usable. One has a roof caved in from heavy snows of hard winters.

We stop at the water's edge.

"This is Upper Saranac Lake. Two boathouses in this bay—both in need of repair and another around the point."

I stand still. How will we even begin? I have so much faith in Jay, he seems so sure, but this? It's huge. Will we get help or try to do it alone? We have Al Tyrol and Chuck Phillips, a native Adirondacker, working as handyman for the Club and family camp, but that hardly seems enough.

We have looked at the three-story Main Lodge with hotel-size kitchen, living and dining rooms, reception area, and dormitory space for the help; the icehouse; the Rec Hall; a laundry house; at least three boathouses; a motor boat and numerous canoes and guide boats; a dam and power house dispensing DC electricity; a caretaker's cottage; an enormous, old barn; a 1955 long-bed Chevrolet pickup truck; a Model 40 John Deere Crawler; and twelve individual houses with two to eight bedrooms each, baths, living rooms, and rudimentary kitchens, one with a caved-in roof. Every one of them screams for attention. Some will need to be demolished. The rest need to be re-roofed, re-wired, re-plumbed, re-stained, and completely refurbished. With the help of Al and Chuck, we plan to do the work. My head swims; I have to go back to our manageable little cabin and take a nap.

V

In the evening we sit in front of the fire, a kerosene lamp between us, and listen to CBS news on our transistor radio. After Walter Cronkite signs off, we sift through stacks of old photos and documents we found here. Jay's eyes narrow slightly, his dark brows come together, not frowning exactly, but in total concentration. The jumbled piles taunt his meticulous Marine training. He has brought several legal-sized, mottled-brown expandable files just for this project. Tonight, he sticks a piece of masking tape on each one, and, in large block letters, writes dates across them: *Pre 1921. June 1921–1936. Post–1936.*

"Okay," he says, looking satisfied. "Now when we find something with a definite date, it goes in the right file."

We look through the photos. "Take a look at this." Jay hands me an old brochure with an etching of a huge, antlered deer.

"That's a ten-point buck. And listen to what it says—*V. C. Bartlett's Sportsmen's Home, Saranac Lake, N.Y. Located in the Adirondack Region, presents An Unequaled Resort for Sportsmen. Trout and venison during the season. Guides and boats at reasonable rates.*"

I hand the brochure back. "What's Virgil Bartlett's story?"

Virgil Bartlett, ca. 1872.

Caroline Bartlett, ca. 1872.

"He was the first guy to build anything here. Back in the 1800s. Before that, Native Americans, I think Mohawk and Algonquin, traveled through, hunting, fishing, maybe camping."

"Look at these!" I hold up two small sepia photographs, one of a man, one of a woman, both dressed quite finely in formal poses. I turn one over.

"Jay! It says Virgil Bartlett! And look at the date! 1872!" I turn the other. "And this must be his wife. It says Caroline Bartlett. I wonder who wrote this on the back."

Jay takes the photos. "That's Gramp's writing. He wrote lots of stuff down. There's a guestbook for the family camp somewhere. I think he started that, too."

"Is that when Virgil Bartlett first came? In 1872?"

"It was earlier than that. We'll find out when."

Years later, through research, I do find out.

Federal Census records vary from decade to decade, but Virgil Bartlett was most likely born in Massachusetts on January 5, 1816. Sometime before 1850, he moved to Jay, New York, "best known for the iron manufactured in its forges and the timbers hewn upon the mighty shoulders of its hills."[3]

It is probable that, after his arrival in Jay, Virgil had the good fortune to encounter a tall, fine-looking young woman teaching in the village school. Caroline Greene, eleven years younger, may well have been smitten by this adventurous man with twinkling eyes, a great sense of humor, and a reservoir of stories. And so, despite her observation of his rough ways, quick temper, and more-than-occasional profanity, she accepted his proposal of marriage and new horizons.

In hindsight, I see such a parallel with my meeting Jay. I was definitely swept away by my adventurous man with fascinating stories, a quick sense of humor, and intense blue eyes.

Virgil and Caroline had a grand vision. They saw in the Adirondacks a magnificent wilderness with vast treasures, many as yet undiscovered. Others had just begun to journey forth there seeking adventures. Virgil and Caroline may have imagined fishermen, hunters, people who enjoyed the out-of-doors visiting this new frontier; even women, families, particularly if there was a comfortable place for them to stay, delicious food on the table, guides to accompany them into the woods. They sensed opportunity.

Over a hundred years later, Jay saw a similar opportunity, and I was willing to support him pursuing it. *Let's go live in the wilderness!* he said.

Let's make this a place people want to come to. He wanted to do something different, exciting, challenging, not yet proven. I accepted even though I had no idea what that meant. I just knew I was ready to follow him. I wonder if Caroline felt anything similar. I didn't have Jay's heritage begun by his great-grandfather or property that went back to Virgil Bartlett, but I did love the idea of living in a wilderness similar to the island of my childhood summers and of restoring a rich, historical tradition.

In early 1850, Virgil, thirty-five, and Caroline, in her early twenties, moved from Jay to Saranac Lake, New York. After a bone-jarring, four-hour stagecoach ride over rocks, potholes, mud, and loose sand across almost thirty miles, they finally reached a small village in the midst of tall pines and majestic mountains at the northeast edge of Lower Saranac Lake.

First settled by Jacob Smith Moody in 1819, Saranac Lake sat in the center of a well-traveled highway of lakes, rivers, and portages that formed a 140-mile transportation route from the hamlet of Old Forge on the southwestern edge of the Adirondacks to Lake Champlain on the east. Algonquin and Mohawk frequented this route as well as travelers of European heritage—trappers, loggers, anyone looking for the least arduous route across this part of the Adirondacks. Lumber had ruled here as the major industry since the early nineteenth century.

Virgil and Caroline made the acquaintance of Captain Pliny Miller, another entrepreneur. Miller had moved to Saranac Lake in 1822 and built a sawmill and dam at the site of the present dam in Saranac Lake. After over twenty years, he saw potential in the village, and in 1848, he sold his mill and, just across the river, built the Pliny Miller House, the first hotel in Saranac Lake for boarding and lodging. Locals referred to it as Miller's Hotel.

Miller leased his hotel to William Martin, another visionary gentleman, during 1849 and 1850. By the end of 1850, just as the Bartletts unpacked their satchels, Martin was ready to embark on his own dream. He ignored "the protests of his fellow townsmen who regarded him as visionary and reckless,"[4] left Miller's Hotel and moved just outside town to erect a two-story building on the southeast shore of Lower Saranac Lake to serve eighty patrons. The building's official name was The Saranac Lake House, better known to locals as Martin's.

Meanwhile, after Martin defected to his new hotel in 1850, Captain Miller needed a new lessee. Virgil and Caroline took on the job and became immersed in the growing interest in the area. They heard stories of more and more sportsmen discovering the joys of sparkling rapids, lush woods, clear air, and the plethora of wildlife for the taking. They also heard frequent grumbling about the lack of comfort while out in the woods.

Just as Virgil and Caroline settled in to lease and manage Miller's hotel, Jesse Corey, yet another adventurous entrepreneur, built his own hotel, Rustic Lodge, on the southern end of Upper Saranac Lake. Native Americans had gathered at the point between Upper Saranac and the Raquette River for centuries to hunt, fish, and smoke their game. Alfred Street, author of *Woods and Waters: or The Saranacs and Racquet*, claimed they named the narrow strip of land the Eaglenest Trail of the Saranacs. Most referred to it as the Indian Carrying-Place or Indian Carry. This portage marked the shortest path between Upper Saranac and the Raquette River, and all boat travel naturally led to this route.

Rustic Lodge quickly became a popular layover for weary, hungry sports and travelers. Virgil must have noted the lack of accommodation in the wilderness. Leasing Miller's hotel was only short term for him. Not unlike Jay, he wanted a place where he could make his mark. Both Jay and Virgil were practical businessmen, able to recognize a good opportunity, and at the same time, they pushed the edge of the envelope, chose to do something different, exciting, challenging, not yet proven to be successful.

In fact, Virgil and Caroline stayed at Miller's hotel in the village of Saranac Lake for only four years. During that time, it is probable they visited Jesse Corey at his new Rustic Lodge. They would have gone by boat through Lower Saranac Lake, Round Lake, and on to the river leading to the portage to Upper Saranac. In 1858, a group from Martin's hotel traveled the same route:

> We make our way quietly through the channels between the fifty and odd islands of the lower lake. Here soars an eagle; there a hawk lights on the tip-top of a dead pine tree . . . In this nook we are approaching, the river covered with lily pads and white waterlilies . . . At a rocky place we must get out and the guides drag the boats over. This is the work of a few minutes . . . We cross the lake and land at the foot of the rapids, on the short river leading from it to the Upper Saranac Lake for a portage . . .[5]

I often paddle this same route now, over 150 years later. I can picture Virgil and Caroline rowing across Lower Saranac, through the river, across Round Lake, entering the last stretch of river—a heron poised to snatch a fish, a doe bending her head to drink, the sound and smell of rapids ahead. Around a bend in the river lies a flat span of mossy ground. Virgil and Caroline recognized the potential of this spot. It sat near two major routes: the Indian Carry from Upper Saranac Lake into the Raquette River watershed and the waterway from Round Lake (Middle Saranac) into Upper Saranac Lake and on to the St. Regis Lakes. Anyone and everyone traveling through the area had to pass by this point. It also happened to have the best trout waters in the area.

In 1854, Virge and Caroline left Miller's Hotel in the village of Saranac Lake and settled on this mossy ground to build V. C. Bartlett's Sportsmen's Home. They envisioned a place where people could stay for months or for a night or two; a place with a stable of guides for hunting and fishing; a comfortable place to eat well and rest in the midst of the wilderness.

Caroline must have been more worried than I was over one hundred years later. They started with nothing; no roads, no buildings. They had to create from scratch with materials at hand. They hefted axes to harvest wood, plentiful and nearby for the taking. They had no stores, but food in abundance: deer, grouse, small game, and a plethora of fish; and vegetables from their garden, although the growing season lasted only a few brief months. When they needed anything else, they climbed in a boat and rowed through Round Lake, carried over the rapids, and rowed across Lower Saranac Lake to the shores of Ampersand Bay. Once they had procured supplies, they turned around and rowed home fifteen miles upstream.

The difficulties they endured eclipsed anything I dealt with when we first came. I wish I'd been more aware of Caroline then, had her as a compatriot as I washed yet another glass chimney and pushed away yet another gnawing pang of loneliness. I was aware of her from the one photo we had, but thought little of her life back then. I know she had long hair just as I did. I had to dry mine by leaning over the kerosene heater floor vent. Now I wonder what she did. I might have found some solace back then had I known of her life and immense challenges in this place.

Was Caroline also overwhelmed by the mountain of work required before they could open their Sportsmen's Home? Did they worry about money? We did. We had to find funds for construction, the inevitable workmen we needed, supplies, bulldozer, a dump truck. We each had some savings, but no idea how long they would last.

Did Virge (a nickname used by many) and Caroline have savings to tide them over? They could get fuel, lumber, and at least some of their food from the nearby woods. Most other materials had to be purchased and rowed fifteen miles upstream. They had to pay workmen and, once they opened, guides and other staff.

I seek more details about their lives. I discover the world of Seneca Ray Stoddard, photographer, naturalist, writer, and cartographer, who published an annual guidebook, *The Adirondacks: Illustrated*, from 1873 to 1914, based on trips he took into the wilderness. Twenty years after Virge and Caroline settled on the Saranac River, he ventured by boat from the village of Saranac Lake and stayed at Bartlett's.

> Bartlett's is at the foot of a short carry, between Round Lake and the upper Saranac . . . the house, which will accommodate about fifty, is a long, low, old fashioned structure with a rambling, uncertain look about it and its outbuildings as though they were dropped down here and there as a temporary sort of arrangement. The interior is pleasant, containing some fine and well furnished rooms; the table is excellent. It is reached principally by the route we pursued [by water] and has no connection with the outer world save by boat or through the wild woods.[6]

Stoddard wrote this in 1874. I wonder how others got to Bartlett's from New York, Boston, and as far away as Philadelphia. Edwin Wallace in his 1875 publication of *Descriptive Guide to the Adirondacks and Handbook of Travel* described the trip as lengthy and arduous. At a time without reliable roads, Lake Champlain served as the thoroughfare: 120 miles long, its narrow waters sliced between New York and Vermont and stretched from Whitehall, New York, to just across the Canadian border. Coming from the south, travelers arrived in Whitehall where they boarded a steamboat, fueled in the first years by wood. Many of these boats, such as the *Phoenix*, perished in inevitable fires. By 1881, new coal-powered

Bartlett's Sportsmen's Home, ca. 1882.

steamboats like the *Maquam*, proudly steered by Captain Holt, assured a safer passage. The trip took seven hours from Whitehall to Burlington, Vermont, and an hour more to cross to Port Kent on the New York State side. James Wood traveled this route in 1865 and described the view: "(We) enjoyed a magnificent sunset with the brilliant clouds softly reflected in the smooth surface of the lake, and the effect grandly heightened by the bold Adirondack peaks which stood against the bright horizon like the teeth of a great Titanic saw."[7]

In Port Kent, after rediscovering their land-legs, travelers boarded a stage coach, possibly painted red with yellow and black filigree, with four prancing horses. After seeing such a coach on display at the Adirondack Museum, I can imagine five or six passengers riding inside on black leather seats and perhaps two brave souls riding atop. Five-and-a-half miles on rumbling, rough-wood-plank roads took them from Port Kent to Taggart's Inn in Keeseville for the night.

After breakfast at 6:00 a.m., they boarded a tally-ho stagecoach, one of several owned by Virgil Bartlett, bound for Martin's. Many hotels in the Adirondacks offered the convenience of stage connections for their guests.

The full day trip took them over fifty miles on stones, dirt, and mud, albeit with grand mountain views.

"Sports," the colloquial term for hunters and fishermen, loved Martin's. Frank Leslie gives a vivid picture of one such group in 1858:

> We rise at early dawn, after a refreshing sleep on Martyn's [sic] fresh, oat-straw beds, still fragrant of the fields, and however rude and simple the furniture and other arrangements of his house, there is a neatness and cleanliness in every nook and corner, always fresh trout and well-seasoned venison on the table and a fresh breeze coming down among the evergreened islands on the lake, bearing with them a balmy sweetness from the pines and fir balsams. As you fling open the sash, on arising, you inhale draughts of this delicious air.[8]

Travelers arriving twenty years later would have had a similar experience. Once they arrived, they still had fifteen miles by water to reach Bartlett's Sportsmen's Home, so they spent the night at Martin's. For many years, the next day they traveled by rowboat or guide boat through Lower Saranac Lake and up the Saranac River as far as the Middle Falls rapids. At that point, they had to disembark, walk around the rapids, and climb into another boat to cross two-mile Round Lake before they reached Bartlett's.

According to author and historian, Alfred Donaldson, in the fall of 1877 Bill Martin, owner of Martin's hotel, decided to make this trip a bit less cumbersome. With his son and some others, he blasted rocks at the Middle Falls and built a dam to create a channel deep and wide enough to accommodate a small steamer. Enter *Water Lily*, a thirty-six-foot steamer capable of carrying forty passengers and the first powerboat on the Saranac Lakes.[9] Donaldson reported that her first official trip was July 4, 1878, and that during that summer, passengers could travel directly from Martin's on Lower Saranac Lake all the way through to Bartlett's.

While this made Bill and Virge and their customers happy, apparently some guides didn't much take to that steamboat being on the lake. Travelers weren't employing them to get from one end to the other, and they had only so long in the summer to make a living before going back to logging. Other folks claimed the boat was ruining the hunting by driving deer and other game back into the woods. Donaldson related that finally, a few men, unnamed by history, but undoubtedly well-storied in dark barrooms, took matters into their own hands, went up to the Middle Falls, and dynamited the dam to bits. End of channel.[10] From that point on, *Water Lily* took passengers as far as the Middle Falls, at which point they were met by Mark Clough, ready to row them in his seven-passenger wooden rowboat, smaller than *Water Lily* but solid and canopied,[11] able to meet the challenging winds of Round Lake.

After crossing two-mile-long Round Lake and entering the river, Mark would have to row harder against the growing current. On this present day as I write, a rich forest of pine, hemlock, and fir lines the shore. Back then, jagged stumps of lumbered trees poked out of bare ground like stubble on a plucked chicken. Both then and now, the din of rushing water grew louder as they approached the rapids. When they rounded the last curve, they would see the first buildings they'd seen all day. Any hope of an attractive resort in the green woods evaporated on the spot.

Nothing spiffy, nothing brightly painted; these weathered gray buildings stood like stalwart old tree trunks. And yet, after three days, the travelers must have been relieved to finally arrive. Several men pulled the boat onto dry land, and they stepped ashore. Henry Van Dyke, author, educator, clergyman, and traveler to Bartlett's, described it in 1895:

> Did you know Bartlett's in its palmy time? It was the homeliest, quaintest, coziest place in the Adirondacks. Away back in the *ante-bellum* days, Virgil Bartlett had come into the woods and built his house on the bank of the Saranac River between the Upper Saranac and Round Lake. It was then the only dwelling within a circle of many miles. The deer and bear were in the majority. At night one could sometimes hear the scream of the panther or the howling of wolves.[12]

I remember thinking, when I first read this paragraph, not long after Jay and I had our exhausting tour of the Bartlett Carry Club, that we may have heard howling coyotes, but at least not the scream of a panther.

In my photograph of Virgil Bartlett, he stands tall, left arm resting on a high-backed chair. He wears a high, white collar, vest with fob chain,

Bartlett's, ca. 1882.

and a jacket. White hair, mustache, and beard, his mouth drawn down in a pensive frown, his eyes looking directly out, not missing a thing.

I doubt he dressed this formally as he greeted his guests. Estella Martin, daughter of hotel owner William Martin, gathered information for Alfred Donaldson as he wrote *A History of the Adirondacks*. She wrote personal observations about the Saranac Lake area. She described the animals Virgil loved: a pet raccoon shuffling down to the shore looking for a handout, a pet fawn, weasel, flying squirrel, and dogs everywhere. As Virge awaited his guests, he may have tossed a fish to an otter wriggling up from the river. Virge once said, as an otter caught the fish and chewed with gusto, "Ah! I told you he was great on fish!"[13]

From the hill beyond, men would have approached, some carrying boats from the Upper Lake or with huge packs on their backs or perhaps carrying strings of fish or some kind of bird. A horse-drawn wagon would have stood ready to carry the guide boat of a passer-through to the Upper Lake for fifty cents.[14] Perhaps Virgil called in his high, nasal voice to several men in red shirts who stood nearby cleaning their rifles. "Now boys! Let's get these satchels up to the house!"

Horse and cart, ca. 1895.

The men who worked for Virge did as he said. At election time, they voted the way he did if they wanted to keep their jobs. No election day closed until the boat carrying the Bartlett contingent arrived in town to cast their ballots. He went out of his way to help those in need who worked for him. One unusually cold winter, he fetched an ailing lumberman from the wilderness, brought him back to Bartlett's, and nursed him back to health.

As Virge stood on the shore to greet his guests, enticing aromas wafted through the air from a pot of simmering venison outside and from bread baking within. Estella Martin wrote of traveling in late fall with a Mrs. Dunning, a frequent visitor to Bartlett's. The wind blew hard that day across Round Lake. High waves slopped mercilessly into the boat, but Mrs. Dunning persevered. "Well," she said, "it will be worth the trip from New York to Bartlett's to go there for dinner and have a meal of Mrs. Bartlett's brown bread."[15]

A formal sepia photograph of Caroline matches Virgil's. Her arm, too, rests on a chair, her hair parted in the middle, a fringe of bangs, the rest pulled back in a rolled braid. Her light eyes look directly at the camera, a half smile playing on her mouth. She wears an elegant, long, fitted dress with a velvet collar and bow fixed with a cameo broach. She holds a fur muff. Estella Martin wrote that Mrs. Dunning, the woman salivating for Caroline's brown bread, also looked forward to seeing what new fashionable outfits and fancy work Caroline might have procured from her annual trips to Albany, New York, or Boston.

In contrast, the every-day, rough-and-ready Caroline is portrayed by Frank Leslie in his article about the group of men who ventured to Bartlett's in summer 1858.

> Mrs. Bartlett, besides being a stirring housewife, is ready to go into the woods and camp as a lady guide if a party of ladies gives her a call, and as she knows the points and name of every guide dog and boat all about the country and will convert a deer, partridge or trout in quick style into roted [sic: roasted] haunch, ramrod-toasted saddle piece, pork fried or baked, and has a multitude of canines ready at her side to fetch the game she wants and is not afraid to pull a trigger if no better hand is near, no one need fear of starvation while in her care.[16]

Like Virgil, as Caroline met their guests, she most likely did not wear her best finery. Her sleeves might have been rolled up as she may have just emerged from the kitchen. I have photos of only the rustic exterior of their hotel, but firsthand observations by Estella Martin describe at the entrance a large picture framed with pinecones and burrs made by Caroline; a fire screen of pressed autumn leaves on glass in the parlor; and nearby, a parrot, perched with one eye open to appraise newcomers. This famous parrot possessed the talent of repeating Virgil's forceful language, and, as the last of the kerosene lamps was blown out each evening, squawking "Good night, Mrs. Bartlett!"[17]

Donaldson gives us an evocative picture of Bartlett's:

> The unchangeableness of their little hostelry was one of its homy [sic] charms. Remote as it was in location, it soon became the connecting link and favorite half-way house between the two great highway lakes of this section. Its patronage was, therefore, largely transient, although some families spent the season there. Mrs.

Bartlett soon established the reputation of setting the best table in the mountains, for both guest and guide. It followed, as the night the day, that guides were always eager to get their parties there for a meal, and were never in a hurry to take them away.[18]

VI

"Listen to this," Jay says one evening, not long after our first tour of the buildings. He reads me the Donaldson quote about Bartlett's.

"I think in our brochure we should use the part about how the guides were never in a hurry to take their parties away. And I do think we should call it Round Lake and not Middle Saranac."

I agree. We just don't have an idea yet of when we will make a brochure. After our first tour of the buildings, we know we have a lot of work ahead of us, sometimes together, but mostly with our separate jobs. One of mine will be housekeeping, no matter how much I think I have evolved from the culture of my childhood when Mom stayed home and Dad went to work. And I have had zero cleaning experience. When I was a kid, it was never my responsibility. Living in a truck for four months on our honeymoon to Alaska required none. And in Tunisia, a woman named Zorah showed up every day for $.25 per hour to sweep, scrub floors, do the wash, and hang it on the roof of our villa in the brilliant North African sun.

Not long after we move into the Guide House, Jay, who had survived white-glove inspections in military barracks, begins to notice our dusty floors, an uncleaned toilet, and a smudged mirror. My housekeeping will have to start with our own home. Jay knows how to break tasks into small steps and how to implement them, so he helps me make a list. Then he climbs on a bulldozer and rips into buildings. That leaves me to do the cleaning. Looking back, I can see that list of chores pinned on the bathroom wall: Monday—shake out rugs, dust, sweep floors (no electricity means no vacuum cleaner); Tuesday—wash kerosene lamp chimneys, fill lamps (this happens every day or every other day); Wednesday—clean bathroom, wash kitchen floor; Thursday—laundry and grocery shop (we both go to town since I've not yet learned to drive the stick-shift Land Rover); Friday—I don't remember. Something domestic, I'm sure.

Looking back, I have a hard time believing I did this, but in 1968, more than anything, I wanted to do my part, prove I could be a good partner in this venture. So every day, I got up, peered in the mirror at my freckly face, gathered my long hair in a ponytail, and consulted my list for the day's chores.

Jay's parents puzzle over his enthusiasm to take on a huge piece of property with a lot of neglected buildings, but they don't say much. My dad typically says little about our move, although I know both he and my mom are grateful we're back in this country and have a telephone, even if it's a five-household party line. My mom wants to see for herself what her fourth child has gotten herself into. Mom knows all about the less-traveled road. She has accompanied my dad, an avid fisherman, to South America, Alaska, and many places in between. So, when Mom visits during our first February, shortly after that hypothermia-inducing, record-cold, ice-booming night, I don't worry about her.

Our little cabin has no room for her to sleep, so I fix up David's cabin, which sits directly on frozen ground with no insulation, twenty steps from our porch. A pot-belly stove provides at least a possibility of keeping the tiny place habitable. Mom loves staying there. On her first night, after dinner, I put on my parka and boots and escort her across the snowy path. Our steamy breath clouds the frosty air. The fire I laid earlier blazes in its cast-iron home. The cabin welcomes us with colorful curtains and favorite knickknacks along window sills. I stir the fire and add as much wood as possible. "Night, Mom! Sleep tight!" I kiss her good night, then sprint back in crisp below-zero air.

The next morning, I arise before the sun, put on every piece of clothing I can find in the semidarkness. My steps in the snow crunch like potato chips. The frigid air stands motionless, waiting for warm fingers of the rising sun to stroke it back to life. The inside of Mom's cabin almost matches the outside cold. Intricate filigrees of frost fill every window pane. The hump under the down comforters and Hudson's Bay blankets hints that Mom has not yet braved the morning air.

"Morning Mom!" Her nose appears above the covers.

"Hi Dearie!" she says cheerfully.

"Stay there," I say. "I'll get the fire going." If I don't say that, she will be out the door in her nightie looking for more wood. The remaining coals help the fire spring alive. I jump onto her bed and wrap myself in a blanket. "So how was your night?"

"Oh, perfect. It was the best night's sleep I've ever had!" While I know she always says this, she clearly loves the whole adventure.

The day Mom leaves, I stand outside our cabin waving until her car disappears down the dirt road and around a wooded curve. I hadn't expected to feel such a void, but with her visit came a flood of memories of my beloved, chaotic family life—my two older brothers always on the move, my older sister trying to keep up with them, me trying to keep up with her, and my younger sister trying to keep up with all of us. In the summer, we had cousins and friends, fish to catch off the dock, a raft to swim around and, oh, the scavenger hunts! Pine sap stuck to our clothes, chirping chickadees and loon calls greeted us every morning, and always the aliveness of that wide expanse of lake.

As I watch Mom's tail lights disappear, I take in the quiet. And the loneliness. I only have access to civilization and other people on our weekly visits to town. Did I ever imagine I would end up in such a place at the age of twenty-four?

I didn't think much back then about Caroline's life in the wilderness. Now that I feel such a kinship with her, I am curious about her daily experience. Was she lonely? Overwhelmed by the work she had to do? Estella Martin writes that Caroline and Virge had no children of their own. They adopted Caroline's niece, Carrie Niles, when a baby. According to the 1880 Federal Census, she was born in 1863. They also brought Kate and Martha Shene when mere children into their household and trained them to help run the hotel. Martha in particular learned well in the kitchen under Caroline's watchful eye and, at eighteen, went to work at Martin's hotel. She became famous as a pastry cook, especially for her cream puffs. Kate married Tom Healy (sometimes spelled Haley) one of Virge's guides, and lived in a small cabin just uphill from Bartlett's Sportsmen's Home. They named their boy Bartlett, nicknamed Barty, the apple of his surrogate grandfather's eye. Virge had a small cot placed near his own bed so Barty could visit whenever he wanted. On trips to the outside, Barty went along. Estella reported, "anything the child did not have was simply because he did not ask for it."[19]

Once old enough, Carrie most likely took guests to their rooms, up narrow wooden stairs to a second-floor landing where a breeze wafted through a low open window framed by white eyelet curtains. Once inside his or her room, a guest might see a wrought-iron bed, painted white with embroidered coverlet, a wrought-iron wash stand, white porcelain pitcher and bowl with a towel hanging below. In the corner, under the sloping ceiling, a small desk and chair with a colorful braided rug on the floor, a window with flowered curtains with a view of the river flowing by and the music of rushing rapids filling their ears. I could easily stay in that room; no wonder guests returned year after year.

And many guests did return year after year. Dr. James R. Romeyn of Keeseville first came in 1854 with his family. Although he had a degree in medicine, he spent his time managing the AuSable Horse Nail Company, started by his father-in-law. With all the horses needing nails for shoes on those rough roads, the business flourished. Dr. Romeyn had streamlined the operation so they could manufacture two hundred pounds of nails for horseshoes in the same amount of time it previously took to make ten.

Dr. Romeyn loved to fly fish. The rapids below the dam cascading down to flat water in front of Bartlett's created the perfect home for brook trout; smallmouth bass; rainbow trout, introduced in the 1870s; and brown trout, introduced in the 1880s. He came for at least three weeks every year, up to three months if he could manage it. My favorite photograph of him shows this dignified man, with pointed beard and sharp nose, balanced on a rock over white rapids, focused on the rod in his right hand, left hand tucked in the pocket of his dark jacket. Perhaps on some evenings trout he had caught graced the supper table along with Caroline's famous brown bread and, in season, fresh strawberries and cream. I would have loved to sit next to him and listen to his fishing stories.

After supper, guests often gathered in the parlor for a bit of entertainment. Caroline had a piano for anyone wishing to play. One evening, according to Estella Martin, during an impromptu concert, a new guest in the audience spontaneously broke into song. Suddenly, from his perch in the corner, the parrot screamed "Shut up! Shut up!" Guests like Dr.

Dr. James Romeyn.

Romeyn, who had been coming for years, thought nothing of this remarkable behavior. The singer, enthralled with her own singing, did not stop, whereupon the parrot flew over, landed on her shoulder, and pulled at her hair. Amidst the chaos, Caroline calmly approached the bird and took him from the room.

VII

One hundred years later, my life in the same place, though less primitive, seems more isolated. Caroline was surrounded by her husband, her adopted niece, Kate, Martha, Barty, guides, a constant stream of guests, and, of course, the parrot. Other than Jay, I have only chickadees and the occasional chipmunk to break the silence of my day.

After Mom leaves in February, 1969, I realize how much I miss my childhood, always surrounded by chaos and noise, joy and laughter. I want to climb on a giant toboggan in my puffy snowsuit, scrunched between siblings and friends, my wooly hat askew, my mittens snowy, tingling cheeks rosy-red as we zoom downhill screaming with delight, toppling over, brushing ourselves off to trudge uphill again.

Instead, I have to buckle down alone. It doesn't take long to realize that completing daily chores on the cleaning list won't fill the long days or fulfill my need to help fix this place up.

"Here's what you can do," says Jay. "Go through all the buildings here at the camp on Round Lake (he uses this and Middle Saranac Lake interchangeably) and make a list of what's here—dishes, furniture, linens, that kind of stuff." Jay loves lists.

Well, this should keep me busy. I silently start counting how many buildings he's talking about just at camp—more than ten.

"I also need you to inventory the twelve houses and the Main Lodge at the Bartlett Carry Club before we start taking some down and renovating others. Can you start soon?"

The Club—that's all the buildings we saw on our first tour, a mile from where we live at the family camp. If I include the boathouses and icehouse plus the twelve houses and Main Lodge, that adds up to more than twenty buildings just at the Club. It sounds overwhelming.

I decide to begin with the fewer buildings at the family camp. While Jay spends his days climbing on roofs at the Club to assess the solidity of chimneys or crawling underneath to examine foundations, I focus on my task.

The Main Cabin where Jay's grandparents stayed seems a good place to start. It stands on a hill overlooking Middle Saranac Lake, under pine trees too big to wrap my arms around. I pull on my beige down parka and heavy winter boots. As I enter the back door, four inches of fresh snow don't mask the unmistakable odor of bat feces. Bats love to nest under the spruce-bark-covered exterior walls of each cabin. Wind whistles through pines, piercing the smothering quiet. The cold bites more inside than out on this chilly morning. Today, I will inventory furniture and linens. Sheets and towels. Hard to manipulate with thick mittens, but impossible to expose bare hands for long. Howl of wind. Expanse of cold, empty white on the lake. No sign of anyone. Hours 'til lunch.

I never met Jay's grandparents. I have no connection to any of this. Who sat on this wicker chair and looked out at the lake? As my breath steams the air, I sink into fathomless quiet broken only by howling trees and creaking windows. I finish listing sheets, towels, chairs, desk, beds, even the intriguing silver filigree wall-mounted cup holder in the bathroom and the tarnished brass dragonfly perched on the door. I can't wait to go back to our snug cabin for lunch with Jay.

One day, I attack the kitchen cabin with shelves of floral-patterned dishes. I take off my mittens and jot on my yellow pad "one dozen plates of Calyx Ware, Adams, England, two dozen of Johnson Brothers Willow Blue, also England." We can use these in some of the many houses at the Club—if we ever get that far. In the middle of taking notes, I slide freezing fingers under my armpits to thaw them.

I move on to the Maid's Cabin. When I enter, a hollow echo whispers of ghosts just beyond my awareness. Did Molly stay in this cabin? I remember Jay telling me she was his grandmother's maid. As I sort through yet again another shelf of sheets and towels, I imagine Molly on her one-afternoon-a-week-off, untying her apron, pulling on sturdy shoes, packing a lunch, and heading down the trail to a flat rock at the mouth of the river. Perhaps on a warm summer's day, in stark contrast to today, the sun would beat on that rock, releasing heady smells of balsam, pine, and possibly a dead fish or two. Molly might have settled into the soft moss, relished rare free and alone time, picked a wintergreen leaf to chew after her lunch.

I wouldn't mind having Molly to talk to. I dodge an imagined whisper here, turn aside from a lonely feeling there, and go into a bedroom. Under the frosted window sits a large wooden trunk, as long as my outstretched arms, thigh-high and just as deep, two key holes in the front, iron corner bars, heavy iron handles. On top, the initials PAS are stencilled in black Even more intriguing, on the front side is painted a huge black number "3." As weak winter sun filters through glass clouded with years of grime (where are the maids now?), my mittened hand tests to see if the lid is locked. It gives. A faint scent of old soap and faded fabric releases into cold air. More linens. It makes sense. No mouse, even an industrious Adirondack mouse, could break the seal of this sturdy trunk. We have been having mouse problems since we arrived. What a perfect mouse-free place to put our clothing. No time like right now to clean it out.

I remove one heavy pile of sheets after another, blanket covers, pillow cases, towels. Jay's mother kept this camp well stocked. Her housekeeping theory included having enough linens for a set on the bed, a set in the laundry, and a clean set in the closet. Even with my long arms, I have to almost climb in the trunk to reach where newspaper seems stuck to the bottom. I take off my mittens, scratch to remove it. The date on the newspaper catches my eye. August 18, 1918. *1918?* I stop scratching and try to loosen the paper in a gentle way. It won't give. Whose trunk was this? Who put this paper in here? And "PAS"? Who or what was that? I don't have time to figure out the answers now. It's all I can do to stay on top of my list of chores. Each day I wake up, my head full of which cabin to inventory next, how many sheets, towels, dishes, where to put them, how will we use them. And when I'm not thinking about those things, I wonder what we will have for dinner, did I get the right ingredients on our last weekly trip to town? Or do we have enough wood to stay warm through the winter? And will I finally master washing a smoky glass kerosene lamp chimney without breaking or smudging it? Only very occasionally do I pause to look at sunlight sparkling on snow or at purple light infusing dusk on the coldest nights.

One crisp winter day, we go on a mission. Jay takes a break from climbing on roofs and I from inventory to investigate the large black safe we discovered in the Main Lodge. As usual, the cavernous building holds more cold in than out. Jay and I, encased in down jackets, wooly hats and mittens, gather around the safe with Al and Chuck, our breaths fogging the cold air. The safe stands over three feet wide, five feet tall, three feet deep; gold letters on the front—"W. F. Roberts." Perhaps I will find the silverware missing from the Main Lodge kitchen during our first tour. Jay's considerable safe-cracking skills haven't worked, so we have brought in an expert to do the job.

This man kneels down, hunches over. His fingers delicately turn the dials, his head cocked for the slightest click. I make fists inside my mittens to warm my hands. I don't want to miss a second. After some time, the expert says "She's not giving. I'm going to have to drill." We didn't want this. This old girl is an antique. It seems a crime to injure her in any way. On the other hand—what's in this safe?

Finally, Jay says "Okay, but do as little damage as you can." The expert chooses a quarter-inch drill, works up to a half-inch. The high whine of the drill combined with the cold shoots shivers up my spine. He puts the drill down, swivels the large handles of the two doors. They turn. Grunting, he pulls the seven-inch-thick doors open. We lean in closer. Another set of doors! At least these aren't locked.

The expert backs up and allows Jay to take over. Jay looks at me with a glint in his eye, a smile playing on the corners of his mouth. He kneels down, takes hold of the door handles, and pulls them open. A creak splits the cold air. I expect to see boxes overflowing with silverware, possibly some silver dishes. I peer over Jay's shoulder. The safe is practically empty. Jay reaches inside and pulls out some rolled up papers, a small box, and one tarnished silver napkin ring. And some books on the bottom shelf. That's it. He hands me the box.

"Maybe this has some silverware," he says hopefully. I unwrap yellowed tissue. One corroded butter knife. That and the napkin ring comprise our silver discovery for the day. Jay unrolls the papers. One is a blueprint map of the Bartlett Carry Club, dated May 25, 1951, showing every house on the property.

"Look at this."

Jay points to a handwritten notation in one corner. "Fireplace—for roasting wild duck, wild turkey [Wild turkeys were abundant in New York in the 1600s, but uncontrolled hunting and aggressive forest cutting led to their demise. They were not re-established until the mid-to-late 1950s. The map maker was likely unaware of this fact.], young hogs—broiling venison, fish and bear steaks." *Really?*

This doesn't distract me. I want silverware. I try to contain my disappointment. Jay draws out the books, three of them. They look ancient with torn leather bindings. He hands one to me. Gold letters engraved in the pockmarked dark red cover—"Minutes of the Saranac Club." *That's nice*, I think, *but it's not silverware. And what is the Saranac Club anyway?*

I didn't know then that these books and maps would become my portal to the world of Bartlett Carry; to the stories of people who came, built, and survived in this place beginning over one hundred years earlier—people who, while I never met them, I would come to consider friends. I had no idea, as I crouched on the cold floor clutching one corroded butter knife and an ancient book, that I held the key to a door into the past, and it wasn't the butter knife.

Chapter 2

Splinters in Our Fingers

I

One day decades later, before I contemplate writing this book, I sit at my desk and consider a long-needed office reorganization. Where better to start than the shelf five feet away? My hand seems to gravitate of its own accord to one of the three old dark-red leather-bound books we discovered in the safe. While many books have come and gone from this shelf over the past forty years, these have remained. Occasionally I have opened one, only to be stymied by the old-fashioned, almost indecipherable handwriting. Back on the shelf the book has always gone, and back I have gone to my busy life.

For some reason, this time I lift the book off the shelf and do not put it back. I hadn't remembered the weight of it, the thickness. My fingers stroke the pockmarked, lustrous red leather cover, trace the engraved gold title—*Minutes of the Saranac Club*. From inside emanates the aroma of old paper, ink dried for decades. It smells of stories. In the top left corner of the front cover sits a tiny faded pink sticker: "from Tower Manufacturing Co, Stationery & Blank Book Warehouse, 306 & 306 Broadway [sic], New York." In the crease, old mottled adhesive tape valiantly holds the book together.

The initial entry starts on the third yellowed page. The signature at the end: "*R. D. Douglass, Sec. pro tem.*" Mr. Douglass must have dipped his pen into black ink and set nib to paper in an undulating wave; first dark script, the black ink having been just replenished, then gradually more faded, then dark again. His grandson, Henry Darlington, has described him as a stately gentleman with bushy eyebrows and mustache, dressed in an impeccable suit with creased pants, high white collar. Perhaps he sat, straight-backed, writing at a desk by a window.

"*New York, Jan'y 17/89*" in an elegant, almost calligraphic hand, difficult to decipher. Intriguing. I read slowly.

"An informal meeting was held at Davies Restaurant, Orange, N.J. on the above date."

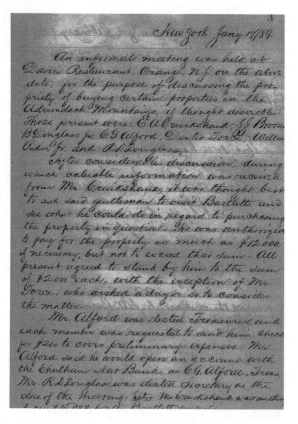

Saranac Club Minutes, written by Robert Dun Douglass, January 1889.

This volume contains the history of this place. It exists nowhere else in the world. The date refers not to 1989, but 1889. Should this book be in a museum? Should I wear gloves?

Before diving into this treasure, I need to understand how this place transformed from the days of Virgil and Caroline Bartlett, congenial hosts of the Sportsmen's Home, to Mr. Douglass in 1889 recording the history of the Saranac Club. To piece together the story, I pull books, documents, maps, photographs off shelves and dive in.

Virgil and Caroline drew loyal visitors to their cozy backwoods refuge until the early 1880s, when Virgil fell seriously ill. Caroline got him to Keeseville, but he never improved. He died there February 27, 1884, and now rests in the Fairview Cemetery in Au Sable Forks.

In Au Sable Forks in August 2011, his gravestone, more like a small monument, stands on a knoll with stately white pines keeping watch. Lichen creeps across huge block letters:

VIRGIL C. BARTLETT
JAN'Y 5, 1816.
FEB. 27, 1884
RESTING

Below, I am surprised to see:

CARLINE L. GREEN.
WIFE OF
V. C. BARTLETT
MAY 9, 1827.

Virgil Bartlett gravestone, taken 2011.

There is no death date, so apparently Caroline is not "resting" here. She most likely died in Glens Falls where she moved to live with her niece, Carrie Niles, in 1887. And "Carline"? Every other record says Caroline. Her last name is sometimes spelled "Green" and sometimes "Greene." My grandmother's maiden name was Greene. Perhaps somehow Caroline and I are related. I certainly feel a kinship with her. At any rate, in February 1884, Virgil made his way to the great beyond.

Rest in peace, Virgil. You were a key figure in making it possible for so many to pierce the edge of the wild Adirondacks. Henry Van Dyke wrote:

> Virgil himself, the creator of the oasis—well known of hunters and fishermen, dreaded of lazy guides and quarrelsome lumbermen,—"Virge," the irascible, kind-hearted, indefatigable, was there no longer. He had made his last clearing, and fought his last fight; done his last favour to a friend, and thrown his last adversary out of the tavern door. His last log had gone down the river. His campfire had burned out. Peace to his ashes. His wife . . . now reigned in his stead. And there was great abundance of maple syrup on every man's flapjack.[1]

Caroline took on responsibility for a major piece of property, multiple buildings, boats, animals, employees, and guests. With her strong face and erect posture, she may have drawn herself up and said; "Well, what do you think our guides are going to do if we don't open? And what about the families who count on coming? Of course we will open!"

They did in the summer of 1884. As the rowboat full of guests rounded the last curve and Bartlett's came into view, no Virge stood by the shore blustering a greeting, no otter slithered up for his handouts of trout.

Caroline, in her mid-fifties, now without her life partner, faced the challenge of continuing the business she and her husband had created together. I imagine the responsibility and loneliness weighed heavily. After three years, in 1887 she leased the property and business to Mr. George Fowler and bade farewell to her thirty-three-year home in the woods. Her agreement stipulated Mr. Fowler would open for business the next summer and give guests the same care they had always received. She would now collect a regular income, but not have to supervise the kitchen, greet guests on the porch, or keep up a strong front—alone. What a relief that must have been.

Mr. Fowler fell ill subsequent to his arrangement with Caroline, and yet he took over for the summer of 1888. Rumors flew. Would Bartlett's survive? Although Dr. Romeyn loved these woods and waters and the camaraderie of other fishermen, he would certainly miss both Caroline and Virgil. Would he, as well as other regular patrons, continue to return? This may have been the moment when Robert Dun Douglass, a regular visitor, approached Mr. Fowler with a plan. He had first brought his family from Llewellyn Park, New Jersey, to Bartlett's several years earlier. They may have come to escape the mosquito epidemic on the New Jersey shore where vicious insects prevented anyone from sitting outside without being mercilessly attacked. Carpenters refused to work. In some areas, typhus and cholera abounded. Mr. Douglass would have found Bartlett's a suitable alternative. His older son, Benjamin, may possibly have suffered from tuberculosis. In that case, the fresh mountain air would have enticed them as well.

During the summer of 1888, Robert (he feels like a close friend through these Minutes, and I hope he wouldn't mind my referring to him as Robert) would have realized that, due to Mr. Fowler's ill health, his haven in the Adirondacks might close. A decisive businessman, Robert called a group of friends together to discuss the matter.

On the evening of January 17, 1889, Robert and his brother, also named Benjamin, gathered with the others at the Davies Restaurant near his home in New Jersey. At this time, Robert worked for his uncle, Robert G. Dun, who had thirty years earlier taken over the Mercantile Agency in New York City and renamed it R. G. Dun & Co. (later to become Dun & Bradstreet). This company now thrived. It provided credit reports to businesses, an important tool in the development of American commerce. Robert would soon be replacing his aging uncle as General Manager, putting him in a most favorable financial position.

Despite his responsibilities, he and his wife, Eva, enjoyed visiting Bartlett's. Their two boys, Benjamin, fourteen, and Robert, fifteen, loved to explore the wonders of that magical place. Robert wanted to ensure its survival.

Possibly the friends who gathered with Robert and Benjamin that evening had also been guests at Bartlett's. After Edwin Cruikshank, Jonathan Broome, Charles Alford, Dexter Force, and William Riker arrived, they may have enjoyed a sumptuous repast, and then, over brandy and cigars, settled down to business. The Minutes, exclusively Robert's entries, reported that because Mr. Fowler could not sustain his arrangement with Caroline, he would relinquish his lease. At this first informal meeting at the Davies Restaurant, these gentlemen hoped to determine if they could step in.

According to the Minutes, Charles Alford and William Riker were especially keen about the idea. They offered to make the arduous trip to Bartlett's to obtain more information from Mr. Fowler toward the goal of purchasing the property. They hoped to attract enough members to each invest $1,000 and offer Mr. Fowler as much as $12,000, but not to exceed that sum.

$12,000—a value of about $316,000 in 2015 terms. From my modern perspective, that sounds like a pittance, even though most of the buildings had aged over thirty years and were in dire need of renovation. The state of affairs greeting Mr. Alford and Mr. Riker reminds me all too well of the situation facing Jay and me when we arrived eighty years later.

The two gentlemen made the trip in February, not an optimal time to travel, but at least by 1889 they had the luxury of traveling by train rather than by steamboat up Lake Champlain. Mr. Alford recounted their train ride north from New York to Plattsburgh in a driving snow and rain storm. They made their connection and caught the Chateauguay train extension to Saranac Lake, built just two years earlier.

Their trip from New York to Saranac Lake took fifteen hours. They had hoped to spend the night at Martin's Hotel on Lower Saranac Lake, but it had burned to the ground the year before. Instead, they stayed at the elegant, new five-story Ampersand Hotel on the northeast shore of Lower Saranac Lake, not far from the site of Martin's. It was "crowned with fantastic roofs and peaks, and flanked with broad piazzas . . . Its battlements, towers, roofs and all are red, and the structure gleams . . . under the morning sun like a garnet in an emerald setting."[2] Even in the middle of winter, guests found much to do—skating, sulky races and a toboggan slide,[3] trips to see a lumber camp and snowshoe trips up Mt. Marcy. Mr.

Alford and Mr. Riker most likely had too much on their minds to go down the toboggan slide.

Next morning, they traveled fifteen miles to Bartlett's. Robert's Minutes don't describe how they got there in mid-winter; possibly by sleigh on a winter road across frozen lakes and through snowy woods, over a bridge arching above rapids running fast and free even at thirty below zero, and at last, Bartlett's.

They met with George Fowler to determine what would be included in the purchase. He knew the property well and had apparently recovered enough to stay on as superintendent.

On March 21, 1889, twenty members officially launched their new organization, the Saranac Club. They each paid a $1,000 initiation fee plus $50 annual dues. Articles of Incorporation included the particular business and objects: "To promote social intercourse, health and recreation among its members; to furnish for its members and such others as the Club may permit, facilities for fishing, shooting and hunting; to provide its members, their families and such others as the Club may permit an agreeable resort in the Adirondacks with a suitable Hotel or Club House, Cottage houses and appurtenances."[4]

In addition to club members, they would open in a limited way to the public to help offset expenses: "The stated objects of the club are, primarily, the health, happiness and pleasure of its members, but while the accommodations of the house will be largely required for the club it will be kept open as a hotel and the public accommodated to such an extent as may be without inconvenience to club members."[5]

Thus began the new Saranac Club. How would this adventure turn out? Robert Douglass and nineteen others were earnestly committed, but did they comprehend the magnitude of what they had taken on?

II

Looking back, I wonder . . . did Jay and I comprehend all that we had taken on in the same place some seventy-nine years later? I know I didn't. On the rare occasions I stopped to think, I felt overwhelmed, so I just went back to work. Looking back, I can see how alternative our lifestyle was, living in such isolation, dependent on each other for companionship. I had blue jeans and long flowered cotton dresses, bare feet and waist-length hair dried over a vent in the floor—a flower child. Not Jay. He was a Marine. Once a Marine, always a Marine.

We both slaved to realize our dream, once only his, now mine as well. Jay's domain involved assessing walls to be demolished, big machinery crashing into buildings, carting heavy things. I gladly deferred to him there. I took care of inside the buildings: did inventory, packed up dishes and linens, and, when the time came, I helped design kitchens—where the fridge, sink and stove went, and what pots, pans, and dishes would go in them. We didn't have to worry about painting walls since they were covered with vertical wainscoting (thin, grooved wooden strips) stained a light brown/green that went with everything. Sometimes Jay weighed in on what color he liked for kitchen counters. I never weighed in on what size drill bit he should use. Together we decided on furniture and on prints from old Adirondack books for the walls. The zillion other details we figured out as they came up. While Jay didn't talk about it much, I think he understood the magnitude of the situation far better than I. That

Jay and Fran, taken by Joe Harley, 1969.

might explain why he often sat silently, swirls of pipe smoke above his head, looking out the window.

In the middle of our first winter, Jay makes another list, this one of buildings to demolish because of irreparable damage or undesirable location:

2 boathouses on Upper Saranac Lake
1 boathouse on the river
3 houses—Cherry, Cedar and Spruce
1 Rec Hall
1 Laundry room
1/3 of the Main Lodge (including top two floors of
    dormitory where help used to stay)
The power house on the dam

When Jay finishes removing these buildings, we will still have to renovate nine houses, two-thirds of the Main Lodge, the Icehouse, and a small boathouse on the Upper Lake. Enough to keep us busy for a while.

In Spring 1889, members of the new Saranac Club had plenty to keep them busy. After drawing up Articles of Incorporation, Robert recorded a report by Mr. Alford after his second trip to Bartlett's in April. His mission—to complete the transfer of the property from Caroline Bartlett and the lease held by George Fowler to the Saranac Club.

Our Committee left the city on Monday, the 15th inst. [abbreviation for *instante mense*, meaning a date of the current month, in this case, April] and proceeded direct to Glens Falls, to meet Mr. Beman, the attorney from Malone. Mr. Beman failed to arrive at the appointed time, and from the commencement of our trip to its finish, extending over eight days, complications more or less serious were of constant occurrence, and if we were to have a regularly appointed historian to the Club, your Committee could give a good deal of interesting matter to be woven into a romance which would make entertaining reading for leisure hours, but we forbear at this time.[6]

Oh, the power of an understated turn of phrase! Mr. Alford, aka spokesman for the "Fowler Committee," discovered they would have to pay more than the originally agreed upon $12,000. Unfounded rumors spread that Mr. Fowler, the holder of the lease, had died. And the travel conditions—well, Mr. Alford says it best:

After spending the night in Saranac Lake, we had to travel to the Club House at Bartlett's by carriage. There was still ice on the lakes so we were not able to travel by water. It was April. It was warm that day. And as the sun grew stronger, the road, some called it the State or Winter road, was a mess of deep mud and ruts. As I attempt to describe our journey, language fails me. But suffice it to say that it will linger in the memory of both myself and our whole Committee throughout the balance of our lives.[7]

Now this story has my full attention. Even though I know the outcome, I eagerly read on. They made it to Bartlett's, met with Mr. Fowler (still living), and spent three days doing inventory. They made lists of buildings, boats, household furniture, stock of groceries and liquors as well as horses, cows, sheep, pigs, poultry, and barn and farm implements. The total value amounted to about $4,500.

Once Mr. Alford submitted the Fowler Committee report, they called for a final vote. Should they proceed to purchase the property? It's possible the air vibrated with their excitement and commitment. After a unanimous affirmative, on April 16, 1889, the Saranac Club purchased from Caroline Bartlett 267 acres of land plus appurtenances for $15,000. My records of land transfers show that Virgil had bought 100 acres of land in 1872 and willed probably that same 100 acres of land to Caroline. It is unclear how the additional 167 acres were added to the property by the time Caroline sold to the Saranac Club.

> All that tract or parcel of land situate in the north part of the southeast quarter of Township 23, Great Tract 1, Macombs Purchase, Franklin County, New York described as follows, to wit: Beginning at a stake and stones north 2 degrees west 24 rods from a large rock on northerly bank of the outlet to Upper Saranac Lake and 2 rods and ten feet below the State Dam called Norton's dam, running thence north 80 degrees east 150 rods to a stake and stones standing ten rods north of the north bank of said outlet or river as it is sometimes called; thence south ten degrees east 214 rods to a stake and stones on a high hill; thence south 80 degrees west 200 rods north 80 degrees east 50 rods to the place of beginning, containing 267 acres of land.[8]

Our current deed also mentions "Norton's dam." I haven't found a recorded date of when this dam was built, but it was possibly in the 1850s when Christopher Norton was active. An astute businessman, he saw vast potential in the virgin pine, hemlock, fir, and hardwoods in this area and bought 100,000 acres, thus inspiring Alfred Donaldson to dub him "the lumber king."[9] He ignored naysayers reminding him that his several attempts to move lumber down the Saranac River to Plattsburgh, New York, had failed in the past. Norton moved to Plattsburgh in 1856 and, after acquiring his mill in Franklin Falls in 1864, he manufactured between 25 and 30 million board feet of lumber each year and claimed his business as the largest of its kind in the State of New York.

In 1865, "Norton's dam" appeared as part of the sale of a 6,280-acre tract by Gerrit Smith to Thomas A. Tomlinson (spelled Tumlinson in some documents). Gerrit Smith (1797–1874) was a man of great wealth and a social reformer, one of the "Secret Six" to fund John Brown's raid at Harper's Ferry. He sold John Brown a farm in North Elba in 1859 and gave numerous farms of fifty acres to Black colonists so they could vote. The same wording about Norton's dam reappeared in the deed of 100 acres (a section of the 6,280 acres) sold in 1872 to Virgil Bartlett, and then in the 267 acre deed sold by Caroline to the Saranac Club in 1889. I send congratulations across time both to Caroline, finally free from this huge responsibility, and to this intrepid group of businessmen from New York and New Jersey.

III

One cold day in late February 1969, Jay and I are due congratulations ourselves. When I emerge beaming from my physical, he takes the pipe out of his mouth and cocks his head questioningly. I grin at him.

"Well, who knew? I'm already pregnant!"

The baby's birth date is early September. Wow. A baby. Where will we put it? We need a crib. A place to change diapers. Is the cabin big enough? Warm enough? It doesn't occur to me to worry how I will deal with a newborn with no electricity. We'll figure it out.

They tell me I'll feel better after the first three months. I can't look at red meat. I eat cup after cup of cottage cheese for protein. I have no one nearby I can ask for advice until I meet Heidi Allen. Jay and I have joined the Unitarian Universalist Church which gathers once a month when Max Coots travels seventy miles from Canton to preside. During one meeting, across the room I spy a woman about my age, with long hair like mine.

"Hi!" she says. "I'm Heidi. Jay just told me you're expecting. We are too!" She and Rip, Bill and Joan, Ilse and Carl become our first friends, even though we see them only once a month. Heidi and I bond over our growing bellies. I'm going to have a baby!

This doesn't interfere, at least for a while, with my work. One day, with a sigh of relief, I report; "Okay! I'm done with inventory of the family camp—all eleven cabins plus that little one down by the water."

Jay gives me a thumbs up and, with a dry look, says, "Great! There are probably twice that many at the Club. We have to clean out the ones I'm going to take down. Ready to do the inventory?"

I have ended my first trimester and feel better. Still, I sit down.

"Sure. Where should I start?"

I know the houses have had hard use and no maintenance for a long time, but I have no real idea of the upcoming job.

"How about Cedar, the little one right in the middle. It's too close to the others and we want privacy for our guests. It has to go. Besides, it's small so it will be good practice for some of the other buildings I have to demolish. But I do like the name, so we'll change Chestnut to Cedar."

The next day I head up to the Club. Cedar is a cute little cabin, but I agree, it's too close to the others. Cheap faded cotton curtains droop off brass rings. I pull them down, salvage the rings for curtains I will sew for nine lodges. The metal beds and wicker chairs weigh more than I want to lift now. I leave them for Jay, Al, and Chuck to cart out. Chuck looks quietly puzzled about our choices. Why take down a perfectly good building? Why keep old claw-foot tubs and porcelain faucet handles when we could go to Casier's in Saranac Lake and buy modern appliances and stainless steel fixtures? He shakes his head and keeps on working.

This first winter, digging, demolition, and destruction fill Jay's work schedule. Day after day, he comes home with stories about a bulldozer broken down or a huge boulder smack in the way of taking down a wall. Countless trips to the dump. Countless ditches dug for water lines, phone lines, electric lines.

"Okay!" I tell Jay. "I'm done with the Cedar inventory."

Jay, Chuck, and Al move out furniture and salvage maple flooring for who-knows-which building renovation. Jay then climbs on the Model 40 John Deere Crawler (on the property since the 1950s), revs it, and rams into the building. He and Chuck hand load splintered remains onto the also inherited 1955 green Chevrolet long-bed pick-up truck. At the dump, tucked away on a dirt road, Jay unloads by hand and returns multiple times to repeat the whole operation. This project might take a while.

Some days when I'm not listing furniture and bedding from one building or another, I take rare time to weave. I have to plan ahead. My loom sits in the back room off the kitchen. Our "central heating," shooting warm air up through a single vent, doesn't reach this far. To take the chill off, I fire up the tiny Franklin stove a couple of hours before I want to weave. I sit at my loom, south light filtering over my shoulder, comforting clack, clack, clack as I step on the peddles, throw the shuttle, pull the beater toward me. Gradually, the design of a brown and maroon pillow cover takes form.

One winter day, I have a rare visitor. Jennifer, daughter of Bill and Joan whom we know from our Unitarian meetings, wants to learn to weave. And I want to learn more about making bread. I experimented with baking bread in a reflector oven by an open fire on our honeymoon trip to Alaska. Now I have a real oven, and Jennifer can teach me a lot more. We agreed to spend a day together and swap info.

While the loom room warms up, Jennifer teaches me how to mix and knead dough. As it rises, I teach her how to fill a shuttle with wool, what peddles to push to raise which treadles, how to beat not too hard, not too soft, how to get a rhythm going; back and forth, back and forth, press the peddles, throw the shuttle, beat the beater, press, throw, beat, rock, rock, rock. The aroma of rising dough and baking bread fills our nostrils and our souls, and ups the ante of our joy factor for the day. Maybe Caroline felt like this about her brown bread. I am sure it filled the Sportsmen's Home daily with its heady aroma.

By the end of our first winter, I have inventoried every house. Jay has removed all furniture, flooring, and fixtures to store in the barn; demolished two houses; begun the jacking and leveling of all salvageable buildings; and commenced basic interior modifications on the first three we will rent out. We are on a roll.

Saranac Club members were also on a reconstruction roll in 1889. They organized the painting and re-shingling of every building. This included the Sportsmen's Home, enlarged over the course of the Bartlett years to now contain about thirty rooms with accommodations for about fifty guests.[10] Members designated the large sum of $1,700 to pay Mr. J. Callanan of Keeseville, New York, for major construction to improve the water supply, plumbing, and kitchen appliances.[11] In addition, he would build a boathouse and drain the buggy swamp so mosquitoes wouldn't drive them insane that first spring.[12]

Robert Douglass and others who had come to Bartlett's for years no longer needed to fear that their haven in the woods might close. The place had not only survived, it had improved for long-time visitors as well as for new members and guests. With the added bonus of renovated buildings with functioning water closets, members willingly paid $2 per day plus $.75 for breakfast and supper [lunch], $1.00 for dinner. Guests paid $3 per day or $17.50 per week. Because of the long trip to travel here, on average most likely they stayed well over a week.

A high percentage of members relished fishing. They lost no time submitting an order to the Chairman of the New York State Fish Commission for 50,000 brook trout and 19,000 lake trout to stock Round Lake as well as 6,000 brook trout for the river rapids and 50,000 lake trout for Upper Saranac Lake.

Members insisted on their comforts. They purchased books and stationery for use at the Club House and cigars for their post-prandial pleasure. To assure evening entertainment, they rented a piano for the months of June, July, and August. Perhaps Caroline had taken hers to Glens Falls along with her parrot. In an effort to stay in touch with the outside world, they established their own post office and telegraphic communication. Robert Douglass may have promoted this idea. During his weeks or months in the wilds of the North Country, he would have needed to communicate with his Uncle Robert in New York about R. G. Dun & Co.

Refurbished Sportsmen's Home, 1889.

Robert and other members also received daily mail via a swift and stable guide boat rowed by Mr. Sheldon. He stopped first at the Alexander House (renamed the Algonquin in 1890) on Lower Saranac Lake and then rowed fifteen miles across both Lower Saranac and Round Lakes to deliver Club mail.

One other item of Club business that first year concerned the dam, the same dam Jay and I stood on eighty years later during our first tour of the property. Robert recorded, "With regard to our correspondence with Mr. Ayres of July, 1889, please see that the dam, roadway and sluice-way are repaired at a cost not to exceed $150. We are in agreement that the sawmill should not be run for any outsiders and used only when necessary for Club purposes."[13]

During my present day research, I find an old photo of this sawmill. And now that I know it existed in 1889 and most likely well before that, I crave more information. I know just whom to ask.

Clarence Petty, neighbor three miles down the road, friend, and avid Adirondacker, entered the world in 1905. He grew up hiking, fishing, canoeing, and trapping. "Not all people feel they need to have wilderness, but I do," he said. "If things go bad and everything seems to go wrong, the best place to go is right into the remote wilderness, and everything's in balance there."[14] Clarence worked to protect that wilderness his whole life. As a pilot, he instructed student pilots in the Navy during World War II, but after that, he came home and worked forty-two years for the New York State Department of Environmental Conservation. In his seventies, he could snowshoe thirty-five miles. At ninety, he still gave flying lessons and didn't need glasses to file his flight plan.

One day in 2007, two years after his 100th birthday, I ask him about the sawmill. He reminisces with a mind as clear as Adirondack air about the camp his dad built on state land in the 1890s. "One of the first portable mills in this area was put in at Bartlett's. That's where my father got some slabs he used on the camp he built."[15] Clarence spent his first three years in this rustic home.

That sawmill at Bartlett's was the closest of the 4,000 existing in New York in the early 1900s. It served the increasing need for lumber both at the Saranac Club and on neighboring properties such as those owned by the Petty family.

Bartlett's Sawmill, ca. 1850–1900.

The successful summer of 1889 inspired Saranac Club members to take advantage of handy construction material provided by their sawmill and to expand. With full coffers, they planned a huge new building, "Hardscrabble Lodge," also known as the "Combination Cottage." Perhaps a combination of several families stayed in that dwelling. The design included twenty rooms, certainly enough for multiple families.

A sepia picture of this building hangs on my wall in a rustic wood frame. The four chimneys, spacious wrap-around verandas, and twenty rooms hardly fit my image of a "cottage." I see no evidence of a kitchen. Without existing facts, I have to surmise that everyone ate at the Sportsmen's Home, newly dubbed the "Club House." By the spring of 1891, the new Combination Cottage rose majestically on the hill, not far from the little cottage where Virgil's guide, Tom Haley, and his wife Kate had lived with

Combination Cottage, 1891.

their son, Barty. How grand it must have seemed next to the weathered, yet comfortable Club House down the hill. Those fortunate enough to stay on the second floor or in the attic third-floor room could look east down the river to Round Lake and Ampersand Mountain and beyond to the High Peaks range.

The enclave built by Virge and Caroline had grown from seven or eight small, ramshackle, unpainted, "uncertain" looking buildings to a compound including the newly refurbished Sportsmen's Home, guide houses, laundry, woodshed, boathouses, Haley's Cottage, and now the crown of their new enterprise, the Combination Cottage.

They purchased extra fire insurance to protect this major expense. Robert's Minutes spelled it out: "And in the case of damage by fire, the amount of insurance received shall be applied to repairing the same; if it is a total destruction the amount of insurance shall be divided among the owners of the cottage in proportion to their respective ownership."[16]

No wonder they insured themselves against fire. Fireplaces, their main sources of heat, opened directly onto a room and often had no hearth. Kerosene lamps and candles with open flame provided light. The swish of a voluminous dress or twigs breaking loose from a dried arrangement invited disaster.

They purchased fire insurance in early 1891, just in time.

On August 16, 1891, at 9:30 a.m., a raging fire broke out. No telling where or exactly how it started. Flames licking dry old wood roared a victory cry as they destroyed the refurbished Sportsmen's Home, now the Saranac Club House. Attached buildings, the laundry, guide house, storeroom, and a great deal of personal property also succumbed. Only the new Combination Cottage and Haley's Cottage on the hill remained.

Those who didn't frantically fight the fire most likely stood on the shoreline safely across the river and watched their possessions and recent hard work disappear in blazing orange flames. The next day dawned vermilion, birds still sang, the sound of rushing water still filled the air. Wild animals cautiously returned to inspect the ashes. The strong scent of burnt wood permeated the air as they gathered to assess the damage and figure out their next moves.

Over seventy years later, in April 1969, the only fires Jay and I have to contend with are those in our cozy, stone fireplace to help keep our cabin warm. Now that spring approaches, we don't need a fire every evening. The receding snow reveals the first bare ground in five months. We have outlasted winter with no electricity, three feet of snow in three days at Christmas, and I still don't know how to drive a stick shift. I can zip up my jeans, barely, over the lump of my growing baby.

One day, Chuck calls on our party line. He has contracted shingles and won't come back to work for several weeks. A few days later, Al Tyrol tells Jay he doesn't want to work here anymore. Within a few weeks, he and his family vacate the caretaker's house. One day, Jay comes home for lunch. Instead of diving into his grilled cheese sandwich, he sinks into a chair in our tiny living room. The stone fireplace frames his hunched body and his bowed head, so different from his usual erect posture. He still has his work hat on, stained hands, muddy boots. I just swept the room that morning, but I don't care. I sit down too.

"What?" I ask.

He can't talk for a while.

"I don't know." I lean forward to be sure I can hear him.

"I'm not sure I can do it. It's so much. It's too much."

I freeze. Oh God. Jay is the motor on this particular boat. His assurance keeps me afloat, allows me to carry on. If he isn't sure, if he doesn't know, we are dead in the water. Without that assurance, how will we go forward?

The time it takes him to rally seems interminable, but within a day or two Jay stands tall again, and I heave a huge sigh. We know Chuck will return, and Jay can relax now that he doesn't constantly worry about whether Al is doing his job. As if echoing our new optimism, the ice leaves Middle Saranac Lake on April 22 after a winter of fifteen feet of snow.

One morning I walk in the glory of sunrise, the sky streaked with hints of colors to come, a preview. The whole way, I crane my head to the left to take in the glory, the unabashed splendor of the sky. First a gentle sort of pinky red, then what? Not crimson, so trite. Not red. Not pink. There should be a crayon in the Crayola box named "Sunrise." The undulating splash, the sense of being lit from within or beyond, is so pure, elemental, so completely itself, it defies description. It opens my heart, turns up the corners of my mouth. I sense the lake, its openness, freedom, sheer expanse, and unending possibility.

Jay and I look at each other in amazement and say for the millionth time—we have a baby coming in August! Our faces light up, but do I see a note of panic in Jay's eyes? Or in mine when I look in the mirror? We push past these silent feelings and get practical. I will need a car. We trade in the Land Rover for a maroon Ford station wagon—automatic transmission—with plenty of room for a baby carseat. For Jay, we buy a spiffy new green four-wheel-drive Chevy truck to plow our mile-long road and cart firewood and construction supplies.

That's not all. A few weeks later, a smile plays on Jay's face when his new 350 Model John Deere Crawler Loader with a 91 Series backhoe arrives. He informs me "all the boys" name their big machinery after their girls. He promptly dubs his machine the "Frances." Chuck, now healthy and returned to work, runs his hand along the shiny yellow finish and grins at the thought of operating it.

How will we manage all these expenses? So much going out, very little coming in. Jay takes charge of finances. I am only vaguely aware of income sources: we have started selling sand and gravel to local contractors from a pit at the end of our driveway; Jay is working with a forester to design a sustainable logging operation where we will cut and sell only one third of marketable trees per season to allow the forest to regenerate and thrive; and every cent Jay saved from his years working overseas has been well invested. Still, our savings dwindle daily. It gives us incentive to keep the work moving. We want to open as soon as possible.

Despite our ever-decreasing bank account, we make a tough financial decision. Will Rogers Hospital in Saranac Lake, a sanitorium for members of the entertainment industry since the late 1920s, has subleased the Club

Jay on the "Frances," 1969.

for the last four years to accommodate summer interns and their families. Some of the buildings are not habitable with caved-in roofs and buckled hardwood floors. The summer interns have used the others without doing much, if any, maintenance.

Now that we have arrived, we need to revisit this arrangement. As Chuck rams the "Frances" into the next building scheduled for demolition, Jay and Dr. Goldman, director of Will Rogers, confer nearby. Splinters fly everywhere. The two men raise their voices to hear each other and quickly reach an agreement. Will Rogers will find another place for the upcoming season, and we can continue our demolition and salvage operation.

How did the Saranac Club salvage anything after the huge 1891 fire? Still, they did have the new Combination Cottage with twenty rooms to house people. They erected a temporary dining room and kitchen and planned to proceed with the summer.

What pluck! What optimism! Over forty guests remained for the rest of the 1891 season. Mr. Foster, the manager, took charge and organized the guides to erect tents for those who had no place to stay. The gardens, barn, and animals on the other side of the river had survived, they had plenty of fish and meat from expeditions, and they knew how to cook outside.

Robert would have felt vast relief as he wrote, "Our prudence in taking out fire insurance has been rewarded as we will be recompensed for $8,085.84. Considering that our initial purchase for all buildings and 267 acres of property was $15,000, this is a considerable sum."

That original $15,000 in 1889 would be worth over $390,000 in 2015, still a remarkable value for the land and buildings. The insurance payment they received would today be about $200,000. No wonder they immediately planned "to design and erect a new suitable Club House upon the Club premises for the accommodation of members and guests at the earliest practicable time." They also considered a new boathouse, laundry, and accommodations for guides and help. Hedding Fitch, treasurer, worked up the expenditure list:

New Club House	$15,000
Furniture & Fixtures	4,000
New Laundry and accommodations for guides and help	2,500
Moving Haley Cottage	250
New Boat Houses	1,000
Grading	500
Total	$23,250

Even with the insurance money, these ambitious plans required a healthy additional influx of funds. Some members balked at the new levies and resigned. In December 1891, Robert sent out a letter stating if they raised insufficient funds from members, they wouldn't build the new Club House that year, and furthermore, they would have to consider selling the Club property.

Apparently, that worked. By the following summer, they increased membership to twenty-four, including one who would figure in the history of the Club for the next half-century. Schuyler Merritt, age forty, was a lawyer in Stamford, Connecticut, for Yale & Towne Manufacturing Company, and a well-respected banker who would, years hence, serve as a U.S. Representative from Connecticut from 1917 to 1931. He and his wife, Frances, and their two daughters, Louise, thirteen, and Katharine, seven, spent their first Adirondack summer as Club members in a tent platform on the shore of Upper Saranac Lake. Not uncommon in the Adirondacks, these semi-permanent structures became popular at camps in the late nineteenth century. Some were simple with a rough plank floor and canvas walls, others were almost like a cabin and quite elegant with wood stove, oriental rugs, and partial walls of wood.

Energized by the influx of new members and new funds, the Club engaged architects Jardine, Kent and Jardine from New York City to design a grand new Club House and A. S. Wright Manufacturing Company of Lake Placid to build it. Total expense, including repairs to the dam and sawmill, came to about $24,700 (value in 2015 almost $650,000), over threefold their insurance compensation. New members had joined just in time.

In fall 1893, only two years after the huge fire, the new three-story Club House opened. Gabled roofs, a round turret in the front; spacious views east to the river and Round Lake; glistening polished lobby floors and ceilings; a broad piazza wrapping around the front side, promising a cool spot to enjoy a summer's afternoon. Inside, over the long desk hung a deer head and several trophy fish. At least one very likely had Dr. Romeyn's name on it. Oriental rugs graced the floors, a long table offered stationery for guests to write letters, and a wide staircase led to the second floor. Beloved old Bartlett's had faded to a distant memory.

When guests arrived, they settled into their rooms in either the Main Club House or the Combination Cottage. Mr. Merritt and his family stayed at first in their tent platform, but dreamed of building their own house. As guests arrived, they greeted each other and renewed old friendships. They rarely went to town. Days sped by with fishing, canoeing, hiking, and gathering blueberries, all their needs attended to by staff who cooked, cleaned, guided, and brought in provisions.

Saranac Club House, 1893.

Interior of Saranac Club House, 1893.

Their only links with the outside world arrived daily with the mail boat. In 1896, young Herb Clark took over the mail run from Mr. Sheldon. Herb had spent two years as the Club night watchman. Now, each day he climbed into the thirty-two-foot-long Club freight boat and rowed fifteen miles downstream through Round Lake and Lower Saranac Lake to Ampersand Bay. Once he had picked up needed items—food, tools, building supplies, the mail—he rowed back in time for lunch. After this thirty-mile jaunt, in the afternoon he served as a guide to members and guests.

His fame grew as a strong man who could row a great distance. Several times, I have paddled ninety miles in the historic Canoe Classic boat race from Old Forge to Saranac Lake and pulled into the finish line proud, exhausted, and full of blisters after three days, not one. I stand in awe of Herb's record of rowing sixty-five miles in *one* day, twenty-four of them in the enormous freight boat. To add to his charm, he had a great sense of humor and a knack for telling creative versions of North Woods lore.

Thus families came to the Club, settled in for their summer vacation, and reveled in a time when they "entered a world of freedom and informality, of living plants and spaces, of fresh greens and exhilarating blues, of giant, slender pines and delicate pink twinflowers, of deer and mosquitoes, of fishing and guide boats and tramps through the woods."[17] Why would they ever want to go home? But threat of frost and winter winds finally signaled the inevitable end of the season, and these families had to bid farewell to their summer haven.

IV

Unlike the families at the Club in the late 1890s, Jay and I had no such option. We had no other place to go. This was our home.

After our first seemingly unending, snowy winter, in May 1969 I revel in the fresh-green first spring of my new Adirondack life. One day I walk down to the lake, newly released from its ice bondage of the past five months. I test the warmth of the air and don't need to pull a parka over my growing belly. Only three months to go. I head down to the generator to crank it up and wait seventeen minutes while enough water pumps uphill for this day's use. Robins, redpolls, and white-throated sparrows now join my winter companions, the chickadees. The earth feels springy beneath my feet. I rejoice in the lightweight sneakers I have donned in place of the heavy, cumbersome rubber boots with thick felt linings of winter. As I walk, my eyes roam, looking for good things to pick and bring into our cabin to brighten the day.

I can't wait for the baby to come, but right now I long for clumps of daffodils here, there, everywhere. Last fall, by the time we arrived, it was too late to plant any spring bulbs. I want tulips. Now. I want apple trees bearing their sweet pink-white blossoms. I want bushes I have planted, but not new bushes, I want them old and a bit gnarled, familiar, so I know just what will produce a flower or an interesting branch and just when.

I have none of that. I *do* have, though I'm not in a frame of mind to appreciate it, ancient towering pines and sacred hemlocks standing guard over us, over our cabin and the lake. I have mosses and ferns, here for longer than I can imagine. I have the rich scent of earth as my foot kicks up a patch of mud. It loosens an aroma that, if I allowed it, might tell the story of this place, the feet that have trod this path before, the tree that fell just so ninety-five years ago and donated its composted self to rich humus now being stirred up.

I focus on what I can plant, what I can call my own in this new home. I still don't feel it is truly home. I am new here, newer than the tiny maple seedling just peeking out from under its grandmother trunk nearby. I have no childhood history in the place as Jay has. I don't know this area. I don't know what plants will like to grow here, what will withstand a late frost this spring or an early one next fall; what will like sun, what will be perfectly happy in the shade. I crave knowledge that only emerges after years of living. I long for a tree I have planted to be tall enough to give shade to my hot body after an hour in the sun while weeding the garden. I want to sit on the bulging root of that tree. I want to pass a patch of ground and say, *uhh, there are my johnny jump-ups! There is that chionodoxa which somehow emerges each year and presents me with its glorious sky-blue divinity as it dances in the new spring grass.* I will not know for another forty years that from the day I arrived, I have been longing for roots.

I reach the lake, pull on the cord. The roar of the generator shatters the stillness. I want good soil, not this sand I have here—sand that requires a lot of devotion and extra work to make things grow. I want rich soil holding a white birch tree I might plant, holding it as it towers above our little cabin and graces us with branches and dappled shade. I want a fertile garden yielding twelve-foot sunflowers and carrots, corn, beans, and lettuce. I want children running around barefoot and digging, getting soil under their fingernails, smudges on their cheeks. While I think about plants, I really want roots shooting with vigor out the bottoms of my feet and furrowing into this Adirondack soil. On this spring day, I don't have any of that.

My Timex watch tells me seventeen minutes have passed. I turn off the generator. A chickadee calls from a nearby tree. I reach in my pocket for sunflower seeds, hold out my hand. In seconds, the bird lands tentatively on my fingers as he has grown used to doing over the winter, plucks a seed and flies off. A plane drones overhead. I cock my head to listen for the loon's warning call I know will come right after. I spot something on the ground. I can't bend over much with this growing baby. Instead, I crouch as best I can, reach down, pick a just-emerged spring leaf of wintergreen, and chew its essence into my throat.

While I dream of roots, Jay contemplates further destruction. After the tedious dismantling of two buildings by ramming into a building and carting the debris away, he comes up with Demolition Choice #2. Burn the building. Some of the structures targeted for destruction sit too close to others to burn safely, but Jay starts looking at two of the boathouses on Upper Saranac Lake and one on the river. Once he realizes how much more efficient a fire might prove, he invites the Saranac Lake Fire Department to conduct some realistic, somewhat alarming training drills for their men. We assume these professionals know their job, but when bright orange flames shoot through the first roof and a huge section of wall implodes, we step back in awe. Within a matter of days, three buildings are gone. Just gone.

Did I have any awareness back then of the history behind those buildings, of the people? Maybe some, but not really. For both Jay and me, each house represented one more item to check off on the list to shape the place up and open for business. I didn't appreciate then that someone chose that particular spot to put a boathouse. Now, looking back, I mourn the loss of those buildings—tangible evidence that others came before us. This dock felt footsteps of people I will never know, that wall soaked in the sound of stories I will never hear of a boating trip just completed, of the fish that got away. *Whoosh*, three boathouses gone in flames. Back then, the fires and demolition made it possible for us to focus on the nine houses we would keep and finally pay attention to in a constructive way.

It sounds tidy now when I write this in a neat paragraph or two, but despite the speedy demolition conducted by the Saranac Lake Fire Department, weeks, no, months of work remained. I have stacks of scrapbooks to remind me of details dimmed by years. From the beginning, I glued photos on one page after another, jotted notes, and tucked one stuffed scrapbook after another under beds, in the corners of this room and that. Now, over forty years later, I have only a blurred image of what we did when, and who was here, and how did we make it all happen. I reach under the bed, pull out a huge dusty black book, 16 × 24 × 3 inches—"December 1968-January 1975"—and open to a snapshot of a roaring fire bursting through a boathouse roof. It takes me right back.

Boathouse on Upper Saranac Lake, 1970.

Boathouse on Upper Saranac Lake, a different view as it burned, early 1970s.

I don't have scrapbooks to take me back to 1893, but, in addition to Robert's Minutes, the New York State 1893 Annual Forest Commission Report fills in details of the Saranac Club then:

> It may be of interest to the travelers and sportsmen of the Adirondacks to know that there is one club whose elegant and commodious house is open to them and whose grounds are not posted with forbidding trespass signs.
>
> The large and handsome structure, erected by the members of the Saranac Club on the old Bartlett Carry, will compare favorably in all its appointments and comforts with the finest hotels in the Adirondacks. It has a charming situation and the architectural design is bold and pleasing. Best of all, the club members who own it are willing to share a good thing with the public, and its doors are open to the weary tourist or sports-man who may pass that way. The traveler may rest upon its broad and cool piazzas and refresh himself at its inviting table; furthermore, if unobjectionable or properly introduced, he can remain and enjoy all the comforts and privileges of this lovely spot by paying the rates usually paid for superior accommoda-tions. Throughout the woods there is many a tourist sportsman and guide who cannot say enough in praise of the hospitable arrangements of the Saranac Club.[18]

The reference to "unobjectionable or properly introduced" travelers suggests the Saranac Club had a policy of banning people with "pulmonary trouble" (TB) and possibly Jewish people, a deplorable practice of exclusion common at many hotels (often labeled "clubs") on Upper Saranac Lake and other places in the Adirondacks at that time.

In addition, the Forest Commission Report describes the location of that grand Club House built in 1893. I want a better understanding of exactly where it was. I set out to follow the clue: "Situated on a slight elevation . . . about 300 feet west of the hollow where the Bartlett House or old club house stood."

Saranac Club, between 1893–1921.

On a beautiful spring day in 2015, I leave my desk, walk a mile down the road and cross the bridge. The rapids run with full force to celebrate the tiny, just emerging emerald birch leaves. I walk into the field through new spring grass, dew seeping into my sneakers, and stand between the buggy swamp and the river, on the spot of the old Sportsmen's Home.

The field thrums with energy, as if at any moment one of Virge's pet raccoons might sidle up for a handout or perhaps a large rowboat might land on the nearby shore, full of supplies, mail, and new guests. I know of an eagle nest high in the pines behind the swamp. Did eagles nest here in Saranac Club days? Part of me wants to rest in this sun-soaked spot and immerse myself in that past. But reconnaissance black flies have emerged. One has already taken an inquisitive bite. I lurch back to the present and begin to count off—what did the Commission Report say?—300 yards west of this hollow where I now stand. That would be about 300 of my three-foot steps. I stride back across the field: 50, 70, 90 . . . across the dirt Bartlett Carry Road . . . 110 . . . and then climb the mossy hill . . . 140,

150, 200. My steps stir up the scent of sun-warmed dried leaves and pine needles . . . 260 . . . Vociferous birds scope out summer homes in tree tops . . . 290 . . . The shoosh of rapids constantly with me . . . 300. Then, yes, right at the top of the hill—a perfect spot to put the new building. The Commission report referred to a fine view to the east. The pines have grown tall in the past century, so rather than a fine view, giant solid trunks surround me like great green-tufted friends. I have to imagine the vista down the hill. In my mind, I scan along the half mile of curving river, out onto Middle Saranac Lake, and across to the range of mountains beyond. What a lovely spot to spend a summer.

The Forest Commission Report also wrote of another building:

> Almost opposite, and a little east of the new club house, on the "Carry" road, stands a large cottage, built in 1891, by a few of the members as an annex to the old house. This is a substantial building with about twenty rooms conveniently fitted up, affording its occupants most comfortable quarters, with somewhat more privacy than the club house itself. It is known as the "Combination Cottage."

The Combination Cottage! Also no longer here, but everything I have read in the Minutes springs to three-dimensional life. My feet stand right where Robert Douglass once stood. I walk a bit downhill and to the east. Here stands a large sloping boulder, about as long as a Volkswagen Bug, not quite as tall, covered with soil and moss. Surely this massive stone existed in 1891, something they had to reckon with as they decided where to build. I flash on a birch-bark-framed photograph hanging in my office.

It shows a mustachioed man, felt fishing hat perched jauntily, holding a fish. On the back, Farnham Yardley, Jay's grandfather, has written: "Presented by Robert Dun Douglass—a photograph taken in front of the 'Combination Cottage' at the Saranac Club—now Bartlett Carry Club—Date unknown but probably about 1890. Governor Patterson [sic—Robert E. Pattison, Governor of Pennsylvania, 1883–1887 and 1891–1895] of Pennsylvania is holding the fish." Directly behind him in the photo stands the same rock and behind that, the breezy porch of the Combination

Governor Pattison, Combination Cottage, ca. 1890.

Cottage. Now I know the exact location of that photo. One more piece of the puzzle falls into place.

In the photo, several people pose with the governor; a group of men with soft hats and rough countenances, women in long skirts and puffed sleeves, and a young girl. I would love to engage in conversation. *That's a beautiful fish, Governor! Did you catch it this morning? Where is Mr. Merritt? What's for lunch?*

I can't identify anyone except the governor, but I have to wonder if one of those women was another potential new member of the Club. Mrs. Pauline Agassiz Shaw of Boston, Massachusetts, would likely have visited the Club several times before the April 1893 meeting when members proposed her for membership.

I sit today at my desk and wonder if Pauline had anything to do with Shaw Island on Middle Saranac Lake. I know from my research that Jay's great-grandfather bought the land where I now live from a Pauline Agassiz Shaw. This must be the P.A.S. who owned those three wooden trunks I found when doing my first inventory.

Time for more research. Pauline Agassiz was born in 1841 and came from Switzerland. She was the daughter of Louis Agassiz, the world-famous Swiss naturalist and one of the members of the Philosopher's Camp of 1858. William James Stillman, journalist, author, and critic, had gathered a group of ten doctors, lawyers, scientists, and poets, including Ralph Waldo Emerson, to embark on a summer adventure in the Adirondack wilderness. They enlisted guides and headed out from Lower Saranac, into Round Lake, over Bartlett Carry, into Upper Saranac Lake, over Indian Carry, into the Raquette River, and on to Follensby Pond. Pauline's father had visited this same spot four years after Virgil and Caroline built the Sportsman's Home. Perhaps he stayed there and partook of Mrs. Bartlett's brown bread.

When Pauline was seven, her mother died from tuberculosis. Two years later, in 1850, her father moved to the United States, accepted a position at Harvard College in Cambridge, Massachusetts, and married Elizabeth Cary, a member of the Boston mercantile aristocracy. Her new stepmother's social position meant that influential Bostonians readily accepted Pauline and her brother and sister into their wealthy circles.[19]

In 1860, when nineteen, Pauline married one such affluent Boston merchant, Quincy A. Shaw. This solidified her financial and social standing. While raising five children, she helped establish the first Boston kindergartens. By 1883, thirty-one free kindergartens throughout Boston benefited from her support. She also started a day nursery school, later expanding it to seven more locations around Boston. And, in the 1890s, she became active in women's suffrage. Again, she not only saw a need, she did something about it. Her accomplishments shone in a time when society rarely considered women first-class citizens. I would like to have known her.

Her father had undoubtedly regaled her with stories of his memorable Adirondack trip in 1858. She must have wanted to experience it herself. This woman, at the age of fifty-two, ventured into the Adirondack wilderness, presumably without her husband, who is never mentioned in the Minutes. His business with the Calumet and Hecla Mining Company and his major philanthropic activities very likely consumed most of his time. Given everything else Pauline achieved, it fits that she would have set out on her own. Those three trunks were her suitcases. What did she pack in them? Linens? Dresses? Hats and shoes? Ledgers about kindergartens? For how long did she come? A whole summer? Did she come alone?

She must have reveled in this place where her father, too, had paddled these waters, inhaled the woodsy smells. Thirty years before, he would have heard the same eerie loon call, the same rush of rapids. The connection with her father might have been why she decided not only to become a member of the Saranac Club, but also to purchase a 700-plus acre tract of land.

Looking back, I wonder if Pauline ever experienced anything like my recent morning walk down our road. It had rained during the night, and, as I walked, the woods shook off the last drips, shiny dewlets flying windswept, crystal-filled with sunlight, slashes of a Cezanne brush of sunlight on the wet dirt road. Everything shone. Each leaf, even the metal tractor shed roof. The smells weren't shiny, but so moist, full of deep goodness, life, and growth. The early song of a hermit thrush reverberated from atop the highest pine, an organ in this sacred space. Chickadees added chorus, and a tiny rainstorm fell on an ant in the brush. Newly washed. As if anything was possible. On that morning I had the whole world ahead of me, full of beauty and promise, full of life-giving sunshine and water, full of quivering possibility. I hope Pauline had a walk like that.

She arrived at a crucial time. The health of the Adirondack forest was in jeopardy for several reasons. As early as the 1870s, visitors had begun to arrive in droves due to a frenzy created by a book. In 1869, William H. H. Murray, a minister from Boston, had written *Adventures in the Wilderness; Or, Camp-Life in the Adirondacks* extolling the undiscovered pleasures and restorative properties of the Adirondacks. Only three years later, "Adirondack" Murray, as he came to be known, divulged in a statement in the *New York Times* that he himself rued the changes wrought by his book: "That once imposing forest solitude is now rather more crowded and decidedly gayer, than the Central Park on a summer's Saturday afternoon."[20]

The threat to the forest itself soon surpassed the threat to a sense of solitude and peace. The ever-increasing demand for lumber downstate resulted in escalating destruction of Adirondack forests. As trees fell, erosion, flooding and a threat to the watershed for the state rose. The forest needed allies to fight for its protection. Verplank Colvin proved to be one such ally.

Colvin, born in Albany, New York, in 1847, had fallen in love with the Adirondack mountains before the publication of Murray's book. Rather than becoming a lawyer as his father wished, he committed to exploring the Adirondacks from one end to the other, publicizing threats to the health of the wilderness, and advocating conservation. While he appreciated the aesthetic beauty of the region, he primarily aimed to protect the natural resources, particularly water, "because of their potential commercial value to future generations."[21]

In 1871 in a report to the New York State Museum of Natural History, he stated:

> The Adirondack wilderness contains the springs which are the sources of our principal rivers, and the feeders of our canals. Each summer the water supply for these rivers and canals is lessened, and commerce has suffered . . . [.] The immediate cause has been the chopping and burning off of vast tracts of forest in the wilderness . . . [.] The interests of commerce and navigation demand that these forests should be preserved, and for posterity should be set aside, this Adirondack Region, as a park for New York.[22]

His focused advocacy along with that of many others contributed to eventual recognition of the threat to the watershed due to wholesale lumbering. In 1872, after ascending Mt. Marcy, the highest New York State peak at 5,344 feet, Colvin launched a state survey of the Adirondack wilderness that lasted almost three decades. In the same year, New York named a State Park Commission to research the possibility of creating a public park to protect the watershed. In 1883, the New York legislature voted to withdraw from further sale all state-owned lands in the Adirondacks. Then, in 1885, the newly enacted Forest Preserve Law declared that state-owned lands in the Adirondacks would be forever part of the public domain, forever kept as wild forest lands, and overseen by a newly created Forestry Commission.[23] However, logging would still be allowed. The goal was to protect the watershed and also allow for continued timber harvest, thus keeping everyone happy.

Indiscriminate lumbering continued and increased to the point that it represented a serious threat to the continued health of the watershed. New

York State had recognized that their residents needed an abundant supply of water more than they needed timber. While the water issue was the main impetus, a growing awareness of the Adirondacks as a recreational and spiritual retreat also influenced the argument for protection of the forests.

In 1892, the year before Pauline considered becoming a member of the Saranac Club, New York State passed a bill establishing the Adirondack Park, governing just over 550,000 acres of state land in northern New York. However, this law still permitted logging on state land as the legislature was more interested in multiple use than in preservation of the wilderness. Still not enough protection.

At this juncture, in March 1893, Pauline Shaw purchased her 732 acres of land from Smith M. Weed "and others"[24] on what was then Round Lake and the river leading up to Bartlett's.

In the summer of 1894, a New York State Constitutional Convention approved Article VII, Section 7: "The lands of the State, now owned or hereafter acquired, constituting the forest preserve, as now fixed by law, shall be forever kept as wild forest lands. They shall not be leased, sold or exchanged, nor shall the timber thereon be sold, removed or destroyed."[25] Thus New York's Forest Preserve lands came under the state's highest level of protection.

When Pauline purchased her property in 1893, she saved it from the fate of so much other private land: development or irresponsible logging which often led to forest fires. New York State owned almost the entire remaining Round Lake shorefront which, under the new rigorous constitutional provision adopted and approved by New York voters, would thenceforth remain Forever Wild.

After the proposal of Pauline Shaw as a member in April 1893, the Membership Committee concluded they would be adding a fine citizen who, not so incidentally, would add significantly to their coffers. She passed with flying colors. The Club officially welcomed her as the first woman member. I can find no record of her voting on Club matters, but her financial contributions would certainly have been critical in keeping the group afloat.

The members of the Saranac Club must have felt a real sense of accomplishment. They now had twenty-four members, improved accommodations, and ever-increasing interest from people searching for the perfect place to vacation in the woods. Despite the setback of a major fire, they were indeed carrying on the legacy of Caroline and Virgil Bartlett.

As Jay and I dig in during our first year, we always have in the back of our minds honoring the work of Caroline and Virgil. To do that, we must get practical.

"Okay." Jay leans back at his desk, runs fingers through his hair, puffs on his pipe.

"We've got to get some income happening. Here's the plan. First, we'll get the three houses at the west end open for business. Then we can work on the other six when we don't have guests. We'll start on Merritt."

We have figured out that Mr. Merritt built not one, but two houses at the Club during his long membership. We think one had the caved-in roof, beyond repair, a candidate for demolition. The other, targeted for renovation and our biggest building other than the Main Lodge, perches at the far end of the property on the shore of Upper Saranac Lake. This "Merritt" was designed in 1925 and built in 1926. Decades of heavy snows and crumbling foundations have taken their toll.

One day at breakfast, Jay says, "Chuck and I are going to plumb Merritt today."

"You mean put in pipes? Isn't it too soon for that?"

"No, different use of the word. It means testing to see how straight up-and-down the building is. We can't do anything else 'til we figure that out."

They crouch under one outside corner of the house, carefully place a jack, crank it up one inch at a time. When satisfied, they set in a just-the-right-height support post in newly poured cement to reinforce that corner. When that's set, they gradually ease the full weight back down on the new foundation. They repeat this on every corner until the huge building is level.

One day, again at lunch, Jay's shoulders sag.

"What?" I ask, not sure I want to hear the answer.

"This is big," he says in a low voice. "There's more work than I can do with just Chuck. I need help."

Oh no, not again. I hate seeing him look this defeated. I simply cannot help him. He needs heavy lifters, truck drivers, people who know about construction. All I can do is listen.

This time, his resilience kicks in by dinner. The next morning he makes plans to bring in seven men from Garwood and Golden Contractors of Tupper Lake. These stalwart workers remove one stone chimney at Merritt and rebuild another, re-roof the entire house, re-side the exterior walls with board and batten, and apply a traditional looking dark-brown stain. Now things are happening!

V

Rebuilding. Updating. Maintenance. True for Jay and me in the 1970s. And true for the Club some eighty years earlier in the 1890s. Some house or dock or barn or shed always needed attention. These items mattered, and so did something else. Fishing. During long winters in the city, they most likely did not dream about repairs and updating. They would have dreamt of gleaming fish pulled from the lake. From their first year, they had annually submitted an order for thousands of fish to the New York State Fish Commission. In April 1896 alone, they ordered 300,000 brook trout and 100,000 lake trout. In June, they received the lake trout (no brook trout available that year) and planted them in Upper Saranac Lake. Fish might have had a hard time surviving the mercurial weather that year. Just before Thanksgiving of 1896, a major snowstorm and numbing chill hit the area. Residents of the village of Saranac Lake skated on Pontiac Bay. Then, on Thanksgiving Day, the temperature reached 70 degrees.[26]

Henry Van Dyke, who wrote about Virgil Bartlett after his death, frequented first Bartlett's and later the Saranac Club and most likely joined Dr. Romeyn in a perpetual quest for the perfect fishing spot. In 1895, he wrote:

> The charm of Bartlett's for the angler was the stretch of rapid water in front of the house. The Saranac River, breaking from its first resting-place in the Upper Lake, plunged down through a great bed of rocks, making a chain of short falls and pools and rapids, about half a mile in length. Here, in the spring and early summer, the speckled trout—brightest and daintest [sic] of all fish that swim—used to be found in great numbers. As the season advanced, they moved away into the deep water of the lakes. But there were always a few stragglers left, and I

have taken them in the rapids at the very end of August. What could be more delightful than to spend an hour or two, in the early morning or evening of a hot day, in wading this rushing stream, and casting the fly on its clear waters? The wind blows softly down the narrow valley, and the trees nod from the rocks above you. The noise of the falls makes constant music in your ears. The river hurries past you, and yet it is never gone.[27]

Club members may have wished they could spend all their time enjoying the peace of wading into that rushing stream and casting a line into the sparkling waters. Alas, one structure or another always seemed to need repairs, and they had to organize the effort as well as find funds to pay for it. High on the list was the dam. Since it maintained the water level, all Upper Saranac Lake residents regarded it as a valuable resource, but ultimately members of the Club bore the considerable expense of repairs. These costs required numerous injections of funds in addition to regular membership fees. By the end of 1897, Club finances had dwindled to a deficit of $1,179.

Once again, some members could not withstand the continually added levies and had to resign and bid farewell to their summer haven. One was Mr. Alford who had been at the inaugural meeting, the one willing to go on a reconnaissance trip to the wilds of the north. I am sorry he will no longer be a part of this story.

I read these Minutes like a well-loved and often-perused novel. I know the ending, and yet at this point in the story, I think, *Oh no, they might have to close the Club.* They had invested so much time, energy, and money, their families had created traditions and a real life here, something to sustain them during long New Jersey winters. They couldn't lose all this!

If they close, the legacy of Virge and Caroline will die as well. If the Saranac Club members give up, what will happen? The guides will move on, buildings will collapse, persistent grasses will penetrate the floorboards. Fishermen will no longer stride up the hill for luncheon in the shiny-floored Club House nor will laughing women sit on the veranda. Raccoon, porcupine, and deer will have free run of the place. I am frantic over this possibility of losing it all, but it doesn't surprise me. This place has always presented challenges no one can predict.

Smudges cover the next pages of the Minutes, the words just legible. By 1899, only four original members remained; Robert Douglass, his brother Benjamin, Jonathan Broome, and Edwin Cruikshank. Mr. Merritt had also survived the latest exodus. What a relief. They persevered! To repair the dam and sawmill, they took on yet more debt of approximately $1,600 to hire H. N. J. Mansfield of Malone, New York.

In spite of major crucial expenses, these gentlemen did not lose sight of their main goal—to have an enjoyable place to spend the summer. The budget of over $1,400 for fishing attests to that. And even with departing members and financial woes, in 1899 they designated $773 in the budget specifically for a golf course. A golf course?

Jay told me about this golf course not long after we first arrived.

"A golf course?" I cocked my head in disbelief. "In the middle of the woods?"

"Actually," he said, "there's not much golf course about it anymore. It's more a bumpy grassy field, about eight-to-ten acres. But an open field is pretty rare around here. I wonder how we can use it. Something to bring in some income."

We knew the Bartlett Carry Club would eventually bring us revenue, but that opening seemed further off than we cared or dared to think. Meanwhile, in addition to revenue from logging and the sand-and-gravel pit, what else could we do? How about the old golf course, perched on a rolling hill looking south toward the Seward Mountain Range? I remember Jay bending over his ledger to figure out how to make it productive.

Back in the 1890s, I think Schuyler Merritt loved to golf. It's possible, not long after he became a Club member, that he accompanied his family on a blueberry-ing expedition and discovered a hill with an open expanse and good view. Perfect location for a golf course. He might have pointed out to members less than enthusiastic about the idea that a golf course would be a desirable amenity, offering an entertaining diversion for summer visitors. Most likely he delivered the *coup de grace* of his argument with his offer to subsidize its construction.

Fifty-nine golf courses sprang up in the Adirondacks between 1890 and 1932 as a "natural adjunct to the 'improving regime' of physical activities pursued by . . . families, such as hiking, fishing and canoeing."[28] Just three miles to the west of Bartlett Carry, at the southern end of Upper

Saranac Lake, the Swenson family built a nine-hole golf course used by lake residents. These courses were rough compared to modern day. "Some of them were laid out with huge rocks and boulders sitting precariously in the fairways . . . A few of the early courses even had animals grazing . . . The construction . . . was crude and simple to our day, utilizing horses, wheelbarrows and dynamite."[29]

Mr. Merritt succeeded in his quest to build the Saranac Club Golf Links. Maintenance presented quite a challenge, but the "greens" were most likely made of sand with no need for watering or mowing, neither of which was possible. In any case, Mr. Merritt and his fellow Club members must have spent many an idyllic afternoon teeing off and playing those nine holes.

Saranac Club archives include an original score card for this course, undated, slightly yellowed with age with some rusty pricks from some long-lost straight pin. It lists the nine holes by number and by name:

> 1. Start 235 yds 2. Knoll 250 yds 3. Ampersand 350 yds 4. Long Road 295 yds 5. Golf House 341 yds 6. Woodside 169 yds 7. Faraway 420 yds 8. Homestretch 568 yds 9. Finish 150 yds

The Local Rules provide a good image of the course:

> 1. 4th hole. A ball driven from tee into road or beyond, if it falls beyond 4th telegraph pole [this proves they did have telegraph service] from tee, may be dropped anywhere not nearer the hole, without penalty.

> 2. A ball driven into the woods at the right of 7th or 8th tee, is out of bounds.

> In all other respects, rules of U.S.G.A. to govern.

Expenses ranged from $300 to $2,000 annually for maintenance. Golf receipts didn't begin to cover that cost. The Club did receive general revenue from fees charged for transient guests who rented rooms for the night, week, or season; carrying boats between Round Lake and Upper Saranac; and postal and telegraph service. The greatest income came from regular membership dues and constant additional levies. The golf enterprise took a hefty chunk, sometimes over fifty percent of the annual income, but members considered golf a highlight and apparently worth the drain on the annual bottom line. At least for a while.

Saranac Club Golfers, ca. 1907.

Saranac Club Golf Course, ca. 1907.

Dr. Romeyn didn't care about golf. He wanted to fish, and so he did for forty-five years. Sometime in late 1900 or early 1901, he sustained a stroke, causing partial paralysis of his right hand. I can't imagine loving fishing as much as he did and having this happen. No longer could he balance on a rock in the middle of his favorite stream or flick his arm and cast an elegant arc of line. And so, after his first summer of missing the Club in almost a half-century, in early January 1902, he took his own life. Years later, Alfred Donaldson paid homage to this iconic figure:

> Dr. J. R. Romeyn was a well-known physician of Keeseville, whose wider fame, however, came to him through fly and rod, and the unique record of having whipped the same rapids for forty-five consecutive years! He made his first trip to "Bartlett's" as a young man in 1855. He made his last, as an old man in 1900.
>
> Every spring in the interim, as regularly as the buds came out upon the trees, Dr. Romeyn came out of Keeseville and wended his way to "Bartlett's" . . . The last years of his pilgrimage were filled with the keen sadness of change, but the routine of a lifetime held dominion over him . . . His recurrent presence became the one thing changeless in the midst of change. He became a last and lonely link with the past—the avatar of "Bartlett's"—perpetuating in his tall and gaunt but kindly person the half-forgotten memories and associations of its heyday.
>
> There is no more lovable or pathetic figure in Adirondack story than Romeyn of Keeseville, for a lifetime casting his fly in the Bartlett rapids—outliving not only the friends on the bank, but the run of trout in the waters. At last, in the spring of 1901, he came no more, and early in the following year he died. Men said he did not come because he died; but we who knew the lonely fisherman will always think he died because he could not come.[30]

Today, those same rapids rush by overhanging leafy branches, lush ferns carpeting giant boulders. Sunlit water crashes from rock to rock on its exuberant voyage downstream. While I never knew Dr. Romeyn, I think of him standing in his favorite pool, rod poised to flash his line into the perfect eddy. Sparkling fish still swim there, sun glinting on wet gills.

With each glimmer, Dr. Romeyn returns. *I have not left this place, I will always be here.*

VI

During our first year, Jay and I have no time to fish. I page through our scrapbooks to remind myself of the extent of our To Do list. Two-dimensional photos glued on flat pages manage to spark rich memories of actual events and give me a hint of the aches and joys those times etched into my being.

Snap: Jay returns from a day of staining, the hood of his jacket and his face, arms, and hands covered with dried dark-brown dribbles after hours of standing on a ladder and reaching up under the eaves to apply stain. I grab the camera.

"Smile!"

He manages to straighten his tired body, gives me a lopsided grin—click! For a casual observer, the photo may give an inkling of the hours he stood on the ladder, the cold seeping into his boots, his neck screaming from leaning back and looking up. For me, this photo shows a triumphant warrior returning home.

Snap: Jay on the roof of a building shoveling three feet of snow from the latest three-day storm.

Snap: Chuck on the bulldozer digging yet another ditch.

Snap: Jay rowing me in a guide boat, my long hair tied back, my round belly proclaiming the coming baby. Baby? Yes, we have other things besides the Bartlett Carry Club to take up our attention. That photo catapults me back to one particular day.

Late August 1969. I stand in my first garden ever, hands on my back, my belly round and full. I planted this eleven-by-eleven foot plot two months ago and now congratulate myself on a two-foot-long zucchini threatening to crush the lettuce and carrots. My innocence and ignorance about deer have kept me blissful this summer. Perhaps they decided to give the new kids on the block a honeymoon period. I gaze with awe at this giant zucchini started with a seed I planted. *Wow!* I really am a gardener! *Ouch!* A new movement in my belly morphs to pain. I lean over as much as I can to relieve it, then make my way to our cabin. Thankfully, Jay meets me at the door.

Jay home from staining, early 1970s.

Jay shoveling snow at Maple, early 1970s.

Fran and Jay in guide boat on Middle Saranac Lake, 1969.

"I think maybe we should call the doctor." We supposedly still have two weeks before the due date.

The doc informs me: "You need to get to the hospital now!" She admits me to the Lake Placid hospital twenty-five miles away. Four bewildering hours later, I give birth to a healthy 8 lb. 2 oz, twenty-one-inch-long baby girl. A girl! Magical information we don't know until her birth. She has long fingers, just like her mom and dad. Tiny perfection. Now what? How will we know how to be parents?

From that day forward, we enter a parental guessing game, a constant hoping-we-are-doing-the-right-thing. We name her Gwyn and bring her home to our little cabin where we tuck her into an antique wooden cradle, a present from good friends. Part of me inside flutters with joy. Part of me shakes with terror. I don't have a clue how to be a mom. Jay nestles his new daughter in his arms, looks down in wonder. I can tell he is proud, but not in his element. He can understand and take care of a bulldozer far more easily than this fragile being.

I have no one nearby to ask for help. Just Jay and me, and every day he climbs in his truck and takes off, still trying to get three houses ready to open before next spring. I fully immerse myself in my new role: Mom.

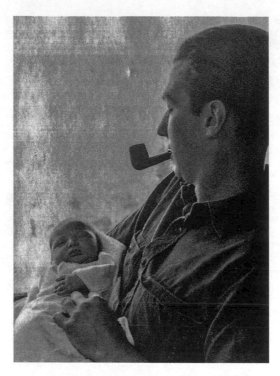

Jay holding Gwyn, 1969.

In our domestic evening scene, after dinner, Jay stretches his legs in front of the fire and tells me about his day's work and upcoming plans. *Thank god the baby is sleeping.* I try to listen as I work on the sweater I have been knitting for months. Knit two, purl two. Jay is explaining about how to level a building. Knit one—*what will we have for dinner tomorrow?* Start a new row. *Did Jay just ask me a question? Oh god please don't let the baby wake up!* The next day, I have a hard time remembering details of what we talked about.

I do remember the conversation about electricity. One night, during dinner, he says, "We can't run these houses on DC electricity from the dam. It's just not going to be enough power." I nod as I jot down how many ounces Gwyn took in at her last feeding. He takes a bite of beef stew, his forehead furrowed.

"I have to get in touch with Niagara Mohawk."

In the early 1900s, everyone wanted electricity. The fashionable Prospect House on Blue Mountain Lake already boasted being first in the world to have electric lights in every room. Wanting to keep up with the times, summer residents on Upper Saranac Lake discussed creating an electric plant at the dam. The threat of fire constantly loomed. With electricity, they would no longer fear the dire results of a kerosene lamp too close to a dried arrangement, and wouldn't it be lovely to no longer fill lamps or wash smoky glass chimneys?

The Club considered it worth investigating and retained an engineer. His report stated that water ran at only seventy-five horsepower over the dam, possibly enough for use at the Club, but too little to supply other camps on the lake. Not to be deterred, Robert Douglass and Schuyler Merritt formed an Electrical Committee. In February 1901, they presented a plan from the Tucker Electrical Construction Company proposing about four hundred lights in the Club House and outlying buildings as well as power for electric launches at the private dock on Upper Saranac Lake at a cost of $5,522.

Bravo Robert and Schuyler! How forward thinking. They could join the Prospect House on the surge toward the future. But no. The majority of Club members agreed to expend large amounts for care of a golf course, but not for this newfangled electricity. Jonathan Broome, Edwin Cruikshank, and Henry Tuck voted to leave the report on the table. It would not be until 1906 that they would accept the idea of this modern convenience, and water over the dam would provide enough DC power to light every house at the Club.

Fortunately, some seventy years later Jay and I don't need approval from anyone to move forward with the daunting project of replacing the existing DC electricity off the dam. The stronger AC electricity will make our work a lot easier. Jay begins negotiations with Niagara Mohawk and considers how to remove the power house.

"We don't need it anymore." Jay's mouth thins, the way it does when he really concentrates on something not yet resolved. "And it's an eyesore. Trouble is how to get near enough with the bulldozer to demolish it."

He narrows his eyes. "Ha! Time for the fire department to have another practice drill."

First, Jay salvages the antique generating system and sells it to the Electrical Historical Foundation in Norwalk, Connecticut. Then, one evening, firemen arrive with their paraphernalia. We sit with friends, Andrea and David from New York City, as we bask in the heat and pink dusky glow of a gigantic bonfire. Loud snapping flames shoot high above the power house roof. We just wish we had brought marshmallows.

To bring in AC power, Niagara Mohawk has to run a submerged cable under Upper Saranac Lake for a mile, from the western shore to the Club. Once ashore, we will bury the wires so they don't interrupt the rustic feel we want. Can we do this? It's an expensive proposition, but essential to our vision of this place. Jay spends a lot of time on the calculator. His savings from years working overseas are the only reason we don't

Power house on fire.

give up on the spot. We bite the bullet. Jay gives Niagara Mohawk the go-ahead.

Late summer, a huge barge travels slowly across Upper Saranac Lake, exuding electric cable like a giant spider releasing silk for her daily web.

Meanwhile, Chuck has spent weeks on the backhoe digging three-foot ditches. It sounds straightforward, but Jay comes home night after night with stories of encounters with underground boulders the size of small cars and ledges showing no mercy. After the barge arrives at the Club shore, they set another 2,500 feet of cable in Chuck's ditches, fill in with soil, and grade, seed, and mulch the ground. Invisible AC electricity finally feeds every building. The Niagara Mohawk semi-monthly newsletter highlights our efforts with an article entitled "New Electricity Service Aids Resort Restoration."

We plan to eventually bring submerged AC cable down river from the Club another 5,400 feet (another mile!) to provide the first electricity ever

Niagara Mohawk submerging electric cable.

to the family camp on Middle Saranac Lake. That means us! We can't justify the expense yet, but I dream of plugging in the Singer sewing machine my dad bought me in 1967, on which I sewed my wedding dress. It's been sitting in a closet since we arrived. I have a lot of curtains to sew. The job will go a lot faster than with the treadle machine I use now.

One day at lunch, Jay says, "Can you bring Gwyn up to Merritt so I can show you what I want to do? It's Sunday and no workers are there. It's a good time."

Is it? What about her feeding? And her nap? Even though I am as determined as Jay to get at least one lodge open as soon as possible, I can no longer just drop everything and go. Jay focuses almost completely on the next steps toward opening. I focus on Baby Time. When to feed, when to sleep (*both* of us), when to get fresh air.

"Um, sure. Let's just figure out a good time for all of us."

We climb in the truck, Gwyn on my lap, and bounce up the road to the Club, past one building after another still needing work, and down to the far end.

I haven't come up here in a while. It looks different now. Jay and the firemen have burned down and cleaned up two boathouses, opening up a great view of Bartlett Bay on Upper Saranac Lake. He has demolished and carted away Spruce, a boxy building close to Merritt, as well as Cherry, just across the road. Now Merritt stands majestically on flat rocks over water, holding its own at this end of the Club.

"Wow. You've done a lot." I say. "This will be beautiful once it's done."

We go inside. Before Gwyn was born, I spent a lot of time here doing inventory. I love this living room with its cathedral ceiling, huge stone fireplace and picture window framing the serene water and graceful evergreens on the far shore. With all furniture and curtains removed, the bare walls and hardwood floors echo each footstep, each word; a blank canvas, waiting for the artist to go to work.

"Okay," says Jay. "We need a kitchen and dining room because right now, we don't have either, and we do have eight bedrooms and seven bathrooms."

"Yeah," I say as I hold Gwyn carefully while stepping over some boards. "And a lot of tiny closets."

Jay shows me how he wants to tear out walls here and here and here and end up with five bedrooms, five baths, a kitchen, a dining room, and the gorgeous living room. He has the 3D visualization skills and knowledge of crucial supporting walls, so I defer to his judgement.

"And while we're ripping interior walls out, we can install new AC wiring."

"What about these floors?" I ask. They're hardwood, dingy, dark-brown from years of neglect.

"We're going to sand them down and coat them with polyurethane."

"And what care will they need?" I know, once all is done, the responsibility for cleaning and maintaining every house will fall to me.

"Just washing and waxing, that's all."

Hmm. Floors in eight rooms not counting the bathrooms, and Merritt is only the first of nine houses. Can I do this by myself?

Looking back, I'm amazed I ever thought of doing it by myself. There were a gazillion hardwood floors. We preserved as many of them as we could. Jay sanded them to their bright natural-wood color and applied at least four coats of polyurethane. By the time I started taking care of them, I had come to my senses and had at least some help, usually two cleaning ladies who appeared sporadically.

For years, I had a recurrent dream. I have to open nine lodges in two days—clean, make beds, lay fires, set the stage for nine arriving families. The cleaning ladies don't show up. One cavernous building after another with tennis-court-size hardwood floors loom in my dream as I grab a bucket of soapy water, get on my hands and knees, wring out a rag, and go to work. Nightmare? Yes. Reality? Not far from the truth.

In addition to AC electricity, we need a new septic system. With Jim Knapp, a plumber from Saranac Lake, Jay designs an ambitious plan. Effluent from all nine houses and the Main Lodge will flow underground downhill to the new leach field at the site of the original Bartlett's Sportsmen's Home. Easy to envision. Making it a reality not as simple. Jay and Chuck take turns on the backhoe and spend two months digging deep, wide ditches linking the houses to the main feed directed downhill. They discover new huge boulders every day.

One day, in the midst of digging along the river, Jay suddenly brings the backhoe to a halt, turns off the motor, stands up in his seat, squints, and stares into the ditch he has just dug. He climbs down, slides through loose dirt into the hole, picks up a black stone, heavy, barely fitting in his palm. One end is rounded and smooth, the other end jagged. Jay spies another near it, same dark color, four inches long, shaped like a shark's tooth. A blunt point at one end and flat, almost knife sharpness at the other. These aren't just any stones; they are tools. Who used these? When? Why are they here? Jay finds six altogether. At the end of this day, he comes home not with a report on ditch digging, but instead with an armful of intriguing stones and a lot of questions.

For a long time after Jay discovered those stones, they sat on our mantelpiece, bookshelves, and window sills along with old foggy-green glass bottles also buried in one ditch or another. It seemed every day Jay brought home a bottle for me to wash, soak in bleach, and scrub. I had two brushes, one for baby bottles, one for the curious bottles encrusted with soil.

But the stones—they were clearly tools. I don't remember that we did any research back then. Today, in the midst of writing this book, I lean across my desk and pick up the black stone I use as a paperweight. It rests heavy in the palm of my hand just as when Jay discovered it. I run my fingers over the cool smoothness, lose myself in light reflecting off dark. Whoever used this had to have been here well before Virgil Bartlett's time. Perhaps Iroquois or Abenaki. History books tell me the river by the Club was part of a well-worn route for both nations. Perhaps they camped regularly as they portaged their canoes from Upper Saranac to Round Lake. They may have buried these heavy stone tools in the soft bank to dig up on their next trip through. Abundant fishing might have enticed them to stop or perhaps the peace of dappled shade gave them respite for a day, or week, or more. They may have come back year after year and known just where to dig up the treasured narrow rock with a point at one end and a flat scraping edge on the other, the one that fit perfectly in a hand to skin an animal or dig up roots. Maybe several clans gathered in this place every year.

I know I need to share these stones. They don't belong to us. One day, I show them to a friend, someone attuned to spirit and the energy of this land. Chris gazes at them a long time. "These are important," he says. "You need to show these to the Faddens." He's right. Ray Fadden created and owns the Six Nations Indian Museum in Onchiota, New York, a mere thirty-minute drive away. This treasure in the Adirondack woods has over 3,000 artifacts with an emphasis on the culture of the Six Nations of the Iroquois Confederacy: Mohawk, Oneida, Onondaga, Cayuga, Seneca, and Tuscarora. Ray's son, John Kahionhes Fadden, accepts with gratitude three of the stones on permanent loan. He tells me they are most likely Mohawk in origin.

After discovering the stones, Jay climbs on the backhoe and digs enough ditches to lay over 1,000 feet of 1½" and 2" plastic pipe to bring water and carry effluents downhill to the new leach field. One day, we pay Hulbert's Tri-Lakes Supply in Saranac Lake a visit.

"We have nine houses to outfit with plumbing." They give us their full attention. We want that old-time charm to make our lodges unique, so we reinstall the old (cleaned up) claw-foot bathtubs, white porcelain sinks, and hot and cold faucet handles.

We do accept the practicality and reliability of modern toilets. Once the plumbing and toilets are in place in Merritt, Jay and I stand in the master barhroom to conduct The Test. We pause, look at each other. He pushes the flush lever. We watch with growing glee as water spirals down and out, through the underground warren of pipes, downhill to the new leach field. Yay! Our first successful flush!

The renovated Bartlett Carry Club lodge in which Jay and I celebrated our modern plumbing was the second one built by Schuyler Merritt, in 1926. His first bungalow was built twenty-four years earlier in 1902 after staying in a tent platform for several years. He was now ready to erect a more substantial dwelling. He engaged William Coulter, a young architect with a growing reputation, who had moved from New York City to Saranac Lake in 1896. Coulter designed the house and witnessed the contract between Mr. Merritt and his builder for $2,800 (about $75,000 in 2015.) Typically, in the early 1900s, the client drew up a legal agreement with the builder, and it was then "witnessed" by the architects, much as someone would witness a wedding.

Kate Babcock also engaged Coulter. Her husband had been an original member of the Club. After he died in 1899, Mrs. Babcock stayed on, and in September 1905, she contracted with Coulter and his new partner, Max Westhoff, to design a bungalow for $1,535. Coulter signed this contract.

It was witnessed by William Distin, a young draftsman in Coulter's office and constructed by Parker and LaBounty.[31]

Coulter came to Saranac Lake as an experienced architect working for the firm, Renwick, Aspinsall and Renwick, and also as a tuberculosis patient hoping to find a cure away from the city in clear mountain air. Tuberculosis had existed for at least five thousand years. Although it began to decline in the late nineteenth century after reaching epidemic proportions in Europe and North America, it still took its toll on many. Another victim of this virulent disease was Dr. Edward Livingston Trudeau. After being diagnosed in 1872, he too had sought the healing air of the Adirondacks. In 1873, half expecting to die, he left his young wife and child in New York to stay at Paul Smith's hotel on Lower St. Regis Lake, twelve miles from Saranac Lake.[32] Instead of dying, he improved. *Why was that?* he must have thought. He surmised; *Fresh air! Rest!* His theory was supported by Dr. Hermann Brehmer from Silesia in Central Europe. He had developed a successful TB treatment with a "rest cure" of fresh air, a regulated life, and exercise.[33]

In 1884, Dr. Trudeau established the Adirondack Cottage Sanitarium, in North America second only to that opened in 1875 in Asheville, North Carolina, by Joseph Gleitsman. Trudeau welcomed recently diagnosed working-class patients with a good prospect for cure who often could not afford to stay in private facilities.[34]

After Coulter arrived in 1896, he designed several buildings for the Sanitarium. TB patients, arriving en masse in Saranac Lake, stayed in the Sanitarium or in local homes transformed into "cure cottages." Here patients could rest on porches with sliding glass windows to maximize their exposure to light and air. Leading doctors and researchers came as well, almost all of them patients themselves. Dr. Trudeau also established a research laboratory to examine the efficacy of his treatment.

It was not until 1944 when Albert Schatz, Elizabeth Bugie, and Selman Waksman reported the isolation of streptomycin, the first antibiotic and first bactericidal agent effective against *M. tuberculosis*. After Dr. Trudeau died in 1915, the Sanitarium name was changed to Trudeau Sanatorium to honor the doctor and to bring the spelling up to modern usage. At this time, the word "sanitarium" (Latin "sanitas" meaning health) was replaced in common parlance by "sanatorium" (Latin "sanare" meaning to heal).[35]

Over the turn of the century and into the early 1900s, Coulter's business and reputation grew. In addition to houses for curing TB patients, he designed a multitude of Adirondack "Great Camps," stunning rustic family compounds for wealthy summer residents. Coulter's flame burned brightly, but briefly. Mr. Merritt and Mrs. Babcock were fortunate to have his artistry and expertise before 1907 when, at the age of forty-two, he succumbed to his disease.

Even as Saranac Lake thrived in its new image as a place of curing and health, the public began to understand the contagious nature of TB. The exclusionary Saranac Club policy to ban those with "pulmonary trouble" may explain why Robert Douglass decided not to build a house for his family on the Club property. If his son Benjamin did have TB, it would make sense to build a summer home in a place that welcomed him, a place conducive to his recovery.

In 1890, Robert had become aware of a parcel of 100 acres of land for sale just west of the Club property. After Club members declined the option of sharing the purchase to protect their boundary, Robert bought the property himself. A little over ten years later, in 1902 when Benjamin was twenty-eight, Robert began construction of a three-story house, complete with seven bedrooms and a third-floor ballroom, designed by an architect with a very different style from Coulter (*New York Times*, July 26, 1903). This resembled more a summer house on the New Jersey shore, with a plethora of windows and wrap around porches to welcome in healing air. Robert named it Blythmere.

Though Robert built outside the Club, he remained committed to it even as its membership began to shift. In 1902, he submitted the name of a good friend who had visited the Club for over ten years, someone who would play a major part in its future and in mine.

3

Rooting and Growing

I

Up to this point, I have been writing of people I can only imagine, people conjured from Robert's elegant, black-inked handwriting and from faded sepia photographs on my office walls. Characters from Bartlett's and the Saranac Club have surrounded me daily. For inspiration, I've gazed at Caroline, well dressed, resting one arm on a velvet-backed chair, or at Governor Pattison, proudly holding a recently caught prize fish. These intriguing pictures have opened doors into the past.

A photograph of Jay's great-grandfather also hangs on the wall. He looks down with discerning eyes, a slight smile behind his bushy handlebar mustache.

While I did not know him any more than I knew Virgil or Caroline, the blood of Alfred Blunt Jenkins runs in the veins of my children and grandchildren. It takes only ten minutes to walk from our house to his grave. We visit it often. Stories of him circulate around our dinner table.

Alfred was born in Boston in 1848, son of Nathaniel and Mary Tucker Jenkins. Nathaniel liked to tinker with things, liked to invent. After one

Alfred Blunt Jenkins.

too many leaky faucets in his home, he had devised a rubber packing to withstand hot water and steam. This led to the Jenkins valve, an invention essential to the facilitation of water flow from that time on, in fixtures from faucets to huge dams. When Nathaniel died in 1872, Alfred and his brother, Charles, took over the Jenkins Valve Co. as partners.

Three years later, Alfred married Adelaide Frances Mullet, and in 1876 their daughter Harriet was born. She would be their only child. Family records show that in 1882 Adelaide died (cause not mentioned) when only thirty-two years old. This must have devastated Alfred and his six-year-old daughter. Not long after, perhaps in an attempt to escape his grief or perhaps for business reasons, Alfred moved with Harriet to Llewellyn Park, New Jersey. This lush, wooded neighborhood near New York City was founded in 1857, allegedly as the country's first planned community.

As it turned out, Robert Dun Douglass lived only a few houses away. Harriet was only a few years younger than Robert's sons. Perhaps the parents bonded over mutual child-rearing concerns as well as discussions about their work and the unique spot where they lived. Alfred eventually remarried. I don't know the date. If he married Annie Grey when Harriet was still a child, Annie would have filled the role of stepmother. In any case, once Alfred and Robert became acquainted, Robert would certainly have regaled his new friend with tales of the Adirondacks and implored him to visit the Saranac Club. Alfred took up Robert's offer around 1890, just a year after the Club had been formed.

It's possible Alfred came without his wife or daughter on that first visit. Perhaps Robert arranged for two Club boats and guides for an outing downriver to Round Lake. Elmer Dockum, one of their best guides, would have held the boat steady for Alfred as he climbed into the stern of a sixteen-foot wooden guide boat. Arlo Flagg, also a highly regarded guide, might well have manned Robert's boat. I imagine an exquisite day; reflection of boats shimmering in glassy water, azure expanse of two-mile-long Round Lake with ever-greened mainland and islands framed by rounded mountains. Not one house or hotel marred the shoreline.

Very likely Alfred became a regular guest at the Club, although he did not commit yet to becoming a member. Thirteen years later in 1903, Alfred had become a man of considerable means after buying his brother's interest in Jenkins Valve. Robert Douglass, with the health of the Saranac Club always foremost in his mind, gave his full support to Alfred to join the Club. In that same year, Pauline Shaw (who had purchased 732 acres on Round Lake in 1893, resigned from the Club in 1898, and then inexplicably renewed her membership in 1902) wanted to sell her land. Alfred jumped at the opportunity. This moment signified the beginning of the direct lineage of Jay's family in the Adirondacks from Alfred Blunt Jenkins in 1903 to the present day. Because Alfred is a part of Jay's and now my family, this history bursts alive for me as if I have opened an enormous, illustrated pop-up book with the major characters in full color.

Members had taken note of Alfred's business acumen, his sociability, his support of organizations and hospitals, including Trudeau's Sanitarium in Saranac Lake. The Club had two looming mortgages as well as impending expenses regarding the Club House roof, the water supply, and other essential repairs. They heartily welcomed him, especially when, as a new member, he lent the Club $3,000.

Alfred's purchase of Pauline's property on August 17, 1903, provided him the opportunity to establish his own family tradition—a place for children, grandchildren, great-grandchildren. The legal transaction mostly likely occurred in a lawyer's office on dry, flat documents. But I like to think Pauline might have met Alfred in the middle of Round Lake and given him a flag or some such symbol representing the magnitude of the moment in the history of this place and in my life. This transfer of property ownership signified the transition from one part of my story to the next—from the end of the Saranac Club (although it stumbles on for another ten years) to the beginning of a whole new era inhabited, ruled, and driven by the Jenkins and eventually the Yardley families.

I savor this moment on the timeline when the lineages intersect and the story becomes more intimately mine. If Alfred had not bought from Pauline, I would not be here today nor writing this story. Thank you, Alfred. Is that why, in your photo, I see a slight smile under your handle-bar mustache? Anyone could write about Virgil and Caroline settling here, about the Saranac Club, about Alfred Jenkins. But no one else has stood on the porch of the cabin Alfred would soon build with Elmer, no one else has listened to the whistle of winter in pines, shivered their way through inventory of the cold, wainscoted bathroom closet, felt the brush of a ghost across a shoulder. I hold that part of this history inside me. I have lived it. Through my present research and weaving past history of this place with my own, I have discovered connections with the past, with people, uncanny parallels I never could have imagined. The one-dimensional knowledge I gained reading about Alfred Jenkins leaps to three-dimensional after I enter his cabin, count the bed sheets he once slept on, and trace my fingers across his filigree cupholder next to the porcelain sink. We share an intimate sense of this place through actual experience of it.

Not long after selling her land, Pauline submitted her final resignation from the Club, but her pioneering, dynamic spirit and stewardship of this land have endured and inspired me.

Once Alfred held the deed, he hired Elmer Dockum, his stalwart, competent guide at the Club. Elmer became Alfred's righthand man and took charge of designing the layout of Alfred's new domain. I wonder, since Alfred had the convenient amenities and sociability of the Saranac Club, why he wanted to build a family compound on Round Lake. Purely for investment? Most other members of the Club were perfectly fine staying within the enclave. Only Robert had built a grand new summer house on the shore just beyond. Perhaps both Alfred and Robert both regarded the Saranac Club as their social club and their separate summer camps as their homes. That seems to be what gentlemen did.

At some point during this time, Harriet, twenty-seven and as yet unmarried, made the acquaintance of Farnham Yardley. We don't know if she met him independently or if Alfred introduced them after he employed Farnham as an insurance agent in the Jenkins Valve Company. In any case, Harriet had spent time at her father's new camp and loved it. Farnham had already become fascinated with the area through a book, *Adirondack Tales,* given to his mother by the author, "Adirondack Murray."[1] William H. H. Murray had ignited a flurry of tourist travel with his earlier book, *Adventures in the Wilderness*, in 1869. Perhaps Farnham and Harriet discovered their mutual love of the Adirondacks through his words: "It is estimated that a thousand lakes, many yet unvisited, lie embedded in this vast forest of pine and hemlock. From the summit of a mountain, two years ago, I counted, as seen by my naked eye, forty-four lakes gleaming amid the depths of the wilderness like gems of purest ray amid the folds of emerald-colored velvet."[2]

Their shared interest might have kindled the nascent friendship. Harriet may have invited him to visit. The second Farnham's feet first felt the softness of pine-needled paths and his nose caught the fresh scent of the river, he was most likely hooked as firmly as a brook trout on the end of Dr. Romeyn's line. He would have found Murray's description perfectly accurate: "The air which you there inhale is such as can be found only in high mountainous regions, pure, rarefied and bracing . . . Many a night have I laid down upon my bed of balsam-boughs and been lulled to sleep by the murmur of waters and the low sighing melody of the pines while the air was laden with the mingled perfume of cedar, of balsam and the water-lily."[3]

In ensuing months, Alfred approved of the budding romance. Farnham Yardley was on his way to joining not only the family, but also the Jenkins Valve business.

II

Jay and I treasure Murray's book handed down from Jay's great-grandmother, but during our second winter, 1969 into 1970, we have no time to enjoy it. Jay is hard at work with Chuck and the industrious contractors as they transform Merritt into a building with a leak-free roof, electric lights, running water, working plumbing, and shiny floors. Meanwhile, I concentrate on my domain—at this moment, curtains. Jay has definite opinions about other work, but he leaves the curtains to me.

Merritt has a lot of windows. So do Maple and Cedar (once Chestnut, now renamed). All three lodges need curtains before we can open. I have heard about Macro's Studio being *the* place to get good fabric. Time to pay a visit. After Gwyn's morning nap, we drive to Tupper Lake. At a small house on a residential street, a narrow path leads to a basement door. The sign reads "Macro's Decorating Studio. Please walk in." A bell tinkles as I open the door. I duck. The ceiling is barely six feet. Rows and rows of colorful, patterned fabric stuff the room. A short, portly woman with frizzy gray hair appears from behind a stack of fabric bolts.

"Can I help you?"

"Oh yes, I think so. I have nine houses I have to sew curtains for."

Mrs. Helen Macro perks up and, from that moment on, she acts as my attentive and helpful guide through the world of fabric choices and measurements. She loves to talk. She beams as she shows me a newspaper article about the elaborate wedding dress complete with hand-sewn pearls she sewed for the wealthy socialite, Mary Lou Whitney. Whitney owns an impressive estate, known as an Adirondack Great Camp, a half-hour down the road.

While the Club has electricity, we still don't. Gwyn has started to crawl, and she loves to stalk bookshelves and the kerosene lamps. At least I don't worry about electrical outlets. While Jay works and Gwyn sleeps, I sew with the Singer treadle machine we found when we arrived. It only operates with a forward chain stitch. If I need to go in reverse, I turn the entire curtain around.

Clickety thump, clickety thump . . . Only the sounds of needle and treadle reverberate in our secluded home. No electricity, no whir of a refrigerator motor, no tiny buzz of an electric light bulb. A mile from the main road, no sound of traffic. When the phone rings, I jump. I do have companions. Every day when Jay comes home for lunch, we have a ritual. Our kitchen window looks out on the roof of the root cellar below. Jay has nailed a small tray to the roof peak, and I put out sunflower seeds. One day, much to our delight, an inquisitive chipmunk appears, stuffs his cheeks

Gwyn Yardley, 1970.

full of seeds, and scampers across the roof, down to the ground, across the small clearing, and into the woods. We decide he is a male, name him Stanley, and buy peanuts in shells for him. He knows a good thing and becomes a regular visitor. He learns to make his way up my arm, stuffing a peanut in each cheek, and leaving with one sticking out his mouth. One day he falls off my arm and onto the floor of the kitchen. I'm not sure who is more surprised. He makes a beeline for the living room, then the bedroom. The cabin is small. He dashes back to the kitchen in no time. Jay has opened the door. Out he goes.

Chickadees visit while Jay or I wait for water to pump up to our storage tank. We stand stock still, holding sunflower seeds in outstretched

Chickadees and Jay, 1970.

hands. One tentative bird alights, then a mate, then a flock. They grow tame, they land on our heads, shoulders, and hands. When friends arrive from New York City and emerge from their car, we welcome them with open arms. A hungry chickadee lands on Jay's hand to snatch a seed, not to greet our friends.

Most of the time, we don't have visitors, and tame chickadees, a chipmunk and a baby don't make great conversationalists. I look forward to going to Macro's. Buying fabric gives me a chance to talk to someone.

I can't sew from morning to evening, and I need exercise. Each day that first winter of Gwyn's life, I wrap her in the peachy-orange blanket my mom knitted, put her on the sled Jay's mother gave us, and walk the half mile down our road and back. The trees accompany me. I learn their names: hemlock, spruce, white pine, fragrant balsam, and tamaracks with delicate feathery needles—the last golden color in fall. Craggy barked maples, papery white birch, smooth beech with yellowed leaves that cling tenaciously through the long winter. Some trees I still haven't identified, maybe one of them black cherry.

I invent stories about the tragic white birch wrapping her thin body around the rough trunk of the ancient pine yearning for the sky. And then there is the shaggy yellow birch, its thin exposed roots spreading out in a hug above a decomposing tree stump.

Over forty-five years later, I still walk past this yellow birch every day. Over the decades, the stump below has completely disintegrated. The tree still stands with those same exposed roots, now as thick as my wrists, clutching the ground.

The tree is dying. It started as a seedling in the rich, nutrient soil of a decaying stump, rose tall and glorious to hold court with neighboring pines and hemlocks, and now is its turn to die. Tenacious roots will no

Birch tree roots, 2015.

longer be able to support the rotting trunk, and the tree will fall. One day a seed will drift down from a nearby maple, birch, or hemlock to lodge in the richness of my birch's decomposing trunk, and it will sprout years later, taking its place in the family of things. Back then, as a new mother living in the wilderness, I wasn't aware of such growth and passing and regrowth. I was consumed daily with how I would survive.

On the days I walk my baby down the road, sometimes I fantasize. *What if . . .* I think, *what if I had someone to talk to, maybe Lisa, my oldest friend . . . We could walk this road and discuss J. D. Salinger and thoughts about the cosmos.* Is this a clue that I am desperate for more companionship? The company of a baby all day and a lost-in-thought husband in the evenings does not fulfill my need for connection.

And First-Time-Mom-dom terrifies me! Who can I find to commiserate with when my baby has a cold and can hardly breathe? My dog-eared copy of Dr. Spock, my best friend of the moment, suggests a humidifier. Great, if you have electricity. I hope for sympathy from my pediatrician.

"What am I supposed to do? We don't have electricity!"

Instead of patting me reassuringly on the back, she says, "Well, we don't either."

"You don't?" I'm not sure if I feel better because I have a compatriot in the No Electricity Club or worse because I'm not getting any oh-you-poor-thing.

"Here's what you can do," she says. "Just fill a pan with water and set it on the floor near your heat source."

Heat source. In our cabin, we have "central heating," a kerosene heater blowing hot air up through a two-by-two-foot floor vent. I place a pan full of water near the vent, and Gwyn eventually survives the sniffles. Somehow I survive too.

Sometimes I need to work at the Club without a baby in tow. Enter Anna Ferree. My doctor, who has twins, gives me her number.

"Hello? Mrs. Ferree? I have a nine-month-old little girl. Could you watch her for a few hours?"

"Why yes, of course!" Music to my ears.

I drive Gwyn into Saranac Lake and follow Mrs. Ferree's directions: park at the bottom of the hill, carry my baby up steep steps. *Is this really a good idea? Can I bear to part with my first born? Will she get good enough care?* I pass a swing—good sign—then a wading pool, three tricycles, a sprinkler, a giant ball, and a sandbox with dump trucks, pails, and a shovel. Maybe this will work out. We arrive at the top of the hill, I knock on the door of the turquoise house. A tiny woman, beaming, opens the door. An intoxicating aroma swirls in the air. Ah, hot cocoa. It smells like home. Something bubbles on the stove. Four small children and a Springer spaniel crowd around and look up, curious to see who their new playmate is. A cat appears from the other room. Gwyn doesn't even notice me leave. Perfect. I have work to do.

Once I have a plan of which curtains will go where, I consider what else Merritt will need. In its new configuration, it has four double bedrooms, one single. I "shop" in the barn where we have stored furniture from every building. I find dark-green stained wooden tables, forty-eight and fifty-two-inch-round, salvaged from the Main Lodge dining room; also several three-by-six-feet rectangular tables. Two of these together will seat at least nine people. We have plenty of dining room chairs. For the living room, I find wicker chairs, end tables, wrought-iron standing lamps. For the bedrooms, wooden bureaus, bedside tables. We didn't keep the old iron beds—too institutional—so I purchase nine box springs, mattresses, and Harvard bed frames which we spruce up with wicker or wooden headboards. Instant rustic, cozy feel.

Okay. Curtains? Check. Furniture? Check. What's left? The kitchen. It needs everything. I have the stock of china salvaged from the family camp, plenty for Merritt and the next two houses to come. But what about the silverware I never found in the safe? And pots and pans more suitable for one family rather than a slew of fifty to a hundred. And glasses and coffee cups. Bert Seiler, restaurant supplier from Albany, comes to my rescue. After I call him, he shows up one day in our driveway in his black Cadillac, tips his felt hat and says "I'm here to help you with kitchen supplies."

I invite him in for tea.

"Actually," I say. "We don't have *a* kitchen, we have nine of them."

Bert sets his teacup down and, just like Mrs. Macro, becomes attentive. "Well, in that case, let's go out to my car. I just happen to have some samples I can show you." He opens his trunk and reveals myriad samples from unbreakable glasses to aluminum pots and pans to Plexiglass cutting boards. And he has silverware! Relief.

"Bert, is that fishing rod a sample too?"

Bert grins.

"Nah. I love to fish. Always have it with me in case there's water nearby." He casts his eye toward the lake. "Mind if I throw a line or two?"

"Sounds like a great way to end our business meeting," I say. And off he goes.

In August 1970, Gwyn turns one. Somehow, in the midst of summer work, I find time to bake a cake with chocolate frosting and plunk celebratory candles in the middle. My sister-in-law has arrived for a rare visit. We prop Gwyn in her high chair and light the candles. Proudly, I parade in with the cake and belt out *Happy Birthday to You!* That morning, I barely had

Gwyn's first birthday, August 26, 1970.

time to braid my hair. By now, one braid has come loose and is flying free. No matter. I set the cake in front of my grown-up girl, say *Make a wish!* and blow out the candles. In less than a second, she plunges both hands into the gooey delight and smears it in her mouth and all over her face.

These festivities don't keep me from the question pecking constantly at the back of my mind. Will we really be able to open for business in a year or two? In addition to Merritt, we want to ready Cedar, with one double and one single bedroom, and Maple, with three double bedrooms and two baths. The men from Garwood and Golden Contractors join Chuck and Jay and get the process down to a rhythm: plumb, chimney work, re-roof, new porch work, re-side and stain exterior walls, rewire, replace plumbing, reconfigure the interior for a kitchen, sand the floors. Then, my turn: sew curtains, choose furniture, throw rugs, lamps, pictures, stock the kitchen. A myriad of jobs happen simultaneously. While the first three buildings progress, Jay and Chuck haul furniture from others, begin jacking and leveling, dig water ditches.

River House after renovation, 1972.

Oh yes, and we begin renovation of the house that will be our new home. Because Al Tyrol has left, we have decided to renovate the caretaker's house downhill and across the river from the Club and move there ourselves. It has electricity! Just as exciting, we will be a tiny bit closer to civilization; still eleven miles from town, but less than a half mile from the Club and on a road other people travel. People I can talk to! At least in the summer. In winter, Carl and Val Hathaway, caretakers for a camp two miles up the road, will be our only neighbors.

We dub our soon-to-be-new abode the River House since it sits by the ever-rushing river running between Middle and Upper Saranac Lakes. Jay rewires for AC electricity, adds insulation, installs new flooring. I sew curtains. In December 1971, we say farewell to our little cabin overlooking Middle Saranac Lake and move one mile down the road to a newly renovated and electrified River House. Two floors! Gwyn walks sturdily now. We put up child gates. In the evenings, rather than adjusting wicks on kerosene lamps, we click a light switch.

At lunchtime, instead of plying Stanley the Chipmunk with peanuts, we gaze at the field across the river where Bartlett's Sportsmen's Home once stood. And now our mailbox is only a few steps from our door. One day when Jay is home for lunch, the mailman delivers a good-sized box addressed to me. "It's from your mother!" When I open it, three beautiful dresses tumble out and a note saying "I hope you like these."

"Oh! I'm going to try them on!" They fit perfectly. I love them. Jay has been silent. Now he raises an eyebrow and says wryly, "Be careful."

Looking back, at that point I had no idea what he was talking about. I was delighted to have new clothes, much nicer than anything I had bought in a long time. Usually if I needed something dressy, I went to Newberry's Department Store in Saranac Lake and scooped up a mid-calf flowy cotton skirt. It took me some years to realize that Jay's mom really wanted to be sure when I visited her, I would have suitable clothing for *her* milieu.

The field across the river that we see from our new kitchen marks the eastern end of the portage known as Bartlett Carry. Canoeists paddle from Middle Saranac Lake up the river, land here and carry their boats up the dirt road, directly by the Bartlett Carry Club houses in the midst of renovation, to Huckleberry Bay on Upper Saranac Lake. Or they do the reverse.

One day the next summer we hear loud voices and the unmistakable clacking of paddles against gunwales. Across the river, we see about ten canoes, full of boisterous boys, pull up to the shore, just about where Virgil would have landed. They tumble out of boats, rummage around, gather backpacks, life vests, paddles, hats, water canteens, you name it, and finally, still calling out to each other with whistles and yells, start their trudge uphill toward Upper Saranac Lake. The path turns into a dirt road taking them right through the center of what we hope will be a peaceful vacation spot for our new guests. With hearty vocal relief and echoing thuds and thumps, they dump heavy boats on the beach we envision our guests using in privacy and quiet. This road is also the only thoroughfare to summer homes past the Club on the eastern shore of Upper Saranac Lake. On busy, dry, mid-summer days, the dust clouds seem never to settle.

"We have to do something," says Jay. He begins negotiations with the New York State Department of Environmental Conservation and offers to build a new half-mile road around the Club (rather than through it) to be used by both vehicles and portaging canoeists. After agreement, Jay designs the road. Larry Mace from Trudeau Sand and Gravel carves it out of a dense pine forest full of enormous boulders and lays a gravel road. It meanders up and down a steep grade we wryly dub "Killer Hill" in honor of trudging canoeists who will traverse it with heavy backpacks and boats on their heads. The job takes two months. Once completed, the reconfigured canoe carry opens for boaters and, in relative peace, we continue our seemingly endless parade of jobs.

We have one more building to renovate before we can open. The substantial three-story Main Lodge looms with its gigantic living room, dining room, kitchen, and floor above the kitchen with bedrooms for the staff—well, the staff that used to work here. Somehow—in the midst of digging pipeline ditches, jacking up buildings, and renovating, designing, and carving out the rerouted canoe carry, installing AC electricity, over-hauling our new house—somehow, Jay manages to oversee the job of dismantling and carting away one-third of this huge building. He and his helpers then re-side and stain the exterior, rewire the interior, and sand and polyurethane the hardwood floors. No wonder he's tired in the evening. We are getting close.

Main Lodge before renovation.

Main Lodge during renovation.

Main Lodge being stained.

Gwyn and I make multiple visits to Mrs. Macro and come home with armloads of fabric. I designate a tiny room in our "new" River House as my sewing room. Piles of colorful material, measuring tapes and window sketches carpet the floor. We have no time to pay attention to the family camp on Middle Saranac Lake. One day we will, but for now, it lies dormant, waiting.

III

If a place could think, could reminisce, would the family camp, during that dormant time hark back to the days when smoke first curled out of its stone chimneys, when bare feet wore a path down to its shore for a daily morning swim? I know Alfred Jenkins and his wife, Annie Grey, and Harriet came in those early years of the twentieth century. Who else? I want to know more about the first days in this spot I call home. I find clues in two wooden crates I haven't gone through in years. A slender book hides near the bottom of one; a guestbook with a worn brown leather cover and "Camp Waubenoo" embossed in gold letters. *Waubenoo?* Jay's family refers to the camp as that. Waubenoo is a character in an Algonquin Indian tale. Jay told me it means "facing east." Perhaps it is the Algonquin word for that. The property does look east across Middle Saranac Lake to the Adirondack High Peaks.

I recognize this kind of book. We had one on my grandmother's island. Ours was dark-green leather embossed with "Eagle Island." Each year, we honored the tradition of signing it: *Name, Dates visited,* and the best part, *Remarks.* Then, what fun to go back and decipher past year scribbles—what my brothers and sisters said and what I said, friends who came to visit—to look through tiny, memory-fogged windows at our rambunctious lives in that magical island getaway.

Inside the Waubenoo guestbook I find a fortune. Over one hundred years ago, 1906, the first signatures of visiting guests; where from, how long they stayed and, when the muse struck, remarks—sometimes simple, sometimes poetic. On the first page, signatures of people from Boston, New York, "Orange"—must be Orange, New Jersey, near where Alfred and Annie lived—and Pennsylvania. They came that year from mid-August to mid-September. No signature by Alfred, Annie, or Harriet. My grandmother never signed our guestbook. Maybe some unwritten rule held that the host didn't sign. After my dad died, Mom was the host, the "grand moobah" as we called her, and she never followed that rule. She signed with a blue felt pen in her clear block writing, mentioned the black Labs accompanying her and dates she opened and closed the island. I wish, as I look at the Waubenoo guestbook, Alfred and Annie had signed it. Most likely they stayed for the whole summer and hosted guests each evening on their cabin porch looking due east over the rosy lake.

Most of the cabins at camp when Jay and I arrived were built by 1906.

- The Guide House, our first home, somewhat winterized. Perhaps Elmer Dockum lived here.

- The main cabin with two bedrooms on the hill overlooking the lake and the dragonfly on the door. Alfred and Annie stayed here.

- Three sleeping cabins for Pammie, Jay, and David, and others who came to visit.

- The dining room and kitchen cabins; after Alfred and family no longer ate at the Club, they needed a place to cook and eat at camp.

- The icehouse to keep food cold.

- The woodshed where Elmer stacked wood in the winter to dry for crackling fires on chilly summer days.

- And the maid's cabin; in those alternate-lifestyle days, the entourage heading north each summer included maids. They needed a place to stay. (I doubt anyone invited them to sign the guestbook.)

Guestbook remarks give me clues into the past. They could just as well describe today: *A place to commune with nature*; and *The most charming place I ever saw*; and one from England—*This visit has added very much to my visit to the Home Land and Camp Waubenoo has to be seen to be fully appreciated.*

They wrote of blazing logs in the stone fireplace, fragrant pines, sparkling lakes, breakfasts of griddle cakes, and always fishing and time outdoors.

More than once, they waxed poetic:

> *Flowers and birds and trees and waters fair;*
> *Mountains, sunshine, bracing air . . .*
> *The bunchberry is red, the closed gentian is blue;*
> *Maple sugar is sweet at Camp Waubenoo.*

No one signed the book in 1907. Harriet, age thirty-one, and Farnham, age thirty-nine, married that year on April 2 in West Orange, New Jersey, and rather than going to camp, the whole family went on a celebratory summer trip abroad. After that, every summer they headed north to the Adirondacks. While they might have visited friends, even eaten a meal, in the grand Saranac Club House upriver, at night they laid their heads to rest in cozy cabins on the shore of Round Lake.

Meanwhile, during this period, how were things going at the Saranac Club? Other establishments on the lake had begun to modernize by installing telephone and telegraph wires and electric plants for light.[4] Club members finally decided they did not want to dawdle in the nineteenth century. In 1906, they took up the tabled recommendations of the 1901 Electric Committee, repaired the dam, and engaged the Adirondack Hardware Company to furnish and install a hydroelectric plant to supply DC electricity to the Saranac Club buildings. The cost amounted to $6,000.

The financial boost from Schuyler Merritt and Alfred Jenkins made a crucial difference, especially since the Club had lost several longstanding members. Dr. Romeyn's death in 1902 had left a gap impossible to fill. Pauline Shaw had resigned. Dr. Henry Tuck, one of the longest serving members and trusted treasurer from 1894 until a few months before his death, died in 1904.

Robert paid Dr. Tuck tribute in the September 9, 1904, minutes: "He was always most genial . . . beloved by us all and most efficient . . . often helping us . . . with his wise counsel. We deeply regret his departure."[5]

To add to the bad news, at the end of 1904, Robert lost his eldest son, Benjamin, only thirty years old, possibly to tuberculosis. Benjamin left behind a young wife and an infant daughter. In his Minutes, Robert never hints at his feelings, but the loss of his son and Club members who had become good friends must have weighed heavily.

Benjamin's death wasn't the end of it. In 1905, Norton Otis, another longstanding member, died, inspiring these words from Robert on April 18, 1905: "Since the beginning, he had been a most worthy and genial comrade, whose companionship was an unending source of happiness and delight."[6]

And then, on Sunday morning, August 9, 1908, Jonathan Broome, president for nineteen years, died suddenly at the Club House. Robert quotes his brother, Benjamin: "The Board of Directors of the Saranac Club . . . do, by this resolution, place on record their sense of sorrow at the loss of a genial, kind and helpful friend, and a member of this Club who was devoted to its interests."[7]

I wish I could talk with Robert. I want to know how Jonathan Broome died, if he had anyone with him. I hope earlier that morning he had cast a fly into the glimmering river.

All these losses. A dark undercurrent coursed even as members struggled valiantly to modernize and maintain a business. 1908 figured as the worst in the Club's history. The treasurer's report stated the income from 105 guests and another 130 passing through the carry did not begin to cover a manager and fifty-nine employees, costing well over $6,000 in salaries. Fifty-nine employees for 105 guests plus members? They did need guides, maids, cooks, gardeners, maintenance men, but with this luxurious ratio of workers to guests, no wonder their finances looked dire. Added to this, in 1907 the New York Stock Exchange fell over fifty percent from its high of the previous year.

How could the original strong spirit of adventure and confidence survive the loss of so many staunch members and the threat of financial ruin? Yet, in early 1909, they made one last-ditch effort to raise money to minimize their indebtedness. They placed a second mortgage on the Club property for $10,000, due to expire January 1, 1913, the same deadline as with an earlier mortgage.

Despite their valiant efforts, the moment came when they had to face the grim fact they could not fulfill the various Club obligations. Their January 1912 meeting differed greatly from the jolly gathering at the Davies Restaurant in Orange, New Jersey, twenty-three years earlier. The few remaining families included Merritt, Douglass, Kingsford, and Jenkins. Farnham Yardley represented his father-in-law, Alfred Jenkins, now sixty-four. Robert, as secretary, issued a letter to all Club members.

January 22, 1912
Office of the Secretary of the Saranac Club
To the Members and Bondholders of the Saranac Club:

We hand you herewith a memo of fire insurance on the Club House properties expiring Feb 8th and Sept 24, 1912, amounting, in all, to $29,600 . . .

    As the Club is without funds, and the managers have no means of paying the premiums becoming due as they expire, this notice is sent to you so that you may take any steps which you deem best, in order to protect your own interests.

R. D. Douglass, Secretary[8]

No matter how many clues signaling the demise of the Club, this letter slams the lid on the coffin. How did Robert feel having to send this letter out? They had failed. I wasn't even a part of this, and it makes my heart sink, my stomach tie in knots.

In Spring of 1913, a notice in the *Tupper Lake Herald* said it all: "The Saranac Club, pioneer of the hunting and fishing clubs of the Adirondacks, is to go under the hammer at a referee's sale on June 12, 1913. The Club, with its 267 acres of land on Bartlett's Carry, will be sold to satisfy the foreclosure of mortgages aggregating $35,895."[9]

Who would want to bid on this property? Only someone extraordinary would have the wherewithal and courage to take on the magnificent Club House and its contents, the Combination Cottage, Haley's Cottage, the barn, boathouse, power house and other outlying buildings, the horses and other animals, the gardens, and the dam.

April 15, 1913—Robert's last Minutes: "In consequence of the absence of the necessary quorum, a regular meeting of the Board of Managers of the Saranac Club, scheduled for this day, at the office of the Secretary, was not held."[10] I turn to the next page. It is blank. I have a moment of shock, feeling indignant and at the same time bereft. What will I do without the elegant writing in these leather-bound, gold-embossed books? Who will be my guide? I have loved this tangible, trustworthy companion. Whenever I stalled in my research, I could open to one of Robert's entries and be re-immersed in the world of the Saranac Club. Without this touchstone, how can I continue writing about the history of this place?

I will miss everyone I have come to know through Robert's writing. I am attached to these stalwart individuals who made a go of it in the northern wilderness. I have pictured them being rowed out to Round Lake for a picnic lunch, whacking a golf ball in the noonday sun, sitting in a wicker chair on an airy porch. Their long dresses, mustaches, and waistcoats have woven their way into my imagination and will not fade.

As I write this, a breeze through the window rocks my office door back and forth with a slow squeak. It feels like Jay's presence. The thought makes me smile. *Let it go*, he says. *Let it go and see what happens next . . .*

Even with Jay in my doorway—*it will all be okay*—I still feel sad. I mourn with members of the Saranac Club the loss of their haven in the woods. No longer would guides take them on the lake, no longer fresh trout, strawberries and cream on the Club House dining table. I lament anew the loss of Dr. Romeyn, such a steadfast presence in this place. And Virge, standing in his blustery way by the shore, about to send his guides downriver to vote as the Bartlett block in the local election. I miss Caroline and Carrie, dressed just so after making sure the Sportsmen's Home is shipshape for the new group of arriving guests. That unmistakable aroma of baking bread permeates my being.

But the story does go on. It changes, of course, but it goes on. Like many times in the history of the Saranac Club, like raspberries springing up on the blackened hillside after a major fire, some members sprang back. They would not see it end. The end of the Saranac Club—yes. But that was just a name. Robert Douglass, Alfred Jenkins, and Schuyler Merritt had each driven a sturdy stake into the soil of this place. They would not say goodbye. Perhaps Jay meant this when he said, *See what happens next . . .* A stronger breeze blows my squeaky office door closed with a definite click.

IV

The dark cloud hanging over the pending closure of the Saranac Club in 1913 contrasts with Jay's and my growing excitement as our huge project moves forward to December 1971. Could three years really have passed since we arrived?

"Okay! It's time to get the word out," says Jay. Finally. Finally, we know we will be ready in six months to open our doors.

"How do we do that?" I say back.

We cook up a brilliant idea.

"Hi Mom! Will you give us the names and addresses on your Christmas card list?" We both approach our parents, and they agree. Surely, we think, as soon as friends hear we have this beautiful place, they will flock to our door. We send our letter out during the '71 Christmas season.

Dear Friends,

When Virgil Bartlett came to the Adirondacks in 1854, he settled by the rapids of the Saranac River between Upper Saranac and Round Lake. With his wife, Caroline, he made history at this canoe carry by providing food and shelter for countless sportsmen and travelers. "Virge" was a congenial host and the meals served by Mrs. Bartlett induced guides to bring their parties there and never hurry them away. Thus the lakes are joined by what will always be known as Bartlett Carry.

Through the years, the Saranac Club and later the Bartlett Carry Club welcomed guests on the hill overlooking the original clearing. We would like to continue this tradition by offering a limited number of lodges for rent during the 1972 summer season.

Situated on 1,000 acres, the Bartlett Carry Club is surrounded by the Adirondack Forest Preserve, yet it is not far from the village of Saranac Lake and its airport. Mount Ampersand, Whiteface and the Stony Creek Range are only some of the nearby mountains. Bartlett Carry itself is a part of the historic eighty-six mile [this letter was written before the advent of the

"90 Miler" canoe and kayak race] Old Forge-Saranac canoe route.

The Bartlett Carry Club has attempted to preserve the atmosphere of the Adirondacks. Our lodges are traditional, comfortable and completely self-sufficient. Each one has a fireplace and from two to five bedrooms. Canoes and fishing boats for guests are conveniently located not far from the lodges on both Upper Saranac and Round Lake. The rates are $2,000 to $4,500 for our season of July 1 through September 30, monthly rates on request.

We hope you and your friends will join us here next summer. But for now, the last of the geese have gone, the deer are moving down from the mountains and the snow has come to stay. It is time to wish you a Merry Christmas and a Happy New Year.

Sincerely, Fran and Jay Yardley
We also enclose our brochure:

(left) Bartlett Carry Club Brochure, 1972; *(right)* Bartlett Carry Club Brochure inside, 1972.

Much to our surprise and chagrin, we don't receive one response. Each day I check the mailbox. Nothing. Merritt, Cedar, and Maple sport new curtains, wood and wicker furniture, throw rugs, claw foot tubs, pictures, and knickknacks. Newly refurbished wood floors shine. Kitchens gleam with new refrigerators, stoves, muffin tins, good quality pots and pans, silverware, and the occasional soufflé dish. And not one reservation.

We resort to placing a display ad in several Ivy League alumni magazines and in *Adirondac*, a magazine for eager hikers and wilderness lovers. The ad has a tasteful pinecone border and etching of a man carrying a canoe—"Adirondack Lodges available by month or season July through September."

A letter in our mailbox! John Roberts, a lawyer for the Atomic Energy Commission in Washington DC, wants to rent Cedar, our smallest lodge, in September. An actual guest. We vacillate from elation to concern. What about July and August? Just before summer, a friend of my parents calls.

Bartlett Carry Club ad, 1972.

"Franny? Hi! This is Jean Knox. We were hoping we could rent Merritt for the month of August. Do you possibly still have room at this late date?"

Um, yes. We may have a lot of vacancies, but we are in business. We invite friends, Bill and Kitty White, and their two children to stay in Maple for a month to make sure everything works. And to make it look like we are open.

One day that summer, I look out our living room window and see one of our guests, nine-year-old Leah White, walking by with her doll baby carriage. Her mother follows not far behind with Sean, age five. Neighbors! Actual neighbors. For a month, I can run outside and say "Hi! Wasn't it warm yesterday? Would you like to play with Gwyn? How are the mosquitoes? I just made some cookies. Would you like one?"

We pause only briefly to relish a delicious feeling of accomplishment. Always more to do, but while guests are at the Club during the summer, we want a peaceful atmosphere devoid of bulldozers ramming into buildings and hammering on a roof. No problem. Plenty of work awaits us at the family camp.

I celebrate the fertile soil around the River House by planting a twenty-five-by-fifty-foot garden with potatoes, beans, peas, carrots, lettuce, four rows of corn, and sunflowers. Jay helps me buy a rototiller, but the garden is all my responsibility and joy. Mid-summer, I go out in the morning and weed until my back is warm and my brow moist with labor. As I feel the first pangs of midday hunger, I move from the not-yet-ready corn over to the peas and pick just enough for our lunch. Then I turn to the potatoes. I know they aren't yet fully harvest-ready, but I have read something and want to try it. I kneel down, certainly in homage to these miracles being born in my garden, but also to dig my hand carefully into the soil under the potato plant and feel around until yes! A one-inch round volunteer for our lunch! After finding just a few more, I take my harvest basket into the welcome shade of the kitchen, wash dirt off the baby potatoes, and set them to steam on the stove. Meanwhile, I shell brilliant green peas and resist the urge to gobble them. At the last minute, I steam peas and potatoes together and add a little butter and cream, salt and pepper. Jay certainly doesn't mind sharing this feast.

Gwyn, age three, asks if she will have a brother or sister sometime. Jay raises one eyebrow at me. I smile. We have been hoping the same thing. No news yet.

At the end of September, John Roberts departs beaming and promises to return. We take about a second to rejoice and return to work at the Club. We want to open three more lodges, each with two bedrooms and a bath, by next summer. Birch needs a kitchen, a new floor in one room, and otherwise the same major overhaul drill as the first three.

In Hemlock, across the path from Birch, Jay applies his exceptional structural visualization skills, takes out one exterior wall, and makes room for a full kitchen. He adds stairs to the back porch, not far from the dam. The rushing rapids sound louder here than at any other lodge. We hope guests will be as mesmerized as we are. Jay reconfigures the interior of Fir to create a kitchen, two bedrooms, bath, and a good-sized living room with a back porch perched above the rapids. Every lodge has a cozy stone fireplace and hearth.

Hemlock during renovation.

We have a Family Plan. Two children, three years apart. Gwyn's arrival in summer 1969 kicked us into gear perfectly. That means Child #2 should arrive about summer 1972. The Plan doesn't unfold that way. Humbling. So much for any illusion I had about how our lives should go. I had hoped we would have at least two children or more, but maybe that won't happen.

Finally, I get up my nerve for a doctor visit. I heave a huge sigh when he looks at me and declares, "Your only problem is you need to relax. Maybe take a nap during the day." I come home to a three-year-old and a house full of toys, books, and toddler energy; floor plans and lists of furniture and dishes for the next three lodges; a sewing machine, straight pins, measuring tapes, scissors, and yards of curtain material for those three houses. I'm not too sure where a nap will fit in.

Looking back, I think about how Caroline and Virgil never had children. Did they want them? They brought Carrie Niles to live with them, and Kate and Martha whom they practically adopted. Kate's son, Barty, frequented their home as well. Perhaps this youthful energy helped to ease the silence, the loneliness of such a wilderness, especially in winter. I just knew I wanted another child. I found time for naps. I can't say enough good things about naps.

"Congratulations! You have a little one on the way!" January 1973. Music to my ears. This baby will arrive in the summer, smack in the middle of our second season of the finally open Bartlett Carry Club. We announce to Gwyn she will have a baby brother or sister. Her face lights up with joy. She pulls out crayons and paper and draws her rendering of this new being about to come into her life—round circle with two lines for arms and two for legs all sticking right out of the head, dots for eyes and a simple smile that says it all. Perfect cover for our birth announcement.

In mid-winter, we send out a letter saying we are taking reservations for next summer. John Roberts immediately replies. This year, he wants to rent Merritt for a month. We must be doing something right! We ditch our naïve thought that the parental Christmas card lists will bring us reservations. Instead, we target Ivy League alumni magazines and publications like *Adirondack Life*, *Natural History*, *Saturday Review*, and *Atlantic*. In addition to Merritt, Maple, and Cedar Lodges, in summer 1973 we will have available Hemlock, Birch, and Fir. For a two-week rental, we charge a range from $480 for Cedar with three beds to $960 for Merritt with nine beds. Is that enough? Too expensive? Will we make it? Will more people really want to come to this kind of place?

Our new ad campaign brings us several more reservations. We still have a lot of openings, but we are heading in the right direction. All six lodges see some activity during the summer. We have families! We have children running down to the beach, climbing a rock, wanting to know where the best blueberries are, playing hide-and-go-seek. I spend time with Gwyn at the Club beach on idyllic sunny afternoons so I can try to handle any problems or questions. I grow attached to our new temporary neighbors. Gwyn makes new friends.

Our baby is due in mid-July. Instead of guests waving goodbye to me as they depart, I leave them as I head off for the hospital. We bid reluctant farewells with a promise to meet again on the beach the following year.

The miracle happens again. The doctor proclaims "She's a keeper!" Indeed she is. We have two girls! We name her Shana and, in a few days, bring her home to meet her eagerly awaiting sister. I had forgotten how exhausted I felt after Gwyn's birth. In the midst of recovering my energy, feedings in the dark-of-night, and utter wonder at this incredible new being, I try not to worry about how I will manage not one, but two kids in the midst of everything else.

To add to the mix, Jay's parents arrive at the end of August for their annual two-week visit. They prefer to stay in a hotel in Lake Placid, but they are on our doorstep every day. I think they need to see for themselves that we are still surviving in what to them is the remote wilderness.

Keeping up with our girls and renovating three more lodges are not short-term or easy jobs. Mrs. Ferree proves once again to be my savior. While Gwyn discovers new friends at nursery school, Shana adopts Mrs. Ferree as a second mom and melds into the menagerie of kids on swing sets and seeking kittens under beds.

In the past four years, four houses at the Club and one-third of the Main Lodge have succumbed to the crush of the bulldozer. In addition, several boathouses and the power house have gone up in crackling flames. Demolition remains a significant part of our lives, but renovation now takes precedence. Only three lodges left to open.

Pine Lodge is next in line. By now, Jay has enough experience to easily design three bedrooms, two bathrooms, and a porch perched like an aerie looking over river rapids. The last two lodges have basements. Jay decides to insulate and offer them for rent year-round. Lake Placid, only twenty-two miles away, will be the site of the 1980 Olympics. Perfect timing.

Or so we think. Once again, we make plans and have no idea what new hurdles await along the way. The chimneys and major renovations in Douglass turn out to need more work than we can finish before the 1974 season. We will have to open with the first six plus Pine Lodge. In

January, I tap out individual letters on our Remington typewriter to each guest who has stayed with us.

Dear Jeanette and Don:

We hope that you have had a very merry Christmas and our best wishes for a happy new year . . . Winter is really here now with the lakes completely frozen and the plow back on the truck; but it won't be long until spring . . . and then again, the welcome summer.

We hope you will be able to be with us again at Bartlett Carry. We are beginning to receive new inquiries about the lodges. If you have any tentative plans about returning, please let us know so that we can make certain you will have the lodge and dates that you wish.

The Yardley family is healthy and happy with Gwyn at school and Shana a bubbly five months. Fran joins me in sending your family warm regards.

Every day, I can't wait for the mail to come. Any new reservations?

Meanwhile, even as we focus on finishing Club renovations, Jay looks forward to the next project—the family camp on Middle Saranac Lake. He narrows his eyes, tries to determine what to do with his great-grandparents' cabin, his own tiny sleeping cabin, and his sister's and David's with their single beds and pot-belly stoves. Also the cozy dining cabin, the boathouse with decorative twig railing, the maid's cabin where Molly and other maids found refuge after a hard day's work. After a lot of thought, Jay makes a decision. "We're going to tear most of it down, including the Guide House."

"We *are?*"

"It's too much to keep them all. Too much work. Too much expense. All this and the Club? It's too much." Jay gets that furrow in his brow and looks off for a minute.

"We'll save things from them—like the dragonfly on the door of my grandparent's cabin. That's important. And we'll keep Windsor, the biggest. At least it's winterized." We have a photo of this one with Jay, as a little boy in shorts, posing on the porch with his father and grandfather.

Al, Jay, and Farnham Yardley on Windsor porch, mid-to-late 1940s.

I remember Jay telling me his grandfather named it Windsor after Windsor Castle because, while it only had three bedrooms and one bath, its size far surpassed the other cabins. It stands grandly on the hilltop, the porch looking directly east across the lake toward the mountains.

Windsor from below.

"Once we get the Club completely open and get electricity down here, we can demolish the smaller cabins, renovate Windsor, and live there. What do you think?"

Back then, what did I think? The Guide House, the first cabin we lived in, the home to which we brought our first baby, would be gone. But over a dozen buildings at the Club begged for our attention. I didn't regret the idea of bidding farewell to these rustic camp buildings full of mildew, bat droppings, and a perpetual chill in the walls. Thirteen cabins meant thirteen roofs, a lot of spruce-bark siding, a lot of chimney repair. Jay seemed so definite about his plan, ready to move on. I could move on with him. "Yup." I said then. "It's too much."

But oh, today, what do I think? Today, many years later, I open a scrapbook to a color shot, taken mid-summer: a spruce-bark-sided building with old stone chimney tucked in the trees, dappled sun playing on the roof green with moss, lake in the background. Caption: "Dining room at camp." The next picture, taken a month or two later, shows the same trees, same lake, but no cabin, no old chimney. Caption: "Dining room gone."

A lurch in my chest—gone, all gone, no way to bring them back. Jay's dad never talked about it, but I'm sure it broke his heart. The gift of this property to his son was perhaps the most generous act of his life.

A jolt of reality wakes me from my nostalgia. If we kept the buildings, I would have cleaned and laid fires in them. Still, the memory haunts me of sunlight splashed on that mossy roof.

dining room at Camp   dining room gone.

Camp dining room before and after demolition.

Guide House before fire.

Guide House in flames.

The Guide House was the next to go. The Guide House! Our first home. Back then, I agreed it should be demolished. When we moved from that little cabin to the River House, I happily said farewell to dark, dingy corners and cold floors, and welcomed a home where I could click light switches on and off, use all the water I wanted, and feel just a little less isolated.

But today I look at a photo of the skeleton of the Guide House engulfed in flames. Forty years later, I have mostly forgotten about wind whistling through cracks, cold feet, dim rainy afternoons. I peer closely—that's the frame of a window, the living room, where Jay looked out as he sat at his desk smoking his pipe and planning the next negotiation with New York State about the dam. And I make out the frame of the kitchen window and the back door collapsing in flames.

I have a sudden flashback to our second summer in that cabin, an early morning, dark and stormy. In the kitchen, as I spooned oatmeal into ten-month-old Gwyn's mouth, four rain-soaked and hypothermic campers appeared at that same back door. I lit a fire, and cooked up a batch of scrambled eggs. Jay got up late, wondering about the noise, and walked into the living room to see his baby on the floor entertaining four smiling, now warm and dry strangers.

Another memory washes in. One day, I looked out the kitchen window to see a black bear with its big hairy front paws propped up on the boulder just behind my tiny garden. Did the bear want some of my zucchini? I would have given it gladly.

I pull myself back to the present, squint my eyes, and lean forward to see the scrapbook photo better. I can barely make out the porch, engulfed in red heat. I can almost feel it. Oh, that porch. One mid-summer afternoon, not long before giving birth to Gwyn, I wandered out in a post-nap stupor, sat in the wicker rocking chair, and breathed in sunny warmth, heady balsam, and sapphire-blue lake. I will never sit on that porch again. No chipmunk will come knocking at our kitchen window for its lunch treat. At the time I just did what had to be done. Now I know I will never again go from room to room at dusk to light the kerosene lamps.

4

One Swipe at a Time

I

When the Saranac Club property went up for auction on June 12, 1913, Henry B. Corey made the only bid—$22,000 for the entire 267 acres, buildings, contents, crumbling dam, and animals. A value today of about $525,000. Who was Henry Corey? And what actually transpired? I have deeds and only partial information from Robert's Minutes, so I surmise the rest. The Club could not pay off two mortgages or bonds held by several members in early 1913. Robert Douglass, his brother, Benjamin, and Alfred Jenkins (represented by Farnham Yardley), all sophisticated, successful businessmen, wanted to keep the property they had committed to for so long. I have to guess, in order to avoid their massive debts, that they devised a foreclosure on the two mortgages and put the property up for auction in June, 1913.

Robert doesn't explain Henry Corey, most likely no relation to Jesse Corey. My research shows a Henry Corey who worked as secretary of the Cary Great Neck Real Estate Co., not far from the Douglass and Yardley homes in New Jersey. Farnham or one of the Douglasses may have employed him to bid on the property in June and, three months later, to sell the same acreage and contents to the Bartlett Carry Realty Co. (BCRCo).[1] This brand new business had been formed by none other than the Douglass/Jenkins/Yardley contingent. Mr. Corey purchased the property for considerably less than the debt owed before the foreclosure. I have to guess he sold it back to the BCRCo for the same amount plus his commission. While everyone took some level of loss, they were able to hang onto their property.

Papers were signed with Henry Corey on September 24, 1913. Robert Douglass, his brother Benjamin, Alfred Jenkins, and Harriet and Farnham Yardley now held legal responsibility for 267 acres of land, a number of substantial buildings including the enormous Club House, and a now manageable debt.

They did not let the infrastructure of their former Club lie idle. Once they took ownership, they renamed the business the Bartlett Inn and began a new era. They signed an agreement to build a new dam with the recently formed Association of Residents of Upper Saranac Lake. These shore owners stood half the expense of the new dam in order to maintain the water level and protect their properties on the upper lake.[2] In 1915, the BCRCo printed a spiffy brochure advertising a nine-hole golf course and a table spread including milk, fresh eggs, fruit, and vegetables from its own garden.

I wonder why their garden wasn't decimated by deer. My relationship with deer who lust after my garden has evolved over the years. For a while after moving to the River House, I had no fence around my new garden. Then one year the deer devoured everything. My *oh the poor deer are just doing their thing* lasted maybe a day. I built an eight-foot wire fence. When the munched remains of lettuce heads and half a tomato with tooth marks continued to greet me in the morning, I upped the ante with an electric fence. No luck. I learned just how high deer were willing to jump for my tasty flowers. I finally added four more feet of fence to the top, slanted outwards, and that (crossed fingers) kept them out for some time. I had begun to forget how delectable homegrown veggies can be.

In 1915, with their own fresh vegetables and opportunities for boating, bathing, tennis, music, and dancing, the new Bartlett Inn was in full swing.

The brochure introduced James Reardon as the new manager.[3] Guests, some new, many returning, could stay in the still elegant Main Club House, the Combination Cottage, or individual "bungalows," the new nomenclature for structures formerly referred to as cabins or cottages.

Between 1914 and 1916, they built at least eight new bungalows, many of them likely designed by William G. Distin, Sr. Distin had been a draftsman for William Coulter in 1901 and may have worked on Mr. Merritt's bungalow in 1902. After going to university and traveling, he returned to Saranac Lake in about 1912 as a rising architect with a distinctive style. The newly emerging Bartlett Inn gave him plenty of business.

During this spurt of activity, a mile downriver the Jenkins and Yardley families led their own busy lives. In the Waubenoo guest-book, Farnham set down black-inked entries of the most notable events.

Bartlett Inn Brochure, 1915.

On October 25, 1911, in West Orange, New Jersey, Harriet gave birth to a baby boy—Alfred Jenkins Yardley, Jay's father. He made his first trip to camp the following year.

No visitors signed the guestbook in 1912 or 1913. Only family came to camp. Perhaps they were preoccupied with their new baby; that and the impending doom of the Saranac Club. Farnham and Harriet must have attended many gloomy meetings as they figured out what to do. A. B.

Jenkins, suffering from heart disease, no longer stood at the helm. I don't know exactly when he became too ill to visit his camp on the shore of Round Lake. I have no doubt that he, like Dr. Romeyn and many others, would have wanted to come always. A sepia picture on my wall shows A. B. sitting, straight-backed and pensive, in the stern of a guide boat. Elmer Dockum, in vest and tie with his hat cocked forward, rows him on a glassy lake, Ampersand Mountain presiding in the distance.

I like to think whenever that picture was taken, A. B. carried the memory home with him, an image to help him hold a steady course until his death on December 29, 1916. His passion for the Adirondacks matched that of Dr. Romeyn. Donaldson's eulogy to Dr. Romeyn holds true for Jay's great-grandfather as well. "Men said he did not come because he died; but we . . . will always think he died because he could not come."[4]

The site of A. B.'s grave symbolizes as much as anything how much he loved this place. In summer, I often take the ten-minute walk from our house to visit it. I wade through thick ferns, head over a knoll. I know I'm close when I enter the gathering of hemlocks, ancestors with old, untold stories and drooping branches, who fold their great-grandmotherly arms around those beneath them. They have witnessed everything, their roots hold this forest together. Sunlight trickles through their branches like holy

Elmer Dockum and A. B. Jenkins, ca. 1916.

A. B. Jenkins's grave.

water, splashes on the great boulder grave. When I come here, I feel I am entering a council of Old Ones. I listen deeply and with respect.

The massive boulder, draped with moss and ferns, presides over the forest. Here lies A. B. Jenkins. Each time I come, I wonder who chose this place, who found this boulder, who placed this circle of smaller rocks, alternating, one pointed, the next round, the next pointed, and so on, circling as if to protect the grave and the soul within. And who chose the poem engraved on the large weather-darkened brass plaque embedded in one side of the boulder?

> *About this boulder are scattered the ashes of Alfred Blunt Jenkins*
> *Son of Nathaniel Jenkins and Mary W. Tucker*
> *born Boston Mass November 25, 1848*
> *Died LLewellyn Park, West Orange, NJ December 29, 1916*
> *"Sweet Mother Earth, this weary child returns*
> *from his short wandering to your dear breast.*
> *Enfold him in your tender arms*
> *Let your green mantle cover him*
> *And give him rest, oh give him rest."*

While I want to mark this moment of Alfred's passing and to say farewell, part of me feels he lives on. I never actually knew him in life, so I don't miss him in the way I miss dear friends who have died. Alfred exists as much for me today as he did a month ago, a year ago. I treasure family stories, pictures, and my own musings about him. He remains with me along with Virgil and Caroline, members of the Saranac Club, many others. I can honor his passing and at the same time continue to enjoy his congenial company.

Alfred made significant donations to libraries, charities, the Saranac Lake General Hospital, and to many friends. He willed to his wife, Annie Grey Jenkins, their house in New Jersey and an annual stipend for the duration of her life. His daughter, Harriet, inherited the bulk of her father's estate, including the property in the Adirondacks valued at about $36,000. Did Annie mind? Did she still want to come to the Adirondacks?

Annie has wafted in and out of this story like an apparition. The Jenkins and Yardley family tree does not officially recognize her, perhaps because she was not Harriet's birth mother. She doesn't appear in photographs taken at camp, but I feel her presence almost viscerally in this place. The other side of the great boulder in the woods holds a smaller brass plaque covered with pine needles and moss.

> *Here have been scattered the ashes of*
> *Annie Grey*
> *Wife of Alfred Blunt Jenkins*
> *Died at LLewellyn Park, West Orange NJ*
> *March 8, 1936*

She died twenty years after A. B. This place was embedded in her soul as much as the plaques proclaiming the lives of A. B. and Annie are embedded in the venerable boulder. I wonder who else in the future might discover this place and see the sun as I have seen it shooting down. Perhaps they will reach out a delicate finger to touch the moss, to be sure such a beautiful thing can possibly be real. If they take the moment to soak in the place, the air, the light, the rustle of leaves, the dead sticks, the two hemlocks growing together by the boulder—if they take all that in, they might ask who is this A. B. Jenkins? Who is Annie Grey? What is their story? Anyone pausing by this boulder might feel, as I do, the unbreakable connection between them despite little evidence of her spending time here after he was gone.

In 1917, the first year in camp without their patriarch, the family most likely felt off balance. My dad held the role of patriarch in our family. When he died, he left a gaping hole. Frozen seconds of wondering who would sit in his porch chair or at the head of the table, who would carve the meat, who would fill gaps in conversation when we fell into a melancholy reverie? When Harriet and Farnham sat down to dinner in the dining cabin, did either of them take A. B.'s seat? What did they talk about? Perhaps they ate silently, glanced at empty places, listened to water lapping at the shore.

Harriet and Farnham now had full responsibility. Elmer Dockum, with the family since 1903, surely grieved the loss of his good friend, but much to their relief, he stayed on. Perhaps he helped Annie find the woodland resting spot for this man he had come to know and admire. As the consummate caretaker, Elmer knew everything about the camp infrastructure—location of water pipes, sewer system workings, chimney maintenance, how to close down and open up. Elmer designed, created, organized, implemented, and managed everything that seemed to magically work during life at camp. With any problem, they turned to him first, and he came up with a solution.

Farnham took over as president of Jenkins Valve Company and still found time to come to camp for two months. Once the snow receded at their New Jersey home, Alfred, now six years old, probably couldn't wait to return to camp to explore the woods, to push his toy sailboat into the smooth waters off the boathouse ramp, and, most of all, to fish. A snapshot from the family scrapbook shows a grinning boy in a sailor middy shirt standing next to two large fish. Caption in the unmistakable hand of Farnham Yardley: *The first fish caught by AJY, Bartlett Carry, 1917.*

Earlier that day, Elmer might have rowed Alfred and his father in the guide boat to the far end of the lake, pierced a minnow with Alfred's hook, thrown it in the still water. I wonder if Alfred asked Elmer, *Did you ever get lost in the woods?* I bet Elmer would have answered, *Naw. Just got turned around a bit is all.*

Once Alfred felt the tug on his line, Elmer would have scooped the fish into the net. Then, later that day, his father aimed the camera at

Alfred Jenkins Yardley and his first fish, 1917.

Alfred, standing next to his catch, a twenty-two-inch pike dangling from a wooden beam overhead. His proud look said it all.

At the end of April, 1974, Jay and I don't have the luxury to fish. Instead, we spend our time juggling who will stay where this coming summer in the seven lodges we have finished renovating.

I ask him, "With this many to get ready by June 1st, when can I start cleaning?"

"Not 'til May 1st. If we turn water on before that, the pipes might freeze."

"Hmm. Seven lodges and the Main Lodge cleaned in one month? I need help."

I line up Ginette and Claudette, French-Canadian sisters from nearby Tupper Lake. On May 2nd, we begin to work eight hours a day. Chuck stocks each porch with firewood. Some days I wish *we* could have a fire. We wear parkas and rubber gloves to combat the inside chill. We're thorough.

Claudette sweeps cobwebs from ceilings and walls, wipes out drawers, cleans bathrooms. I go through every kitchen drawer and cabinet to make sure each dish and glass sparkles. Ginette washes windows inside and out and makes beds. I straighten the curtains since, as the one who sewed them, I am the ultimate critic. We vacuum dust balls and bat droppings. We fluff cushions on wicker chairs and settees. Finally, the three of us get on our hands and knees to wash and wax hardwood floors. For my birthday this year, Jay gives me knee pads and hand lotion. I couldn't ask for better presents.

Since we don't have reservations for the first part of June, I have extra time to plant flowers in boxes on each porch. Local lore says I shouldn't plant anything before the first full moon in June anyway. One day I climb in the green Chevy pickup (I've finally learned to drive stick shift) and go into town to Phil Wolff's greenhouse. I pick up fifty-four red geraniums, thirty vinca vines, browallia, impatiens, and coleus for shady boxes. Phil teaches me how to prepare a flower box, how to plant and tend flowers. I lose all sense of time as I disperse bright reds and trailing greens from lodge to lodge.

Spring sifts a thin layer of dusty yellow pollen onto every window sill and somehow sneaks inside all seven newly cleaned houses and the Main Lodge. Just before first guests arrive, I arm myself with bucket and rags, fling open windows to fresh air, wipe pollen off every surface, and sweep up last-minute bat droppings.

We're ready! And excited. John Roberts returns for his third year, and we have several new families. They arrive at the River House where we greet them and then escort them to their lodges.

One hot late afternoon in July, a couple pulls into our driveway.

"Welcome!" I say. "You must be the Malins. I'm so happy to meet you!" Mr. Malin looks haggard and road-weary. He doesn't remove his sunglasses.

"Well, that's about the slowest trip I've ever taken! Stop and go traffic for four hours."

Oh dear.

"Well, let me take you up to your lodge. Just follow me."

I lead the way to Cedar, perched on the hill above the calm water of Bartlett Bay. I talk cheerily and keep an eye on Mr. Malin. He continues to look grumpy as we enter the spotless and well-equipped kitchen. He strides over to the refrigerator and says, "Well! I just hope this place has some ice!" He yanks the door open to see two trays and a bin full of ice. His face lights up, his shoulders go down. He makes a beeline for a chair on the porch overlooking the quiet bay. Meanwhile his wife inspects the cozy wainscoted living room with wicker chairs and Waverly-print curtains, and bedrooms with chenille bedspreads and extra blankets. I think they will return.

Ed and Louise Bennett come for their first visit. They have answered our ad after seeing it in both *Adirondack Life* magazine and the *Princeton Alumni Weekly*. They rent Birch for a month with their two daughters. Boyfriends visit. One day on the beach, Louise tells me, "You know, Eddie used to camp in the Adirondacks as a boy. He told me I would love it and I do! The peace and quiet, the beauty. Do you know, I saw a raccoon, and yesterday I heard a bittern for the first time. And this air! It's so pure!" I have a feeling they, too, will return, and indeed they do, for over thirty years.

Ed starts a ritual his first year that repeats each time he comes. On their first evening, he strolls downhill from the Club, across the bridge, and to the River House to inspect my garden. I have been swamped getting the Club open. I squirm as Ed examines the quack grass triumphing over my carrots and potatoes. I learn for the future. In the midst of tending guests' needs, managing turnover from one group to the next, and caring for two rambunctious girls, I will need to steal precious minutes to yank resolute weeds. Then I can proudly present marching rows of corn stalks and saluting fringes of feathery carrot tops for his review.

The Bennetts adopt us in a way. This place becomes a fixture in their lives, a month each year blocked out on their calendar. Louise writes me many years later: "Sitting by the stream—rushing water over enormous rocks evokes a deep sense of the ancient. At night, lying in bed, I listen to the rushing current and I feel I am listening to the drone of human voices of generations of people passing through . . . Thanks for special memories."

Barbara Starfield and Tony Holtzman, well-respected doctors in Baltimore, also come in 1974 for the first time. They rent Pine *and* Fir for themselves, their four children, ages five to sixteen, and Barbara's parents. We like that. They are mountain climbers in pursuit of becoming "forty-sixers," those who have climbed all forty-six peaks in the Adirondacks over 4,000 feet. They have sixteen to go. This summer they have their eyes on Donaldson, Seward, and Seymour mountains, all relatively close to us.

Looking back, I realize Jay and I never even considered climbing a rock face or scaling a peak. In summer, we focused on how to get chimneys pointed or what color shingles to put on the next new roof. In winter, we shoveled three feet of snow off said roof, carted another truck load of splintered wood and stone rubble to the dump, or figured out how many yards of fabric to buy for a house with five bedrooms and three bathrooms. We didn't have time to join the ranks of the sporting leisurely. But we did have time to breathe in the utter beauty—sacred, clear-water, high-mountain, rocky, craggy, mud-season, black-fly-and-mosquito, gentle breeze, and pine-scented qualities—of this place that enveloped us. We always took time to notice the water.

I gravitate toward water. I love the sound, the light, the movement, the sense of openness, how when I see it I take a deeper breath. My body responds. Our house practically sits on it. On dead-calm days, the water is so smooth, I think it might be possible for the brush of a swooping eagle's feather to cause a ripple to the outer edges of the lake. In late fall, I know the sparkling water will soon be encased in its icy prison for four or five months. Until then, it vibrates with the sound of seagulls and circling geese and mournful loons, here until the last possible moment. And the whistling squeal of a high-flying eagle ogling a fish just snagged by a black-and-white merganser. No boats on the lake. This is the time for the wild, a time we witness without interfering.

The Holtzmans are one of many families who understand this too. They love the outdoors, mountain summits, day-long canoe trips, exploring the rapids. The kids discover "ancient ruins" under water at the dam. We know these ruins remain from our power house bonfire, but to them they present a delicious mystery. They fish off the bridge, go swimming, wander in the woods. By the end of their stay, they accomplish their mountain-climbing mission and much more and, as they leave, they say "We'll be back!"

They have come back, with expanding families, every year since then. Tony wrote to me: "The beauty of the Club, the friendliness of you and Jay, and the array of other activities are what brought us back."

In the summer of 1974, we have a passel of young kids at the beach; perfect ages to match the one- and five-year-old Yardley contingent. Water wings and plastic pails all around. Young parents to talk to. Community. Kids catch frogs in the marsh by the beach; dig holes in the sand, fill them

Bartlett Carry Club beach and kids.

with water over and over; find great hiding spots behind a huge boulder or up a small tree. Some sit in a circle and tell stories as they sift warm sand through their fingers, afternoon sun stroking their backs.

On Sunday mornings, Jay dons his Captain's hat, revs up the antique mahogany Garwood inboard inherited with the family camp, and ferries guests to the nondenominational Chapel on the Island on Upper Saranac Lake. Guests feel quite grand and make this a favorite ritual.

I figure out ways to be unobtrusively available for anyone with questions or problems. We want to respect the privacy of each family. I only go near the lodges to water flower boxes or bring fresh linen and towels. Each morning I appear at the Main Lodge to sweep or tidy up. In afternoons, I pack up Gwyn and Shana, bathing suits, snacks, and water, and we head for the Club beach. A pod of playmates surrounds my girls. I bask in adult conversation.

Jay at Chapel Island with Garwood, mid-1970s.

One evening when most of the lodges have guests, a knock-down, drag-out, thunder-and-lightning storm strikes. All the houses, including ours, go dark. We hadn't planned for this. Jay and I don raincoats, slosh from one lodge to the next, deliver candles, matches, and flashlights left over from our no-electricity days (we didn't have to worry about power outages then). Our wide-eyed, mostly city-dweller guests heave sighs of relief when they see us emerge out of the drenched darkness, dispensing welcome light and reassurance that electricity will soon come back on. We sound more sure than we actually feel. We make a note to stock every lodge with candles and matches.

Eventually lights go back on. Everyone leaves this year with stories of how they survived the storm. They can't wait to return. Only two years ago, in the mire of digging ditches and sewing curtains, we had no idea if anyone would want to come here or if they would enjoy it. We may still have two lodges to open at the Club and a lot of work at camp, but now we know. We have guests who can't wait to return.

II

In the early 1900s, despite rumblings of war in Europe, guests at the Bartlett Inn and the family at camp on Round Lake enjoyed a few last halcyon days. Then, in June, 1914, with the assassination of the Archduke of Austria, war broke out in Europe. The United States tried to mediate peace to no avail. On April 6, 1917, after Germany sank seven U.S. merchant ships and tried to ally with Mexico, the United States joined Britain, France, and Russia, and declared war on Germany.

From that point on, everyone in the United States focused on the war effort and coped with gas and food rations. To increase the food supply for both civilians and soldiers, over five million gardens sprouted across the United States.[5] Women, students, retirees, and unemployed played a major role as they moved into jobs vacated by departing soldiers. A time of change, a time of goodbyes, young men scooped into the military, families adjusting to the loss of a father, son, husband, brother. We can only estimate that of the over 42,000,000 mobilized around the globe, about 4,300,000 came from the U.S. and over 300,000 of those were either killed, wounded, taken prisoners, or reported missing.

With no reservations at the Bartlett Inn, the doors closed. Amazingly, the family camp buzzed with activity. More signatures appeared in the guestbook in 1917 and 1918 than in any previous year. I have to guess the war affected those who came as much as everyone else in this country. For part of a summer at least, they escaped to this remote spot and snatched precious, idyllic moments; early morning swims, boating expeditions, luncheons with cheese soufflé and iced tea. Thousands of miles away, helmeted, smudge-faced soldiers in trenches squinted at the advancing enemy. The United States was geographically isolated from the war and the Adirondacks more so. Even as battlefields abroad were strewn with the fallen and Mata Hari was executed as a spy, life here went on.

Somehow, in spite of or due to the raging war, progress marched on as inexorably as soldiers in the fields of Germany. People grew accustomed to telephone, telegraph, electricity, and new and improved roads. A decade earlier, only a few knew of "horseless carriages" to take on those roads. In 1905, two brothers, Norman and Howard Scholle, drove their Winton touring car from Williamstown, Massachusetts, to Blue Mountain Lake in the Adirondacks. En route, after the small hamlet of North Creek, they left behind relatively navigable roads, garnered quizzical looks from bystanders, and occasionally had to unload the car and carry their gear.[6]

A little over ten years later, as the global conflict intensified, the local scene changed. Tourists in automobiles now had the option to travel to the Adirondacks on at least some paved roads as well as by steamboat and train. In 1915, Seneca Ray Stoddard, photographer and promoter of the Adirondacks, recognized the growing automobile trend in his new book, *Picturesque Trip Through the Adirondacks in an Automobile*. "It is truly a new Adirondacks. From the early days when travel was undertaken in devious [meaning circuitous] ways by primitive means, it has become a wilderness traversed by magnificent state highways, forming a network as fine—the major portion at least—as the boulevards of our cities."[7]

Robert Bogdan cited the above quote in *Exposing the Wilderness: Early-Twentieth-Century Adirondack Postcard Photographers* and clarified that those "magnificent state highways" took a bit longer to make their way into the challenging Adirondack interior. Bogdan continued, "Although we should take into account Stoddard's tendency to exaggerate, by the early 1920s, automobile travel to many places in the Adirondacks was common."[8]

My friend and neighbor, Clarence Petty, witnessed one of the first cars to show up in this part of the Adirondacks. Clarence was the one whose dad got material from the Saranac Club to build their home in the woods in the early 1900s. In 2007, one-hundred-and-two-year-old Clarence described how he, at age seven (in 1912), and his brother worked as caddies on the Indian Carry golf course, about three miles from the Bartlett Carry golf course. He shook his head and said, "I just can't figure out why in tarnation there would be two nine-hole golf courses so close to each other." The boys earned thirty-five cents an hour. They did that for about five years and eventually decided to start saving money for a car. Here's Clarence telling the story at a talk at the Bartlett Carry Club August 4, 2007:

> That was in 1918 thereabouts. At that time there was no cars
> up here, you know, it was just dirt roads—that's when the

Douglass people had a chauffeur, and we heard that they were bringing a car from New York and were going to bring it up to Douglass Point on the Bartlett Carry road. That's the first car that we saw. We heard that it was coming, so we hid in the woods and watched the thing go down by, and it got stuck in the sand, and the chauffeur was sitting way up high. The rear wheels were driven by a chain outfit. There was brass on the front of it. And he'd get stuck there on the sand, and he'd get out with a shovel and he'd shovel. Well, he got along the place where we were, and we were hiding in the woods watching all this, and about that time, Ernie Woods . . . came along with a team of horses, and the car was stuck in the sand, and they wanted him to unhook the horses and turn the dog-darn thing around so they could go back to Douglass Point because that road was just all sand and they were going out of sight.

Clarence Petty at Bartlett Carry Club, August 2004.

So we come out of the woods when we saw Woods, you know, because we knew him and when he got them turned around—cuz he unhooked the horses, pulled the car out of the sand, got them turned around and they were headed back toward Douglass Point, where they came from—and Woods stood up on the wagon that he had there, and he lit his pipe, and he looked down, and he give an eye, and he said, 'Them things will never amount to anything here.' That was in 1918.[9]

Finally, after drawn-out years of fighting, at 11:00 a.m. on November 11, 1918, Armistice was declared. Negotiations for the terms of peace took a while, but the war was over, and survivors could return home.

The country welcomed its heroes. It also recognized the role of women who, during the war, had taken jobs on the home front formerly reserved for men. Among other things, they fought fires, worked in banks, and ran heavy, precision machinery.

As of August 18, 1920, the Nineteenth Amendment guaranteed American women the right to vote. During the next decade, people turned from the austerity of war to celebration and excess. Girls with short skirts and bobbed hair shocked older women as they puffed on cigarettes and sipped a prohibited drink or two. The words of F. Scott Fitzgerald, Willa Cather, and Ernest Hemingway enriched imaginations. Louis Armstrong and Duke Ellington kept the nation hopping, Charlie Chaplin kept them laughing. The United States, now the richest nation on Earth, used resources to build roads to remote places and designed cars such as Ford's new Model T to drive on them. A frenzied sense of gaiety and escape permeated many lives.

The Adirondacks did not exactly qualify as an exotic new place for frenzied gaiety. However, it did become known as a more and more accessible spot for taking time away for vacations. In 1919, the Bartlett Inn reopened with Mr. Reardon and his wife reclaiming their managerial positions. They sent out a new brochure extolling the virtues.

Bartlett's is surrounded by a beautiful park containing 3,000 acres of lake and woodland. There is trout and bass fishing in the streams and lakes, while the forests contain all game common to preserved Adirondack lands.

The rooms are light and airy and have polished floors and rugs and all the rooms have open fireplaces. There are the post office, long distance telephone and telegraph offices in the hotel. Connected with the hotel are cottages and camps of typical Adirondack architecture and containing modern plumbing and electric lights.

The grand Club House built in 1893 reigned on the hill with its glistening lobby, spacious dining room, and second-and-third-floor guest accommodations. After standing silent during the war years, it recovered quickly, a perfect locale for special events. The *Tupper Lake Herald* noted a young couple, Anna Sloane and Joshua Zoller, were married on September 2, 1919, at the Chapel on the Island on Upper Saranac Lake. They then left in launches for the nearby Bartlett Inn, a memorable spot for a bridal breakfast. The bride and groom looked east toward Ampersand Mountain, toasted each other, and shared the first slice of bridal cake. Perhaps the sun shone that day, leaves hinting at soon-to-be glorious reds, yellows, and oranges.

III

Jay and I have only a little time to savor the fall colors as we wave goodbye to guests on the final day of the 1974 season. We throw each other exhausted grins and slump into wicker porch chairs. We had a good summer. We do take the kids for a boat ride through mirror-calm water reflecting brilliant reds and oranges. But winter fast approaches. We need to close up before October 1st so pipes don't freeze in an early frost.

Ginette and Claudette arrive each morning for the final push: wash linens and towels; gather every blanket, cushion and anything else a mouse might find nest-worthy and stack them on shelves in a room lined with tin; scrub every dish, glass, pot, pan; drain water pipes; drape old white sheets on beds in darkened rooms. We pack up our cleaning supplies, lock doors, and leave shrouded buildings to the cold of winter.

Even with everything put to bed, more work lies in wait as well as the perpetual, nagging question: will the income we are now bringing in plus our savings keep us going? We need to get Douglass and Ampersand winterized. We want to offer them by next summer to guests year round. "Ampersand" is our new name for Yardley, the house Harriet Jenkins Yardley built fifty years earlier. It has a sweeping view of Ampersand Mountain from its porch. In addition to the routine with other buildings, we will have to install baseboard heat, lay deeper water pipes to protect from frost, and insulate walls and ceilings. This means instead of wainscoted interior walls, we will have sheetrock, so I can choose what color they will be!

"Just don't choose blue." Jay says. "It's not rustic enough." I love blue, but I'm willing to keep the peace and save that color for our house. Forest green for a bedroom and yellow for the kitchen.

My scrapbooks hold only a few pictures of work at the Club at that time. Mostly I have family pictures—baking Christmas cookies, Gwyn's first school concert, visiting friends. It makes sense. I took the pictures, and the majority of my life centered around family and my work at home. The routine: get the girls up and going—one off to school, keep the other from toppling down our wooden stairs; measure, cut, and sew two last housefuls of curtains; type letters, get ads out; parent conferences; Christmas pageants; play dates; box up maple syrup to ship.

Ah. Maple syrup. In spring, 1974, we had decided to bring the old sugar house back into operation. I don't know the history of this weathered grey shack in the woods, but possibly A. B. Jenkins decided to wholeheart- edly embrace the Adirondack way of life and built it. For years before we arrived, each spring someone hung buckets on maple trees, collected and boiled sap, and poured rich golden syrup in jars. We want to honor that tradition and send a half gallon in mid-winter to each former guest along with a letter saying *You can make a reservation now!*

Jay enlists Frank Dorchak, our district Forest Ranger and a good friend, to manage our sugar house. His main job will be to boil down the sap. Jay salvages any still-useable equipment and stocks up on other supplies from the Leader Evaporator Company in Vermont. We drag five hundred galvanized metal buckets from the shed and wash and rinse all of them. Gwyn, now four, explores every mud hole she can find. Shana, only one, stays safely at home with a sitter. Just like sap in maple trees, we rise to the scent of spring in the air. Jay and Chuck drill about five hundred holes in three hundred maple trees and hang a bucket at each tap. We don't seem to do things in small ways. The sun grows warmer every day. We wait for the first perfect sugaring day, below freezing at night, climbing into high thirties or forties in the day. The first plink plink plink sounds reverberate from the bottom of buckets. The sap has started to run.

Sugaring, 1970s.

Jay, in his red, grey, and white check wool jacket and blue navy wool hat, drives the "Little John" bulldozer, pulling a sled with a fifty-gallon galvanized tank. Gwyn, in matching plaid-wool jacket, sits in his lap for a while and then "helps" Frank in the sugar house. Chuck and I gather clear sap from each tap into larger buckets, lug them to the bulldozer, and dump the liquid into the tank. When not with a babysitter, Shana comes along, strapped to my back.

After the collected sap reaches the top of the tank, Jay drives to the hilltop above the sugar house and empties fifty gallons into a pipe that gravity feeds into a two-hundred-gallon tank outside the sugar house. Frank trickles sap from the tank into long, shallow, flat sheet-metal pans sitting on the wood-fueled "arch," or firebox. The fire blazes. Hemlock smoke billows up. Frank gradually releases sap from one pan to the next as the clear liquid bubbles, boils, evaporates, and thickens. Outside, mountainous clouds of sweet steam swirl with wood smoke in the springy air as we negotiate a steep patch of snow here, a piece of muddy ground there.

My favorite moment comes when I stand stock-still in the woods, my buckets filled, and I wait for Jay to return with the dozer. I raise my face to welcome the warmth of April sun and listen; chickadees discussing where to nest this year, a far-off squirrel scolding, and then plink plink drops of sap hitting the bottom of a newly emptied pail. It will overflow again before the end of day.

Frank carefully transfers sap as it boils off from one pan to the next to the next. It takes about forty gallons of sap to make one gallon of syrup. He has to boil the sap just the right length of time. If too short, the watery syrup will quickly spoil. If too long, the dark, heavy syrup will eventually crystalize. Finally, he pours golden-thick-sweet liquid into bottles, ready to be capped and marked with our Round Lake Sugar House label. We use "Round Lake" to honor the history of this land. We end up with about eighty gallons—plenty to send to guests as well as Christmas presents for every family member we can think of.

We send our annual letter in January 1975 to previous guests with a half-gallon of our new maple syrup:

> The fall has been a busy one here at Bartlett Carry as we are finishing up the renovations on Douglass Lodge. We think that with baseboard heat and four fireplaces, it will be pretty cozy for those who want to venture north to Bartlett Carry in the winter.
>
> Even though we pounded a lot of nails in Douglass, there was always enough time to watch the five Canada geese which ate from Fran's garden for a solid week.
>
> We also had a chance to buy all the equipment in another sugar house so we will now be able to increase our "taps" this spring from 500 to 700 or so. If you are able to join us this summer at Bartlett Carry, please let us know so that you may have, if you wish, the same dates and lodge as last year.

We enclose our rate card. Ampersand Lodge requires too much work to open by summer, 1975, but with Douglass finally ready, we have eight lodges to rent. Prices range from $540 for two weeks in sweet little one-

and-a-half bedroom Cedar to $1,350 for Douglass and Merritt, each with five bedrooms. That averages out to less than $100 per day for one to ten people. We don't know if we're asking too much or too little, but once former guests make reservations, we celebrate. A true mark of success.

Did life go as perfectly as it sounds when I write this? It's easy to forget the hard parts as I look back years later. I do know we had an overwhelming amount of work to do. We just kept going, kept tackling the next job. Occasionally I indulged in taking the girls to Mrs. Ferree for a full day. Other days, while Gwyn made new friends in kindergarten, Shana and I holed up and sewed curtains/played with fabric scraps. Sometimes I took her for walks, tiny two-year-old-step walks. "Okay, honey," I'd say with a tinge of impatience as she bent, yet again, over a fascinating rock or puddle. "Time for us to get going now." I had Things To Do. Oh, how I regret that in retrospect—not glorying in every single second with her no matter how slowly we went. I didn't understand "slow" then. Not for many years did I understand slow.

In the back of my mind, still the resolute refrains: Will we ever finish it all? Will we have enough money? Will people still want to come next summer? Will my life look like this from now on? Cleaning, typing, taking reservations, tending my kids, greeting people, sweeping, taking kids to the beach, grocery shopping, watering the flowers, being sure everyone is okay, and in the winter going back to such quietude and no neighbors, although by this point that didn't bother me because I was busy with the kids. If my life *did* look like this, would I mind?

I loved it when Mom came to visit. She always arrived with dinner in her green Coleman cooler—lamb chops, frozen peas, creamed potatoes; my all-time favorite meal. Jay's parents came to visit too, but he never felt at ease with them, and he dreaded those visits, so I did too. Their end-of-August trip coincided with precious end-of-summer days when we were busy with guests, and I had no time to worry about having our house, the kids, and me sparkling clean and perfect. Of course the clothes Jay's mom sent me periodically came out on these visits.

I remember thinking, *I have to figure out how to grow my nails so they will look good.* Hard to do when every two weeks I scrubbed the floors of eight buildings on my hands and knees. Right before they arrived, I inspected our house as minutely as Jay's Marines running their white-gloved fingers along tops of doors to ferret out every last dust speck. I held myself to this standard. I can't say I always, if ever, lived up to it. I'm not sure Jay's mom ever even noticed. If she did, she never said. In fact, I have only a minimal impression of what either of Jay's parents said or felt about our work here.

Winter, 1975 ends; spring arrives. Last fall, I dug holes in the soil and planted bulbs. Now daffodils pop up around our house, dancing yellow light in the cool, fresh breeze off the river, newly released from bonds of winter. I pluck a flower, breathe the spring-ness into my chest, down into my toes.

On an irresistible spring afternoon, I walk down the road with the girls, accompanied by the chortles, knocks, chitters, and thumps of birds deciding which twig goes where in their new homes for the summer. We run smack into a pillow of apple-blossom-scented air. Since about mid-April, the trill of the hermit thrush has entranced me. I didn't know they came back this early. White-throated sparrows sing in unison, a hairy woodpecker knocks out percussion over by the sugar house, and a ruffed grouse thrums away, looking for his sweetheart. The sun warms my back, blinds my eyes. The pond just through the trees sends up steam like a hot cup of tea, our dog rolls around nostalgically on the last mound of dirty snow, nuzzles his nose in, says goodbye in his own way, and moves to some grass to continue his back rub. We don't need mittens today. I stand in my fleece jacket, cool cheeks warmed by the sun, and allow the song of awakening spring and the warmth of renewing earth to start the sap inside me flowing.

One ordinary, yet memorable day—Gwyn has come home from kindergarten. Shana and I are upstairs finishing some curtain or other with spring sun flooding in, warming up the earth after a long winter. I hear Jay's truck in the driveway. He appears at the bottom of the stairs, looks up at his three girls.

"How 'bout we go out for dinner?"

"Oh!" We grin down at him. Especially me. I had just been thinking *Oh dear, what will we have for dinner?* We go to Roy's Diner, our favorite hangout at the Junction in Tupper Lake, and order Chicken in The Basket, in a plastic basket with paper-towel lining. We drive home with smiling, greasy faces.

Reservations, most for two-week rentals, stuff our mailbox. In addition to even more returning families, we have new guests. Jane and Mark Maxwell arrive with their one-and-a-half-year-old daughter and rent Fir for a month. A month! Good. One less time to clean a lodge. Vicki and Bill Boies come with two small children, ages one and three. More kids close in age to mine.

Looking back at these vignettes, I think, *Well, how about that.* I was no longer lonely, and I didn't even realize it. We had two beautiful children; a good, solid, winterized house; electricity; most of the renovations done at the Club; and a burgeoning business with both new and returning guests. Again we didn't stop, step back, and celebrate just how far we had come. We were immersed in the day-to-day work, and we never paused to notice. How does one Wednesday run into the next Wednesday, and what happened in between? Only now do I see how time slips past and then it's gone, irretrievable.

IV

Sometimes seasons slip one into the next, and sometimes one is marked indelibly. In mid-June, 1921, the Bartlett Inn welcomed guests for their vacations. It looked to be the beginning of a busy summer. Despite extremely dry weather, no one suspected what would happen next. Rainfall that May had fallen 47 percent below average.[10] Low water levels made for poor fishing. As high winds and low precipitation persisted, the tally of forest fires grew. In the past, locomotives using spark-spitting wood or coal for fuel had been the culprits, but in 1921, diesel oil posed less of a threat. Instead, visitors, some of them tobacco smokers, careless fishermen, or both, arrived in droves and with them, a greater danger of fire.[11]

While no firsthand report exists of the night of Wednesday, June 22, at the Bartlett Inn, the *Chateaugay Record and Franklin County Record* published a notice on July 1, 1921.

> Bartlett Inn, established 75 years ago by Virgil C. Bartlett, a pioneer Adirondack woodsman, and about which much legend of the mountains clings, was destroyed by fire Wednesday night. Five cottages were also consumed. The original building erected by Mr. Bartlett was burned about 24 years ago, the structure that was destroyed by [sic] last week being built by New York sportsmen. The flames broke out in one of the rooms at the hotel and fanned by a strong wind, swept through the building.

After destroying the hotel, the fire spread to adjoining cottages, and despite the efforts of volunteers from Saranac Inn and from the camps on upper Saranac Lake who scurried in motor boats and cars to the scene, five were burned to the ground.[12]

Dry weather had sucked moisture from the wooden structures and kept green vegetation from growing until late June.[13] It may have been something like this description of another forest fire: "a bright light pierced the darkness and a moment later a sheet of flame flashed from the woods."[14]

Men, women, whole families must have fled into and across the river. Cries, screams, panic, racing to save something, anything. Flames rushing through branches, the heat itself a scorching breeze, roaring, crackling, crashing of burning timbers, sparks flying, choking smoke, hard to breathe, the acrid smell. . . .[15]

Men dashed down the lake in boats from the Saranac Inn and from summer homes on Upper Saranac Lake with shovels, hoes, pails, and axes. The fire had spread to adjoining bungalows Perhaps they used the Double Forester backpack pump and maybe even the new gasoline-fired pump equal to a crew of seventy-five men with shovels and axes.[16] Whatever they used, it was too little, too late. Fire trucks from Tupper and Saranac Lakes had to rumble across rough gravel and dirt roads over eleven miles. They had no hope of arriving in time. The Club House, the Combination Cottage with its twenty rooms, and four other bungalows burned to the ground. Three of the four had been built within the past six years.

A bleak landscape of blackened stone chimneys jutted out of gray ashes once the fire and heat subsided. One year earlier, Robert Frost had written a poem almost prophetic of this moment. It begins: "The house had gone to bring again to the midnight sky a sunset glow. Now the chimney was all of the house that stood, like a pistil after the petals go."[17]

Gone were the airy rooms and polished floors of the Club House, gone was the Combination Cottage with the sound of rapids just outside, gone was Haley's Cottage dating back to the days of Virgil and Caroline Bartlett. All that remained were the chimneys.

Combination Cottage, Haley's, Club House, pre-June 1921.

Combination Cottage, Haleys, Club House, taken by Farnham Yardley, July 14, 1921.

The danger of fire has not diminished in the 1970s as Jay and I renovate the Club. In his role as Forest Ranger, Frank Dorchak, when not presiding over our sugar house, brings us posters of Smokey Bear with the slogan "Only YOU Can Prevent Forest Fires." He takes his job of trying to prevent them seriously. He appoints Jay as an assistant fire warden. In our garage, we stack a row of five-gallon Indian tanks—kidney-shaped galvanized backpacks to strap on and hand pump water while moving through the trees. They are full of water, ready to go. On the wall above hangs a line of shovels, helmets, stiff-bristled rattan fire brooms, and axes: all waiting.

On July 12, 1975, we attend the wedding of a dear friend at the north end of Upper Saranac Lake, about twenty miles away. A wild Greek wedding, a delicious moment away from our usual work. After the bride and groom kiss, we push chairs aside for dancing, the music tempo picks up. I sip wine and contemplate dancing on the table, even now in the middle of the day.

"Jay! You've got a call!" How odd. His face turns grave as he listens.

"We've got to go," he says. "Someone reported seeing smoke near Weller Pond." We do have to go. Weller Pond is a remote offshoot of Middle Saranac Lake, accessible only by boat. We live the closest, have the best hope of getting there quickly. We have a boat, and we have the fire-fighting equipment.

We bid hasty "thank yous" and farewells and race down curvy Route 30 to our house as we wonder. Where is Frank? Why isn't he responding to this? Maybe he's there already. We give our bewildered kids a kiss, explain to the babysitter, shed wedding clothes, and don old shirts, pants, and hiking boots. We pile tanks, brooms, axes, shovels into our small aluminum outboard and head downriver, into Middle Saranac Lake, across Hungry Bay, through the narrow slough into Weller Pond.

"There!" Jay says as we break into the pond. I see it too. On the right, a plume of smoke rises over the trees. We see no one. Jay pulls the boat into shore, a low wetland area. Smoke fills my nostrils as it rises from the mossy rooty undergrowth. I squint to keep it out of my eyes.

"I've got the pump!" says Jay. "Get a shovel, bring the ax. Looks like a root fire."

Frank has told us about this kind of fire. Long after a surface fire has been extinguished, it can smolder for months underground, travel along roots, and spring up somewhere else. Really hard to put out.

Jay grabs the harness of the Indian tank, whirls it onto his back, and begins pumping as soon as he turns around. I grab the shovel and ax, drop the shovel, and start chopping blindly, trying to sever unseen roots to stop the path of the fire. Dirt flies around me, the smells of damp moss and smoldering leaf mulch rise and circle in the air.

"Up here!" Ahead about eight feet I see more smoke billowing out of the ground. I chop at the line of roots toward Jay, ahead of me with the blessed water.

We alone fight the fire, probably started by a campfire, built where it never should have been, and not put out properly. The fire had smoldered in the underground roots and was slowly working its way along, popping up above ground, then under again 'til it could find a big tree to set ablaze. We stay until we're pretty sure it's really out.

Back home, we hug the kids, call Frank so he can follow up, pay the babysitter, give her a ride home, and collapse on the couch. I wonder wistfully if people are still dancing on tables at the wedding. The smell of damp moss and smoke lingers in our clothes for weeks.

After the fire at the Bartlett Inn in 1921, the smell of smoke must certainly have lingered. I think with awe of the resolve of those there that day who had been members from the beginning, through a plethora of ups and downs. Once again, they didn't quit. It was June, the beginning of the season, and they were determined to carry on.

Imagine the meeting at Bartlett's not long after the fire. They might have convened on July 14, the day Farnham Yardley took graphic pictures of the barren hillside where just three weeks earlier those grand buildings had stood. James Reardon, manager for at least ten years, may have contemplated resigning because he had not stopped the fire. I can almost hear Farnham saying to him; "Really, James. We all wish we could have done more. What is done is done, and we need to be grateful we lost no lives. It is my feeling we do not give up, but instead figure out our next steps." I can see Schuyler Merritt and Robert and Benjamin Douglass nodding their agreement.

The wind must have been blowing from the west the day of that June fire. The Club House and all buildings to the east burned to the ground, yet a number of bungalows to the west, including Mrs. Babcock's, survived. The summer had just begun. Guests still arrived and expected accommodations. Mr. Reardon rose to the challenge and placed them in bungalows still standing. Only a few weeks later, they built a long, low building for additional guest accommodations and a temporary dining room. And once again, they engaged William Distin, the architect who had designed several of the new and now lost bungalows between 1914 and 1916. He was commissioned to design a new Main Lodge to replace the former Club House.

Really? I marvel as I think of them standing on that fire-swept hillside, the smell of smoke lingering in the air, saying *All right! Let's get going! We need a new Main Lodge!* rather than tucking their tails and heading back to the city. Something kept them here.

Beauty and wildness. They responded to both. Even in the aftermath of the fire, they remembered that, in this place, they could relish the challenge that wilderness posed, immerse themselves in the wonder and peace of the natural world, and then return to the comfort of a warm meal and a place to lay their heads. Whether from fires, world wars, or new ownership, the circumstances of this place have frequently changed, and yet the place itself remains. Despite the instability of a world where wars might break out or financial institutions collapse, the continuity and familiarity of this wilderness provides a sense of belonging. This may well have held true for the Native Americans who came here. And for Virge and Caroline and the "sports" at Bartlett's, for families of the Saranac Club. I do know this place claimed Jay and me.

1921 heralded the beginning of a decade of hope, of almost irrational optimism. Farnham Yardley, Schuyler Merritt and the Douglass brothers apparently had the financial capability to recover and to pursue their vision of the Bartlett Inn including building a new Main Lodge.

Over fifty years later, in the mid-1970s, that Main Lodge, envisioned in 1921 and finished in 1923, remains a gathering place. Jay and I don't offer meals in the dining room, but two spacious rooms welcome our guests: huge stone fireplaces, floor-to-ceiling windows, inviting wicker chairs with soft cushions, a bear rug, old area maps on the walls, bookshelves crammed with novels and other reading for adults, piles of children's books. Guests borrow some, donate others, a vibrant, ever-changing library.

On rainy days, kids smack Ping-Pong balls, plink out tunes on the old piano, pluck a book and settle into the seat of an old sleigh tucked in a far corner. Or they gravitate to another corner where sits a huge antique maple bureau. They don't know that it came from the house of Harriet Jenkins Yardley in Llewellyn Park, New Jersey. They do know about the games heaped on top—Sorry, Chutes and Ladders, primary-colored plastic stacking rings, a small doll house, and a small red car with fat blue wheels. Inside the wide top drawer are more games—Scrabble, Rummikub, something called Aggravation. Other drawers yield a 250-piece nature puzzle and more cards than even a passel of bored kids could use. I wonder what its drawers held when it lived in Harriet's house, what conversations soaked into the weathered grain of its wood, what little hands tried to yank open that bottom drawer to discover its contents. The bureau stands silent.

Main Lodge exterior, 1923.

Main Lodge interior, ca. 1950.

Our only telephone for the club, a black dial model, crouches in the back of a small closet off the lobby. Most guests love this. The days of computers and cell phones have not yet arrived. If someone needs to be contacted, the phone call comes to our home, and we run up to the appropriate lodge with the message. One day, I get a call from a secretary trying to reach her boss.

"I'm sorry," I say. "I happen to know he's on a canoe trip and won't be available 'til the end of the day."

In her best city attitude, she says "Well, can't someone go out on the lake and get him? This is important!"

"I'm afraid not," I say gently and firmly.

Our guests don't come to the Bartlett Carry Club to be on the phone. They come to get away from it.

The only washing machine and dryer sit against one wall in a small sunny room near the phone closet, available for any ambitious soul who seeks a clean shirt. Often on a sun-splashed morning, a guest might wait for clothes to dry as she sprawls in an Adirondack chair on the patio just outside, cradling a steaming cup of coffee, chatting with new or old friends, raising her face to the sun like a flower absorbing the warming rays.

Meanwhile, after countless hours on hands and knees making the tennis-court-sized hardwood floors shine, I maintain them the best I can. One morning I have just started with a push broom on the old dining room (wryly renamed by me "Tennis Court #2") when one guest, Jane Maxwell, appears with a large laundry basket of clothes. Once the washing machine begins to whir, she joins me.

"Want some help?" she asks.

I smile, hand her another broom, and she starts to sweep the opposite end of the room. Dust flies. Jane starts humming, I hum back, and before we know it, we sing, tentatively at first, then with more gusto as the dirt piles up. We belt out opera, some existing, most we make up on the spot. A moment of no-separation between the one who washed and waxed the floors and the one here for a month's vacation with her family. Two women share a chore and create a new form of music to be appreciated only by us, and that's just fine.

In 1975, with full reservations in July and August, we have forty-eight hours between guests to clean and prepare eight houses with anywhere from two to five bedrooms. Forty-eight hours. A marathon, just like the Adirondack Canoe Classic I have entered multiple times, a ninety-mile, three-day race across lakes, rivers, and arduous carries. I still wonder—how did I do that? One paddle stroke at a time. No other way to do it.

During the forty-eight hour Bartlett Carry Club Cleaning Marathon, I get through with a rag. One swipe at a time. We have it down to a system. As the last car makes its dusty exit out of the parking lot, we spring into action. Chuck carts and stacks firewood. Jay takes care of outdoor work—straightening up canoes and beach furniture, raking the beach, touching up staining, minor repairs. His list never runs out.

The stalwart Ginette and Claudette help me clean each lodge, change beds, wash towels, and transform the kitchen to mother-in-law acceptability. A repurposed yellow plastic laundry basket stuffed with my favorite cleaning rags accompanies me everywhere.

Old cotton sheets with no lint make great window rags. I use flannel shirts, morphed from go-to-town to go-camping to my rag basket for dusting and washing floors. Brasso squirted on Jay's old red-checked flannel shirt spiffs up the medley of copper dishes we salvaged from the Main Lodge kitchen. I save my tattered blue-and-green-plaid flannel shirt for Zud. I discover this miraculous cleanser one day in the local Grand Union when faced with how to clean corroded rusting pipes at the back of toilets and claw-foot bathtubs. It does the trick. I spend hours on my hands and knees, my face inches from the toilet pipe, with my trusty flannel rag in my right hand, the can of powdered Zud in my left, scrubbing and scrubbing. Most of the pipes end up looking pretty darn good. I wonder if anyone will ever notice.

Zud and Brasso live in my second laundry basket with other choice cleaning supplies; powdered Ajax, toilet brush, baking soda for cleaning glass or just about anything, Windex, Spic and Span, and a gallon bottle of floor wax. We use a lot of wax. Also scrub brush, whisk broom, dustpan, spare lightbulbs, electric tape, scissors, straightedge, hammer, screwdriver, thumbtacks, and a few spare nails. I never know when I might need a few nails.

I save thin flannel rags for the primo job of washing and waxing hardwood floors, always on hands and knees, the only way to really get into corners and around immovable furniture. First dip a terry-cloth wash rag in a bucket of hot soapy water, wring it out, wipe across the floor in a big arc. Once the floor dries, then comes the thick, milky wax.

Gwyn and Shana often come with me. I position them outside whichever huge room I'm about to wax.

"Okay!" I say. "Here are some books, here is a game, here are papers and crayons—and here is an invisible wall you can't go through. You can see me, you can talk to me, but you can't come in this room, okay?"

This works. Sometimes. I choose the perfect rag and start at the far end of the room. Swish goes the wax-soaked rag across the floor in a rhythmic arc. Crunch go my knees. I inch my way over the endless floor. I know I will get through if I go one swipe at a time.

After the huge fire at the Club in 1921, I doubt anyone worried about a clean floor. Farnham Yardley wrote in the guestbook: "Arrived July 8 by motor . . . Left New Jersey July 5 . . . 388 miles from home. Bartlett Inn and other buildings burned June 22, 1921. Water lower in lake than for a number of years. Fishing poor. Two hot weeks in July. Kept chickens, no garden."

In August, most likely jolted by the enormous fire devastation at the Club, Farnham commissioned a detailed appraisal and inventory of the family camp on Round Lake. It included the cabins and boathouses here when Jay and I first arrived as well as a chicken house and outside toilet.

The Club focused on rebuilding and repair. In 1922, while architect William Distin conferred with builders about construction of the new Main Lodge, the dam sprang a major leak. Eight years earlier, in 1913, it had been repaired without proper supervision amidst turmoil surrounding the demise of the Saranac Club. Just before summer 1921, members had planned on further repairs. Once again, unforeseen events, this time the big fire in June, sidetracked them, and no work occurred. Now, the dam had sprung leaks that couldn't be ignored. This time they had to build a coffer dam and make repairs for $7,039.23.[18]

Even though the Upper Saranac Lake Association of Residents shared in the cost, the project took an enormous financial toll on the Club. In addition, debits that year included the expense of a new Main Lodge as well as ongoing taxes, insurance, labor for cutting ice and wood; also myriad annual capital improvements, a new turbine for the power house to upgrade electricity, and regular maintenance of the bridge—the only automobile access.

The Bartlett Inn Ledger shows no record of income from guests. In any case, it wouldn't have covered the extensive annual costs. Benjamin Douglass had died in 1922 and Robert, almost eighty, was slowing down. Harriet and Farnham and possibly the Merritts contributed what they could, but the books still showed red ink.

Fortunately, at this moment, a third Douglass brother stepped in. As younger brother of Robert and Benjamin, William Angus Douglass must have known of the Adirondacks. He may have visited occasionally, but he lived in Chicago where he managed that branch of the family-owned R. G. Dun & Co., started by his uncle in 1858. Perhaps he turned his attention to the Adirondacks in the early 1920s because Benjamin had died and Robert could no longer attend to this family investment. William's involvement may have started as a business decision, but when he arrived, he most likely fell in love with the place just as his brothers had.

I can't know his full story. He has left me no Minutes as Robert did, no writing on the backs of pictures or in a guestbook as Farnham did. Personal records show by 1924, William had become president of the Bartlett Carry Realty Co., the entity that regained the property at the 1913 auction. He joined Harriet and Farnham Yardley as official owners of the Club. During 1924, together they "loaned" the Club over $100,000, the equivalent today of well over a million dollars. For several ensuing years, they each loaned the considerable amount of at least $8,000 annually. Perhaps it had something to do with the war being over, the optimism of the 1920s in full swing. Most likely, they hoped to get bungalows built and the property in good repair so they could start a successful enterprise where paying guests would support it all.

Eleven years earlier, in 1913, William, then age sixty-one, had married forty-year-old Lillian Pollock McNutt and adopted her son, Donald. In 1924, Donald was twenty-five and a respected architect. William engaged him to design and build a sizable bungalow above the rapids not far from the new Main Lodge. As William pored over the blueprints, possibly his nine-year-old son, Benjamin (yet another Benjamin in the Douglass family), looked over his shoulder. Benjamin was born three years after William and Lillian married.

Douglass Lodge.

The design showed an arched stone doorway, a great stone living-room fireplace, enough bedrooms for family and guests, and four additional fireplaces.

Years later, when Jay and I first arrived, the daunting size of this same Douglass Lodge, rising out of the pine-needled forest floor just above the rapids, impressed us. I remember standing on the Douglass porch during our first tour. Jay wiggled a filigree key in the lock, the door creaked open. The cold, dry, air inside shriveled my skin. I sniffed. A hint of mothballs and fireplace ash. I could almost hear the faint echo of once-upon-a-time bright voices, crackling fire in the grate, creaking on the stairs. A craggy grey stone fireplace in the living room matched the stone arch doorway. Plastic curtains hung unevenly, as if a child had been swinging on them. I bounded up two steps to a hall and a bathroom.

"Look, Jay! A fireplace in the bathroom!"

From the bedroom, Jay called, "One in here, too." We discovered a total of five fireplaces.

I remember thinking, *Oh, for a hot bubble bath while watching a fire blaze merrily in the grate*. Well, if not I, at least our guests could enjoy this. One evening a few years later, when Jay was in the midst of insulating the house and putting up interior sheetrock walls, he said, "We're making real progress in Douglass. We walled up one of the bathroom fireplaces today. Think we'll do the other one tomorrow."

I put down my fork.

"No! Oh no! We need to have a fireplace in a bathroom. Just think. I bet not one guest has ever taken a bath with a fire in the bathroom before. We have to keep it!" I rarely expressed opinions about the structural side of the business. Jay kept the fireplace.

V

By June 1924, thanks to the infusion of money from William Douglass, construction on the Douglass bungalow, complete with five fireplaces, moved along. And with additional funds from Farnham and Harriet, major repairs to the infrastructure of the Club were completed, and the new Main Lodge and two new bungalows were almost ready to open. This new surge of activity inspired a change in name from the Bartlett Inn to the Bartlett Carry Club. The new manager, Miss Barnum, sent out a brochure and letter:

Miss Barnum's Brochure, 1924

In view of the fact that we are receiving numerous inquiries in regard to the accommodations and the new conditions at Bartlett Carry, it has seemed wise to send out the following statement to some who have been interested in the Carry in the past.

The ownership of the Carry has passed into the hands of Mr. William A. Douglass and interests represented by Mr. Farnham Yardley. A development policy has been decided upon and every effort is being made to make the Carry in all respects—what it is geographically—one of the ideal spots of the Adirondacks.[19]

Miss Barnum described the new Main Lodge, complete with a charming lounge, spacious dining room, and the addition of steam heat. Also, plenty of hot water and, best of all, a complete new sewerage system. As Miss Barnum stated: "This together with pure spring water removed two serious drawbacks."

This makes me wonder about the condition of the sewer system before 1924. Possibly, effluents drained right into the swamp downhill from the

Club. I found no actual documentation about the new system. Her brochure boasted of good plumbing, fresh drinking water, and amenities such as fireplaces, linens, bedding, and electricity. Some fifty years later, these same conveniences are taken for granted by our guests.

The rates in 1924 certainly differed from ours. Guests could stay then for the month of August, the preferred and therefore more expensive month, for between $350 and $600 plus $35 per week for "Table Board." In the 1970s, we charge $800 to $1,800 per month, and we do not provide "Table Board."

According to a Westhoff & Distin drawing, Donald McNutt Douglass designed the Douglass bungalow to face Ampersand Mountain, but an improperly supervised construction crew mistakenly oriented the house ninety degrees off. This meant when the family sat on the front porch, instead of a glorious mountain view, they faced a hillside and the site for another bungalow. The family still came in droves. William's wife, Lillian, and young Benjamin came, of course, and also family members from his first marriage to Eliza Kingman.

One day during my research, a former Bartlett Carry Club guest tells me of a friend from Washington, D.C., who came to the Club at that time.

"Really?" I say. "Who is that?"

Duncan tells me, "His name is Ev Shorey. I think he came in the 1920s."

I give him a call. No journals, minutes, or notes this time. Ev Shorey's eighty-nine-year-old mind shines bright and clear. I discover he is the grandson of William Douglass and his first wife, Eliza. Ev started coming in 1926 at the age of five. He describes vividly his memories of the five years he visited, the same families every year, all the kids about the same age.

Ev could be talking about the Club back in 1893 or in the 1970s when Jay and I ran it. Our families also came every year, most for two weeks, always stayed in the same lodges. A pack of kids seemed constantly to roam the woods, climb rocks, play games in the Main Lodge, splash endlessly in the water. Ev remembers:

We played together every day. We all went up to the mail dock and while we were waiting for the mailboat to come, we swam off the dock. There was even a float with a slide on it! I remember the last few years. Alfred Yardley came up all the time to go swimming. He was a lot older than I was, maybe by ten years, but he was pals with Ben and they let me and Sam tag along.

Alfred Yardley—this was Jay's dad. He was in his early teens then and probably paddled up the river to the Club from the family camp on Round Lake.

We used to go all over the place. There were paddle boats on the river we took down to Middle Saranac. And there was a minnow pond down the road. That was great for exploring and finding new trails and climbing the rocks. We picked blueberries and every night we played kick the can. One time Ben dared us to walk across the rapids on a wet log. I never knew just how slippery a wet log can be! I guess that tells you I fell in! I don't think there was a day when we didn't go fishing for something and whenever we could get an adult to drive the boat, we went aquaplaning. I loved that!

Oh, and then there were picnics on Middle Saranac on an island and then the tennis tournaments! We even had a silver cup and the winner got his name engraved on it every year. Ben was really a good player. He won in 1927 when he was only eleven.[20]

When Jay and I first arrived, we discovered seven tarnished silver cups on one of the massive half-log mantle pieces in the Main Lodge. Ben's name is engraved on one for tennis in 1927 and on two others for the Bartlett Carry Club Annual Golf Tournament, 1927 and 1929. These historic emblems of bygone sports prowess still hold a proud place on that mantle.

I *almost* met Ben, missed him by a sliver of time. In about 2004, just before I started my research and delved into the history, Ben, in his mid-eighties, visited the Club to show his daughters his childhood summer home. His grandniece, Jamie Douglass, told me about his report on that visit. He thought the Douglass house looked very different. The towering pines he saw then had most likely grown from saplings he had known as a child.

Now, through Ev's stories, I know Ben Douglass and Jay's father were friends. Al, as Ben called him, was about six years older and an only child. He would have set out from Round Lake and paddled or walked a mile to the Club to see his summer friend. Knowing this, I have a more vivid image of Jay's dad.

I did meet Ev's mother, Elizabeth Douglass Shorey. At the time, I didn't know her relationship to Ev or that she was the daughter of William Angus Douglass. Once again, a rare opportunity just out of my reach as I had not yet begun to ask questions and had no idea I would be writing a book. I met her one spring day in 1975 when Jay and I were putting finishing touches on Douglass Lodge. As I washed outside windows, I saw, walking over the hill, a small white-haired woman in her mid-eighties, a look of wonder on her face. She introduced herself as "one of the Douglass family who had stayed here long ago."

"I remember this place!" she said. "The trees are much taller, but I do remember it." Well over thirty years had probably passed since she had last visited.

I couldn't miss this opportunity. I climbed down the ladder to hear better. She told me, "My father was William Angus Douglass. He was here at the beginning, you know. His brothers, Uncle Robert and Uncle Ben, were as well. Oh, our whole family was involved!"

Elizabeth craned her neck to gape at the tall pines. "Why, when I was here, they were just little saplings. And you know, I remember the time when I was sitting in the bath, the one upstairs with the fireplace, when there was a crack of thunder and I swear I felt a shock in the water. I was out of there so fast, I almost forgot I had no clothes on!"

I never did get to soak in a bath by a blazing fire, but at least Elizabeth could see the fireplace I saved as I took her on a tour through the house.

"Oh, my!" she said as she looked out an upstairs window. "What happened to the view? I used to see all the way to Round Lake and Ampersand Mountain. Now it's just trees!"

I wish I'd been curious about the past much sooner. Instead, I focused on getting yet another lodge ready to open. I had little time to think of anything else. Years later, when I appreciated the significance of William Angus Douglass, I would have gone out of my way to focus on Elizabeth as well as Ben, to delve into the treasures of their memories. *What was your favorite thing to do here?* I might have asked. *What was it like to be here with three young children? Who did the cooking? Did you have favorite traditions? Why was this place so important to you?*

I also wish I could interview Schuyler Merritt in person. His ongoing support from the day he arrived in 1892 helped save the Club. *Why did you decide to build a new house in 1925?* I might ask. He and his family had stayed for twenty-three years in their bungalow on Bartlett Bay near the boathouses on Upper Saranac. By then, his two daughters had grown and moved on to lives of their own. Perhaps he observed the construction of William Angus Douglass's house and wanted something more substantial for himself.

Whatever compelled him, in 1925 Merritt moved his old bungalow across the road and drew up an agreement with the Bartlett Carry Realty Co. (BCRCo) to lease property and build a new house right by the water. He contracted with William Distin and Arthur G. Wilson Associates of

Merritt Lodge.

Saranac Lake to design and build his new summer home at a cost of almost $15,000 (about $194,000 in today's currency.)

The lease Mr. Merritt signed on September 7, 1925, stated that the BCRCo would provide "furnishing and caring for bed linen, blankets, comfortables [warm quilts], and towels: sweeping and care of cottage, electric light, water, wood for open fires."[21]

Electric light. In the 1920s, the DC power came from the power house at the dam. Fast forward to the 1970s—at "our" Bartlett Carry Club, in addition to supplying furnishings, bed linens, towels, and firewood, Jay and I provided the AC electricity we had brought in to support modern needs.

If I could talk to Mr. Merritt, perhaps he would tell me how much he enjoyed Mr. Distin's elegantly designed house perched on giant boulders above the waters of Bartlett Bay, the same house Jay and I renovated some forty-three years later. Perhaps he would also tell me about visits he made in the 1920s to the Yardley family camp a mile away. I long to interview those here then, to get a sense of this place on Round Lake almost fifty years before I came.

Other than the entries Farnham made in the Waubenoo guestbook, my only other clues of camp life come from signatures and comments by visitors. They may have traveled by train on the New York Central Adirondack Division to Tupper Lake, where Elmer Dockum would likely have met them in the camp Ford station wagon. Old black-and-white photographs in a family album help me fill out the picture: a new float on Round Lake with ladder and slide for children to play on; a blur of four-legged black fur careening around a corner—Blacky, the family dog (in every photo); a kerosene lamp on a wicker table reminding me of no electricity at camp in the 1920s, although the Club had it by 1906.

What a delight it must have been to arrive, dust off travel dirt, and settle in . . . Evocative wood-smoke aroma, sound of lapping water, gentle glow of kerosene lamps; two luxurious months to enjoy this magical spot.

For breakfast, Mrs. Downing (the cook) might have served griddle cakes topped with maple syrup from their own sugar house, the same sugar house most likely built by A. B. Jenkins and restored many years later by Jay and me. In the spring, Elmer Dockum made about five gallons of syrup a year; Jay and I made eighty. Instead of a bulldozer, Elmer used a sled pulled by a horse.

During the day, Ampersand Mountain issued an invitation to climb. To get to the trailhead, guests paddled two miles to the eastern shore of Round Lake. On their hike, they might have met Walter Rice, the "Hermit of Ampersand," who had lived halfway up the mountain since 1915. Each day, from April to October, he climbed to the summit to keep a watch for fires. In his first year, he reported twenty-one to the rangers. Mr. Rice could point out every tree and animal by name to the hikers. And if anyone was of a mind, they could discuss with him some of the books he had brimming on his shelves, among them the complete works of Dickens, Tennyson, Shakespeare, and O. Henry.[22]

After a mountain climb, maybe they took out the new boat with a double sail. Of course, they fished every day. Farnham made it into the local paper with a pike he caught weighing an even fifteen pounds, measuring 39¼ inches, the largest fish caught in Round Lake that season.[23] I bet Mrs. Downing created a masterpiece for the dinner table that evening.

Schuyler Merritt, Farnham Yardley, ca. 1923.

Schuyler Merritt visited the family camp often. Sometimes he would have come by guide boat, other times in his new Ford touring car. In 1923, Schuyler, then seventy years old, and Farnham, age fifty-five, had plenty to talk about. They both loved to golf and most likely shared many rounds on the Bartlett Carry golf course and maybe even on the Indian Carry course three miles away. They very likely discussed the bustling activity at the Club, especially the news that Harriet wished to build a bungalow there.

Mr. Merritt may have puzzled as I did over Harriet's decision to build. She already had the family camp a mile away on Round Lake. Possibly she wanted a handy place to stay "in the country" (meaning the Adirondacks) after camp closed in the fall, and a place for any overflow of friends at camp during the summer. Also, as partial owners of the Club, Harriet and Farnham may have wanted to have a physical presence. For whatever reason, she had a perfect spot in mind, on the hill looking east toward Ampersand Mountain, neighbor to William Douglass's new house. They built "Yardley" Cottage in 1926.

Farnham's 55th birthday, August 8, 1923.

I go back to the black-and-white photos for more vignettes from the family camp: August 8, 1923. Farnham, dressed in knickers, sitting in a chair on the wooden walkway between cabins, grinning widely, holding Blacky the dog, a parasol, two baskets, and a handheld fan.

They were celebrating his fifty-fifth birthday. Several other photos fill in the story. Everyone at camp, including Elmer Dockum, donned a costume and put on an impromptu play. Other photos show aquaplaning or being pulled on a board behind the boat, feeding chipmunks, playing bridge in the evening.

And then a special entry in the guestbook: early September, 1923. Annie Grey Jenkins, wife of A. B.

Jenkins and step-grandmother to young Alfred, came for a brief visit. This was her only signature in the guestbook. Possibly she came more than once, but only signed this time. Her comment was "Alfred, Julia, June and I are left alone, but we are not in such pain, As Hattie and Farnham who went off in the rain." She may have come this time to wander with Elmer through the woods and determine where the best resting spot for her and her late husband would be. The past swallows up the facts and leaves only a hint of what might have transpired.

Julia Abbe, just out of college, visited for two months and signed the guestbook on September 10th. She left her thanks and memories on the white page:

> Mr. Yardley's morning French
> All my questions could not quench;
> Blacky's scuttling to the grove
> when into sight I softly hove;
> Distance swimming in the lake;
> Mrs. Downing carving cake;
> Elmer in dramatic guise
> saying "them bats is thick as flies."
> Most exciting bumpy rides
> Most enthralling slippery slides;
> Dives deep to amphibian-kind,—
> How can I leave you all behind!

So much I will never know about those days and those people . . . so much left to my imagination.

5

Unraveled

I

One lodge to go. Fall 1975. Jay tackles the winterization of Ampersand. We write our winter letter and send it with maple syrup to sweeten memories and encourage resolve to return.

We don't mention our bat issue in the letter. We have dealt with them since our first days when, even in February, I could smell excrement behind spruce-bark exteriors at the family camp. Colonies of bats also roost in the old houses of the Club. As we have renovated building by building and disrupted their peaceful existence, they have moved from one house to the next. By 1975, when we are closing in on the last structures, the tenacious bats have taken up residence in Ampersand.

"Jay!" I say as we contemplate methods to get rid of them. "Do you have any more of those smoke grenades?"

"Nope," says Jay. "All used up. Remember?"

I did remember. When we first moved into the Guide House, a plethora of bats apparently thought of it as *their* Guide House. One day when the bats were especially feisty and smelly, Jay said "That's it! I've got just the solution!" From his Marine Corps days, he had squirreled away a few smoke grenades, used in the military as signaling devices. He climbed a ladder outside our bedroom to a small hatch opening into a crawl space above the ceiling. I stood below, fascinated to see what would happen next. Jay expertly pulled the pin on the grenade, opened the door, hurled the grenade in, and scrambled down. Almost immediately, plumes of red smoke poured out the small opening followed by hordes of red bats scattering in every direction. For quite a while after that, we occasionally saw a swooping red bat at sunset.

The bats (not red) we now have in Ampersand don't seem to be going anywhere, and we have no more smoke grenades. Ah well. As a friend said when I told him this story, "Everybody needs a home."

In our continuing goal to have this property support itself, we search for environmentally responsible income. We already have our sustainable selective logging operation, the sand-and-gravel pit, and maple syrup sales. What else can we do? Jay ponders how we might use the old golf course. One day, his face lights up.

"Hey! We could grow Christmas trees. It's open, unused land. It'll grow back to woodland anyway. We can do it! Who wouldn't want to buy a fragrant Adirondack Christmas tree?"

I love the image, and it sounds simple. We know nothing so, in early 1976, we join over two hundred attendees at the New York State Christmas Tree Growers Association annual convention in Syracuse. We take workshops on "Getting to Know Your Field," "How to Boost the Health of Your Trees," and a useful talk on "Frost Pockets." Armed with new information, on a cool, early fall morning we walk the old golf course to see where fog has settled, the sure sign of a frost pocket. We don't plant in those spots so our seedlings won't freeze.

We start small with "only" 2,000 trees. A lot of tree growers we meet have farms with over 10,000 trees. I can't imagine. What kind of tree shall we grow? We ignore the fact that white pines grow naturally in our field with gusto. We want balsam! The thought of that heady fragrance conjures up images of early Christmas mornings lit by multicolored bulbs, me in flannel pajamas reaching under the tree for the last present. Our family loves balsam Christmas trees, and we imagine others do too. We order 1,000 balsam and, for some reason, 1,000 white-spruce seedlings from the NYS Department of Conservation. While Jay and Chuck spend days preparing the two-acre field we will plant, I tend three- and seven-year-olds and sew curtains for one last house at the Club.

Finally, May and the exciting pick-up-the-trees day arrive. As Jay considers the three-hour drive to Saratoga, he says, "Not sure if I should take the pickup or dump truck." He has just bought a used three-quarter-ton dump truck we have dubbed the Black Beauty.

I envision trees piled high in the truck, spilling over maybe. I say, "Take the dump truck." and wonder if he'll need to make two trips. Later, after hours of waiting, I see the truck finally drive in, but no trees overflowing the back. *What? Didn't he get them?* My heart plummets. I run outside with the girls and, jumping up on the running board, I see two long fat rolls of what look like cardboard. "That's all?" I say. "That's it?"

"Yep. We were thinking about full trees, not seedlings."

We open up one of the rolls, the one marked balsam. It's lucky they are labeled. The three-to-four-inch seedlings, wrapped in layers of peat moss, are so small we don't know which bundle of spindly little twigs is which.

Black Beauty dump truck, early 1970s.

"This is all of them?"

"This is it. We have to keep the roots moist 'til we get them planted."

Hmmm. Will we ever get a Christmas tree from this? In spite of my doubts, we lay a grid on the two acres Jay and Chuck have prepared and plant a tiny seedling every six feet to allow plenty of room for growth. We plan to stagger our planting; 2,000 trees this first year, and then 2,000 in each of the next two years. Our goal is 6,000 trees. It will take at least seven or eight years before we can harvest our first Christmas tree.

The spring and summer of 1976 include more than just trees. Ampersand Lodge still won't be ready this summer, but we can see the end in sight. We greet former guests and new families: the Plummers from Mexico City with three kids and the Lewis family with six. I welcome the built-in entertainment. Saul and Ethel Greenspan and Dottie and Alan Rogers come from New Hampshire. For years before this, they had vacationed on Lower Saranac Lake in a tent platform.

Since the 1920s, families like the Greenspans and Rogers had taken advantage of a ruling by the Forest Commission allowing private individuals to rent a site for about two dollars a year on state wilderness land. Renters could not build an actual cottage, but could erect a canvas tent or a more substantial structure made partly from wood for about $1,000. They had to observe New York State Park regulations and allow seasonal inspection by a State ranger, but minimal maintenance and no property tax made for an ideal vacation setup.

Renters purchased a permit and returned many summers to the same tent platform. As in most summer homes, traditions evolved, stories grew with each fishing trip, and sociability thrived. This permit system, however, allowed use by only a few even as more and more campers and wilderness lovers discovered the Adirondacks. In an effort toward equality, by the 1960s, the New York State Conservation Department had begun "to phase out uses of the Forest Preserve that denied full public enjoyment of these highly valued recreation lands."[1]

The platform permit holders, firmly entrenched, did not go down without a fight. Our friends, the Greenspans and Rogers, were most likely in the thick of it. The permit holders formed the Tent Platform Association and mounted their defense: they served in essence as "watchdogs" for the State and had many times prevented forest fires from spreading; they had aided in searching for lost persons, and provided headquarters for crises in the woods;[2] they cleaned up after transient campers; with almost six hundred tent-platform holders in this rural area, they had a huge economic impact as they spent thousands of dollars annually in stores and for services catering to people who loved the outdoors. They iced their defense with the offer to pay $100 each annually to the state of New York for continuance of the present system.

None of these arguments convinced the State of New York that one person could enjoy a tent platform for little expense while another could not. Landowners who regularly paid property tax, including Jay and me, understandably supported the abolishment of the law. Of the almost six hundred platforms eventually razed in the Saranac Lake region, more than half had existed in Wilderness lands on Middle and Lower Saranac Lakes. Thus, in 1976, along with many former tent-platform dwellers, the Greenspans and Rogers needed a new summer home. They heard about the Bartlett Carry Club from Harry Duso, a mutual friend who in the 1950s had bought the only other private land on Middle Saranac Lake.

We welcome the Greenspans and Rogers when they rent Pine Lodge for the first two weeks in July. What a change for them—electricity, running water, beds, clean sheets and towels delivered to their door, even candles during a lightning storm. As they arrive, fishing gear, picnic paraphernalia, and lots of summer clothes tumble out of their cars.

They spend almost every day fishing, but one exquisite sunny day, I find them in the Main Lodge crowded around our only TV with its twelve-inch screen. Mrs. Greenspan sees my puzzled look. "Oh!" she says. "It's the finals of the Wimbledon Tennis Tournament! We can't miss this!" It turns out tennis comes just behind fishing on their "Passion List." This TV brings in one station, WPTZ out of Plattsburgh, with a healthy dose of fuzz and static. It's a mystery how they can distinguish the tennis balls from the snowy reception. They certainly couldn't do this in a tent platform.

In 1929, if the Greenspans and Rogers had been around, they might have sat in that same Main Lodge, albeit without the TV. The Lodge had been built only six years earlier along with several new bungalows which now graced the Club grounds. In the late summer of 1929, a year well known in history, all seemed rosy. When the Dow Jones Industrial Stock Average boasted a three-hundred-point gain over the past five years, no doubt a wave of optimism rippled through the country. Douglasses and Yardleys would have envisioned families continuing to fill the bungalows—paying guests renewing the strained coffers.

No boom lasts forever. In later 1929, black cracks began to creep through the promising picture. Businesses across the country faltered. Confidence flagged. Then, during a five-day period in October, investors dumped stocks en masse, rocking the financial world to its core. The market collapsed, companies failed, and workers lost jobs.

The next summer, families once looking forward to vacation in a new Bartlett Carry bungalow now counted their blessings if they still had a home and food on the table. Sunshine might have flooded the flagstone patio, but no one sat in the Adirondack chairs. The economy collapsed. Optimism plummeted. The Douglass and Yardley families had to make a big decision. They could try to hang on and hope people would recover and return so they might make a profit. Or they could walk away.

Once again, they did not walk away. First fires, then a world war, then more fires. And now this. Why did they stay this time? Maybe they really had no choice. The disastrous economy ensured that few, if any, would be interested in or capable of purchasing the property. So they hung on.

While iconic images of the Depression show people jumping out of windows and waiting in food lines, a certain echelon of society seemed to sail above the tragedy around them. During this tenuous time, at least two such families began their own enclaves not far from the Bartlett Carry Club.

In 1929, at the former site of Jesse Corey's Rustic Lodge on Upper Saranac Lake, the Swenson family employed William Distin to design a mansion with fireplaces decorated with Dutch Delft tile in each of seventeen bedrooms and bathrooms. In the early 1930s, on the western shore, William A. Rockefeller II, built "Camp Wonundra," including a main lodge with three wings and eight large stone fireplaces. These fortunate few could enjoy iced tea on airy porches overlooking the lake. The Douglasses and Yardleys may have hoped one of them might purchase the Club, even with its attendant problems. That didn't happen.

Meanwhile, in the Real World, some thirteen-to-fifteen-million Americans had no jobs, and almost half the country's banks had failed. The 1920s gaiety and self-assurance fell as flat as yesterday's champagne. In the words of F. Scott Fitzgerald, "The utter confidence which was its essential prop (had) received an enormous jolt, and it didn't take long for the flimsy structure to settle earthward."[3]

The Douglasses and Yardleys did not match the economic level of the Rockefellers, but they could withstand the collapse. In 1933, William Douglass guided R. G. Dun & Company into a merger with its competitor, John M. Bradstreet, to form Dun & Bradstreet. The Jenkins Manufacturing Company, led by Farnham Yardley, thrived because of numerous new government-sponsored programs created to offset Depression disasters. Expanding oil and gas companies demanded ingenious valves, invented decades earlier by Nathaniel Jenkins. They were essential for wastewater treatment and chemical processing, and they were used in major dams built in the 1930s such as the Shasta in California and the Hoover Dam on the Colorado River.

Farnham and Harriet benefited enough from this success to meet the Club's financial needs and to reside "in camp" on Round Lake from early July to mid-September, with full enjoyment of their chosen lifestyle.

It was quite a lifestyle. The chauffeur drove, the cook prepared meals, and maids took care of daily needs for the family. In 1930, Harry and Lena Cummings moved into the Guide House on the hill overlooking the family camp as year-round caretakers. Guests arrived, pulled on bathing suits, ran down to the new dock, and jumped on an aquaplane to be pulled by the new Luddington boat. At the end of the day, the boat landed in the new boathouse, guests dressed in the new guesthouse, and enjoyed drinks on the porch with ice from the new icehouse. And before they left, they signed the guestbook. These comments show no noticeable sign of concern about the times. *It is a very nice place . . . Rain or shine, you always find happiness at Waubenoo. . . .*

To me this is stunning. How could they not feel any ill effects from the financial disaster? For their brief time in this magical spot, they dove into the joys of the moment . . . *Nowhere is it possible to obtain such complete relaxation both mental and physical as that which is found at Waubenoo.*

Since Alfred, known to his friends as Al, never signed the guestbook, I don't know how much time he spent at camp. An entry does tell me that in 1932, when he was twenty-one years old, he invited a special new guest.

Augusta Harper Lynde Du Val—which means 'Kim.' Arrival: July 27th—by myself. Departure: Sept. 1st—not by myself!

This is Jay's mom! A moment in my research I want to celebrate. I have an intimate connection to this history. But by the time I began my research, she had died. I want her at the other end of the phone line to answer my questions: *Why did you come alone that first summer? What did you do when you were here?* At the time I knew her, my own life consumed me, I didn't yet burn with curiosity about what had happened before. I often sat across the table from delicious information and didn't know enough to ask the questions.

If I had thought to ask, Kim could have told me how long she and Al knew each other before her first trip to camp. Over a month was a long time for a casual visit. It turned out she and Al were married less than a year later in April 1933. Did they know the previous summer that they would be married? Since neither of them is here now, I try to answer for myself what they did that summer. Perhaps they climbed Ampersand Mountain, went fishing, and played tennis on the rustic, yet serviceable court in the field where once stood Bartlett's Sportsmen's Home. Kim had a mean serve, and few could beat her when she put her mind to it.

In the evening, no television or probably even radio. No electricity. Perhaps they played card games and board games and read books. In our boxes of old papers, I find a yellowing book with no date, *One Hundred and One Queries* by Daniel Stern,[4] with questions like "If a banana and a half cost a cent and a half, what will a dozen and a half cost?" and "If the earth were a pin cushion, how many pins could you stick in it?" In the waning evening light, someone in the family would have read these questions by kerosene lamp, others with heads cocked, pencils poised to write the answer.

And then they had the clothespins.

In our first inventory, Jay and I discovered an old box with fifty-two wooden clothespins, each one uniquely designed. "I remember these." Jay told me then. "Every time a guest came, they got a plain clothespin and made whatever they wanted out of it." He never mentioned if he made one of his own.

Clothespins, 1930s–1950s

Some are simple and straightforward: a blue clothespin with a tag—*All good things come to an end and so I leave feeling berry blue.* Some elaborate: an angel in a gauze outfit with pompoms, wild steel-wool hair topped with a halo, gold metallic wings, and a huge purple satin bow. Dates from 1932 to 1962. A hula girl, a soldier, a crocodile. Each tells a silent story of the guest who created it and of his or her time at Camp Waubenoo.

The oldest date is 1932, the year Kim first visited. She may have started the tradition. Perhaps she knew she would marry the following year. A flamboyant bride clothespin lies in the old box, complete with a tissue dress, bouquet of tiny dried yellow wild flowers, veil, and train of gauze. A dapper fisherman clothespin lies nearby. Al loved to fish. Perhaps either he or Kim made this to accompany her bride. A bit of black paint for legs; yellow crisscross lines on top for suspenders; a pipe cleaner wrapped around his neck for arms; in one tiny hand, a long, wire fishing rod; and attached to the end, a tin fish.

These two could have started the Clothespin Tradition. Farnham would have loved it, and perhaps declared that from that time on, he would give newly arriving guests plain wooden clothespins to make their own creations. For years, until Jay and I discovered them, these treasures lay abandoned like old toys left in a closet long after the child has grown up and moved away.

II

At the Club during 1933, 1934, and 1935, the Depression took its toll. The Merritts, Douglasses, and Yardleys came to their own private bungalows, but the doors of the other cabins and the Bartlett Carry Club[5] Main Lodge did not open to the public. The deserted place would have felt much as it did when I first counted pots and pans in that old, cold building. At that time, in 1968, we had great hope our work would bring the Club back to life. In the early 1930s, little hope existed.

Robert Douglass had reached the age of ninety, a time to tidy up his life. He leaves me a clue. During my research of the Saranac Club Minutes, on the day I come to Robert's final entry of April 15, 1913, I discover one more treasure—a loose piece of stationery with the letterhead "Dun Building, 290 Broadway, New York," yellowed paper, frayed at the edges, the folded crease in the middle threatening to rip; a typed letter from Robert to Jay's grandfather, written twenty-one years after his last Minutes entry.

September 17, 1934

My dear Farnham:

I am sending you herewith Two Minute Books of the old Saranac Club. There were other Minutes kept by the Chairman of the House Committee, but thought they were of no particular interest to you, so I am not sending them along.

Truly yours,

R. D. Douglass[6]

A signature in black ink, the familiar forward elegant scrawl, a bit weaker—"*R. D. Douglass.*" Aha! This letter refers to the books of Minutes I hold, the Minutes Robert kept faithfully for twenty-four years, the same leather-bound books I held on that chilly February day when we first opened the safe; the books that have guided me through the story of the Saranac Club.

Farnham had the same sense of history and posterity that Robert had. Objects from the past and old photos Farnham has annotated show up wherever I turn in this house where I now live: a black, carved, soapstone Native American peace pipe; a rustic wooden frame with a sepia picture of a mustachioed gentleman proudly holding a fish; a wooden clock with a quail painted on the glass door. If I remember to insert the old key to wind it, it still tells time pretty accurately and fills the room with its comforting tick tock.

Indian pipe of peace presented to Farnham Yardley by his Sunday School teacher, Mrs. Samuel W. Whittemore of East Orange, NJ, ca. 1880.

Wooden clock, said to have been purchased by Elmer Dockum for the camp from a peddler who drove through the Adirondacks in a horse and wagon, ca. 1910.

Each intriguing object has a careful notation in Farnham Yardley's familiar hand. Because of these notes, I catch a glimpse of the stories. The peace pipe was given to Farnham by his Sunday School teacher, Mrs. Samuel W. Whittemore, in 1880, when he was twelve years old; the sepia photograph is of New Jersey Governor Pattison in 1890 at the Club the year before the big fire; the clock was purchased by Elmer Dockum for the camp from a peddler who drove through the Adirondacks in a horse and wagon about 1910. Each detail enriches my sense of the past.

No doubt Farnham recognized the significance of Robert's Minutes. One day, he must have opened the heavy safe doors and carefully deposited the books. Perhaps he thought, *Well, there have been fires before and there could be again. Here they will be safe until some day, someone will discover them.* There they stayed until thirty-four years later on a winter day in 1969 when, once again, the thick doors of the safe slowly opened as I looked over Jay's shoulder. Could Farnham ever have imagined his own grandson returning to put the Club back to its original use?

Over Christmas, 1976, we get our first winter visitors. Still warmed by memories of their summer stay at the Club, the Lewis family, complete with six kids, rents insulated and cozy Douglass Lodge. For a brief winter moment, we have close neighbors. One early afternoon, we head out in search of a perfect wild Christmas tree. A line of colorful parkas, wooly hats, and skis etches a single track in the deep snow. On the hill just above where the Sportsmen's Home once stood, Josh and Jordie Lewis build a slalom course with scary turns and icy jumps; we shovel snow off the ice and skate on Huckleberry Bay; red hands wrap around mugs of hot cocoa in front of a blazing fire.

It goes by far too fast. Fleeting neighbors depart, we return to our solitude. We dream of next summer and get to work. Our late January '77 letter to guests gives our annual update:

> Winter came to Bartlett Carry a bit sooner this year as the first snow fell early in October. But then, we often say that the Adirondacks has two seasons—black flies and snow flies.

Skating on Upper Saranac Lake, 1976.

Work goes on regardless of the weather. We cleared several acres of land for more Christmas trees which will be planted in the spring. A few months were spent cutting timber in the northwest corner of the property.

We urge guests to let us know if they want to return as we are already beginning to receive inquiries. Construction, rather than demolition, occupies Jay as he puts finishing touches on Ampersand. After almost nine years of work, we will finally have all nine lodges open this coming summer. It would be nice to grab even a moment to savor, to take stock, but Jay allows little time to rest.

Back then, I was swept up by Jay's intense focus, his capacity to work relentlessly. It never occurred to me to pause. But now, looking back, I think *What was the rush? We had the Club open.* Jay never let up. Why was he so driven? He always seemed to be working toward some mysterious deadline.

Jay turns his attention to remodeling Windsor, the one remaining building at the family camp, the house we hope to make our new home. This one seems newer than the rest of the cabins. "Oh, it is!" Jay tells me. "This wasn't built 'til my sister came along." He tells the story:

One day in 1937, Harriet—you know, my grandmother—called Elmer Dockum in for a meeting. Mom and Dad had just told Gramp and Harriet that they were expecting a baby in October. Harriet said, "Elmer, the children are having children. We will need more room by next summer."

Elmer had already helped my great-grandfather lay out the first cabins in 1903. So he just broke a dead branch off a nearby tree, bent down, drew a detailed design in the dirt, and said "I think this might work."

By the next summer, the house was built. Mom told me Gramp referred to it as a commodious bungalow and dubbed it Windsor Castle. That was perfect. It looked pretty majestic on top of the hill, much bigger than any other cabin at camp. When they came up the next summer, Gramp wrote in the guestbook: "Pamela DuVal Yardley—born October 11, 1937—to record that the fourth generation greeted Waubenoo."

Four generations! I think. And our children are the fifth.

Now, many years after Jay tells me this story, I still marvel at the longevity and persistence of the Yardley, Jenkins, and Douglass families. Robert Douglass was the first of them to stake a claim at Bartlett Carry. Fires, war, depression, and severe weather did not keep him from his cherished Adirondacks for forty-four years. Old age, however, finally disabled him. After 1933, when he could no longer make the trip, Robert's second son, Graham, who did not share Robert's commitment or passion, sold the gracious home on Douglass Point. Robert lived for another five years, but no longer played an active role. As he slips gradually out of this story, his words and images remain in my heart and mind. His minutes opened a window for me onto the people of the Saranac Club, the people who kept this place going after the Bartletts, and for that rich glimpse into a bygone landscape, I am so grateful.

By the 1930s, other staunch Club supporters had also made their exit. Robert's brother, Benjamin, had died in 1922. William, the youngest brother, had enjoyed a halcyon eleven years at the Club, but he too had advanced in age.

In February 1935, William passed on. While some of his family still wanted to visit the Club, William's passing signified the end of any Douglass financial support and left Harriet and Farnham Yardley with total responsibility. I feel a lurch in my gut. What would happen now?

By the following August, Farnham arranged with Clinton J. Ayres of Saranac Lake for a thorough inventory and assessment of Club buildings and their contents. He might have been considering selling. No matter how well the Jenkins business succeeded, no matter how much Farnham and Harriet loved the land, drastic times and economic realities had finally taken their toll. For exactly that reason, even if Farnham had wanted to sell, very likely no one interested in purchasing this large property existed.

Looking back, in the winter of 1969 when I inventoried the Main Lodge linen room, I had no idea of the crisis Farnham and Harriet faced thirty-four years earlier and no idea that I would discover a clue to their solution. Back then, I had my own much smaller crisis—to stay warm enough to sort the linens, stack them into boxes, and label and move them out of the Main Lodge so Jay could demolish one-third of that enormous building.

I faced shelves of puckered seersucker and white chenille bedspreads, stacks of towels. And sheets. Mountains of heavy, surprisingly cold sheets. One day, without taking off my woolly mittens, I shook one open. Aroma of faded bleached cotton sprang into the cold air—instant fleeting vision of childhood sleepless summer nights when the sun seemed never to set. In one corner of the twin sheet, I noticed printing stamped in faded grey on the fabric—"Treadway Inn."

Treadway Inn? I knew this name. I spent three school years in New England in the 1960s where long-established Treadway Inns dotted the bucolic towns. In 1909, L. G. Treadway, recent graduate of Dartmouth College, had moved to South Williamstown, Massachusetts, to manage and then own the Williams Inn—shades of Virgil Bartlett. From that modest beginning, L. G., his informal name, founded a national chain of Treadway Inns offering comfort, good food, efficiency, and old-fashioned rural hospitality.[7] By the mid-1930's, fifty-five Treadway Inns spread across the country. But how had "my" Bartlett Carry Club in the mountains of the Adirondacks come to have some of their sheets?

Only now, years later, I piece it all together. In 1935, once William Douglass died, Harriet, fifty-nine, and Farnham, sixty-seven, didn't know what to do with the property. I can't be sure what led them to Treadway, but my best guess is their good friend, Schuyler Merritt, helped them. While not a legal or financial partner of the Club, he and his family had been coming to Bartlett Carry for over forty years, since 1893. His daughters had spent idyllic summers growing up wading in the waters of Upper Saranac by day and star gazing by night. At the age of eighty-two, he remained committed and could provide wise counsel.

Because Schuyler lived in New England, he would have known of L. G. Treadway and his chain of successful country inns. Harriet and Farnham must have felt relief with the potential of this new possibility. L. G. visited the Club property, succumbed to its charms, and ordered a full inspection and appraisal. He commissioned Charles Hart, Treadway vice president, to travel north in the winter of 1935–1936. In his follow-up report, Mr. Hart stated, "Many details will, of necessity, have to be omitted in this report, as the season of the year was not a particularly good one to inspect things as closely as one could wish."[8]—echoes of the February 1889 reconnaissance trip endured by the gentlemen of the future Saranac Club. It is likely Mr. Hart's first impressions reflect those of many others who came before and after him. They reflect mine. "It is seldom one has occasion to view property with a setting that so aptly combines the varied charm of Mountain, Lake and Stream, all bounded by acres upon acres of timber, mountain trails and lake expanse. One cannot but enthuse about the property itself for what it has to offer to those who enjoy nature."[9]

As an astute businessman, L. G. had survived the Depression. He saw potential and had the financial wherewithal to take on this addition to his bevy of inns. He would need the economic buffer his established profitable enterprise could afford. Overhead expenses of the Bartlett Carry Club from 1930 to 1934 had averaged $7,138.94 annually. Mr. Hart stated this was exceptionally high for this form of property. The owners had been investing an average of $6,360 per year. This clearly shows the unwavering commitment of William Douglass and Harriet and Farnham

Yardley as they subsidized the whole operation. All other reported income averaged $501 per year.

Mr. Hart stated frankly he did not think large summer resorts had much of a future, but he did describe the Club's potential perfectly:

> We do believe in the future of the small Inn if properly located, and if having a definite background, whether the background be of historical, educational or natural interest.
>
> We feel that there is a definite swing of the pendulum of human interest toward the simpler manner of living . . . If it is the owner's desire to make the enjoyment of this property available to that portion of the public who would be most likely to appreciate it, and as a secondary objective reduce their own annual out-of-pocket expense and gradually eliminate it, we believe there is an opportunity afforded if the property is handled in the right way.[10]

Mr. Hart's assessment came close to describing Jay and me over thirty years later as we, against all odds, began to revive the Bartlett Carry Club. We had no idea if we would succeed. We held on to our vision—to restore these buildings and honor the history for which they stood; to open the doors to those who sought respite in the woods; and to eventually offset our expenses and make a profit. Along the way, we watched peace wash over guests as they allowed tension from the long drive and life's responsibilities to melt in the sound of rushing water and the tranquility of no phones or TV. The most important thing in a day might be to take blueberry muffins out of the oven and eat them warm, with lots of butter.

In 1936, Mr. Hart recommended reopening the Club with the understanding it would not be a stellar moneymaker, but it could eventually take care of overhead expenses. Harriet would remain owner of the property, and the Treadway Inn would lease and manage it. On January 17, 1936, Mr. Hart submitted his report to Farnham and Harriet for their consideration.

They wasted no time. Within four days, Farnham gave the go-ahead. That spring, the L. G. Treadway Service Corp. signed a five-year contract with Bartlett Carry Realty Co. They hired Russell Wayne[11] as manager, and they were ready to open.

Brochure Treadway Inn, 1936.

III

In 1977, with the help of a couple of construction workers, Jay progresses with the renovation of what will be our new home. Elmer had designed this house in the dirt for Harriet almost forty years earlier, just as the Bartlett Carry Treadway Inn had opened. Jay now has his routine down to a science; gut the interior, put on a new roof, re-side the exterior, re-wire for AC electricity (we will finally have electricity on Middle Saranac Lake!), build a new porch, install thermopane windows. We give "Windsor" a new name—the Lake House—to distinguish it from the River House where we still live.

As I look back now at one scrapbook photo after another of the Lake House under construction, I want to screech to a halt. I look away, but my mind flashes forward to a frozen image of a house half-done, standing in the warmth of summer sun, no one there. Mid-July, 1978. All work suspended.

Windsor renovation halted, 1978.

I try to stop my zooming mind and focus on the actual pictures. They seem innocuous. Here's one from May 1977, the year before the work stops: in the midst of an unusually late snow fall, we set out two thousand more Christmas trees seedlings to brave the rough field.

And a picture from June: construction of two stalls in our barn. We welcome the arrival of two aging horses, Bud, a chestnut thoroughbred, and Silver, a portly Welsh pony, given to us by my horse-trainer sister from Maryland. We bring in the requisite barn kitties, Coal and Cinders, who perch, black-furred, on Silver's white back. He doesn't mind at all. I fret about where to find 350 bales of good hay that won't go rotten or mildew.

How naïve we were. How small the problems that seemed so big. As I flip from one page of photos to the next, I have this visceral sense of a locomotive: I stand on a track, behind me a huge unseen train belching black smoke, picking up speed, rumbling down the track, still far off, the dark unfurling plume etched in the sky.

Coal the kitty on Silver's back, Bud and Fran in background, 1977.

For this year anyway, all goes blessedly smoothly. Summer 1977 arrives. Celebration! Nine years after our arrival, finally, every lodge ready. July and August merge in a blur of old guests, new guests, watering geraniums, sweeping the Main Lodge, frantic forty-eight-hour change overs, making sure everyone is content.

Guests congregate on the beach, sit in a soporific daze as they lift faces to mesmerizing late-afternoon sun. While little hands build and destroy sandcastles and bigger hands slather on sunscreen and administer to skinned knees, a lawyer for the Justice Department discusses Washington antics with a lawyer for the Atomic Energy Commission. The conversation proves more interesting and informative than reading the *New York Times.* Then we all go for a swim.

Occasionally, Jay takes a rare moment away from his current demolition or reconstruction project and sits in the shade, long legs crossed, chatting with a guest about our logging operation or old machinery once in the power house or how he took down the Main Lodge.

Jay also helps families embarking on day canoe trips. They pack picnics, climb in boats, and head downstream through Middle and Lower Saranac Lakes, stopping for lunch or a swim. At an agreed-upon time, Jay meets them at the state boat launch on Route 3, loads them and their boat, and brings them back to the Club.

Back then I didn't truly comprehend that we had succeeded in honoring the legacy of Virgil and Caroline Bartlett—to provide a comfortable place on the edge of the wilderness where guests wanted to return again and again. At the time, I was completely immersed in the day-to-day routine of my children and running the Club. I was in a doing phase, not one of introspection.

But now, one day I receive a letter from Turhan Tirana, a guest who came with his wife and two young children in 1977. Turhan writes; "My best memory was my first. After a long drive from Pittsburgh, we spied the green oar blade along the road, adjacent to a dirt road leading into nowhere. No words on the blade, just the initials BCC. I was ecstatic. *My kind of place*, I thought."

He also remembered "catching a landlocked salmon; Peter hitting a bat with the tip of his rod while fishing one evening; Ellie catching a small sunfish, her first one, with her Uncle George—*Good catch!* he exclaimed; Peter catching and releasing frogs in the water grass at the little beach; Ellie watching Peter playing hearts while she read C. S. Lewis; the bear rug in the lodge. Peter summed it up. *That was a fun place.*"

Back then we suspected we were doing a good job because people came back. Now when I read a memory like Turhan's, I see clearly we really had achieved our goal. Turhan's voice from the outside helps me understand how good things were and to appreciate what I could not appreciate back then.

Jay and I ran our business quite simply. Besides the non-stop work we each did, we had only Chuck to help with firewood and repairs and two indispensable, part-time cleaning ladies to keep everything spiffy. No dining room serving meals, no guides to be found. People loved hiking and fishing by themselves and, at least ostensibly, didn't mind making their own beds or cooking their own meals.

Back in the 1800s when the Bartletts ran their Sportsmen's Home, many more people were involved. It took a sizable staff including guides, cooks, maids, and gardeners to succeed. (I think back to that astounding figure from 1908, during the Saranac Club era, when a staff of fifty-nine took care of 105 guests plus members.) Boat boys helped guests into their boats, guides took them fishing and into the woods, maids cleaned up, and a full staff cooked and served in the dining room.

By the late 1930s, the new Treadway Bartlett Carry Club did not need the extensive staff of a few decades earlier, but they did need more than Jay and I. One of those staff members, Elsie Hughes, joined Treadway in 1936 and was grateful for work in those tough times.

I first met Elsie and her husband, Phil Wolff, in the early 1970s when I walked into their florist shop in Saranac Lake. "I need flowers for nine houses and a big Main Lodge." I said. I immediately had Phil's attention.

"Geraniums," he said. "You can't lose with geraniums." He was right. From then on, those bright-red flowers graced Club flower boxes every year. I spoke to Elsie infrequently back then, and if she mentioned anything about being at the Bartlett Carry Club, I just wasn't ready to hear it. I didn't know for a long time of the trove of information both she and Phil held going back to the 1930s.

One evening, about thirty years later, I saw Elsie at a party.

"Fran, what have you been up to?"

I told her about the book I am writing.

"Did you know I worked at the Bartlett Carry Club?"

I was finally ready. I wanted to know.

"Oh my. Would you be willing to be interviewed?"

I interviewed her the next week. At the age of ninety-one, she possessed enviable clarity and candor. She told me she rode into Tupper Lake on the Adirondack Division rail line from Remsen, New York, one spring day in 1936 to work as a waitress at the Bartlett Carry Club Treadway Inn. Nineteen years old, fresh from her first year at Cornell, she had never traveled this far north and never had a job so far from her home in Utica, New York.

She worked in the dining room and bunked with eight other staff in dorm rooms over the boathouse on the river. In her words:

> I do not recall how much I was paid, but it was enough to get me through another year of college. In those times, forty cents an hour was standard. I remember bread was ten cents a loaf.

Boathouse on river.

Some of the families my first year came for most of the summer, others came for a week or a month. The guests went hiking, canoeing, and boating, of course—the usual things you do in the Adirondacks. We had an interesting chef—French Canadian. He had a very short temper, but he was kind to all of us, protected us and helped us learn what we were doing. So he had two sides. One morning, he was cooking Cornish game hens. He pulled the tray out of the oven and they went flying all over the kitchen. He picked them up, put them back in the oven and they were served anyway.

It was an ideal place to spend the summer, meet people from different walks of life, and make some money . . . a wonderful place.[12]

During the two years Elsie worked at the Club, her sweetheart, Phil Wolff, worked in Lake Placid and lived in Saranac Lake. In 1936, to court Elsie, he drove regularly to Bartlett's over State Route 3 which had been under reconstruction for over two years. The alternate, more established road around the north end of Upper Saranac Lake was ten miles longer, so, despite the extensive potholes and delays, he preferred the gravel Route 3 shortcut, at least for a while. He remembered it well:

> The contractor was a fellow by the name of Frenchie . . . they were right in the middle of building the road . . . they started digging out stumps and suddenly there'd be big holes in the road. Few people realized it, but once they dug up the stumps and made those big holes, they filled them with the decaying stumps and then put cement on top. That's the reason the road didn't last very well.
>
> I remember one time I was going along at night [in his 1928 Ford Woodie station wagon he had bought for forty dollars] and I had to stop quick. Everything was black in front of me. I got out and looked down into a huge hole—and that was the last trip I ever made that way 'til the road was done.[13]

Frank Casier also remembered that road. A local businessman and long-time friend, he first came to Saranac Lake as a TB patient. At the age of ninety-three, he told me with a smile:

> Did you know I worked on that road? In 1937, I was just out of high school . . . I had bought a new truck and they paid me $1.25 per hour for my labor and me using my new truck.
>
> People thought the job was almost impossible. The road took two years to build and had five different contractors. There was so much swamp land! By the time we got close to Bartlett Carry, I remember the sandpit. That part of the road building was easy—there was sand available and no blasting.
>
> The road was built of cement blocks from the quarry on the Bloomingdale road. It was high tech to have a cement road. My job was to dump my truck full of blasted rock in the swamp part of the road to fill it in. I can claim I dumped the first load of cement on the Saranac Lake Tupper Lake road.[14]

When Jay and I arrived in 1968, it didn't occur to me that Route 3, our main artery to civilization, did not exist in the days of Virgil and Caroline. Depending on the season, they traveled to the outer world mainly over water or ice or through the woods on a rickety wagon road. Virgil saw the potential of a road linking Saranac Lake and Tupper Lake and conveniently passing close to Bartlett's. In 1872, he joined an effort to lay out and construct a highway, but given that "Saranac Lake was a straggling little hamlet then and Tupper had a population of 'mostly spruce and hemlock,'"[15] this early road project failed.

Decades later, in the 1920s, the villages had grown, roads were laid out, and automobiles became the preferred method next to trains for travel to the Adirondacks. A rudimentary gravel road ran from Tupper to Saranac Lake, but it remained a difficult passage until the work in the 1930s.

Today, with my new awareness of the road's history, when I jump in the car to drive eleven miles from Bartlett Carry to the grocery store in Saranac Lake, I think of smooth blacktopped Route 3 differently; I feel a distant connection with those who worked at a wage of $1.25 per hour, and those who jammed on their brakes at the edges of black holes. Over my almost fifty years driving this same road, I have seen it cracked, rebuilt, repaved, cracked and repaved again—a seemingly unending cycle.

IV

One day in 2005, as I continue my research about the Treadway years at the Club, my phone rings. When I pick up, a quavery voice says, "Fran Yardel? Is this the lady of Bartlett Carry? This is John Sennott." He has called me completely out of the blue.

"I began working at the Bartlett Carry Club during the Treadway years," he says. "I wanted to reconnect with my past." John is eighty-seven years old, living in Pennsylvania, and has recently lost his wife. He begins to call me regularly. I recognize him as a treasure and drop everything to talk with him.

In April 2007, the phone rings. "Fran Yardel? Is it time to roll the tennis court?" I recognize him immediately. No one else calls me Yardel. He is clearly living in his memory when there was a tennis court. "Oh John! Hello! How are you?" I grab a pad and pen to take notes.

"The ice is about to go off the lake!" He is living in his memory and calling from far away, and he is right. It is mid-April, and I look out at ice growing blacker by the day. Every time we talk, he fills in more of his story.

John tells me that while in college in 1941, he came down with an illness that seriously affected his eyesight. His memory of the dates may have been foggy. Facts show the year was more likely 1939. At any rate, he ended up in Massachusetts General Hospital for five months and five operations. With college no longer an option, he needed a job.

"My father had done a lot of business with L. G. Treadway, and they were friends. He said, 'Maybe L. G. can help you. He's had a place for a couple of years in Saranac Lake. Head on up there.'"

John did. In early May (most likely 1939), after hitchhiking from Massachusetts to the Adirondacks, he took on the job of boatman and chore boy. He remembered well the manager, Russell Wayne, who, behind his back, was referred to as Pinhead Wayne.[16] John told me:

> Over the next two years, I got to know him better than I might have wanted to. He was a fly fisherman. That part was all right. But he was a very bad manager, a thief at heart, robbing everyone. He was despicable, especially with women. If you were a handsome lady, he'd try to 'feel of you' in his private office right away. He was a disgrace to Treadway. Couldn't even get along with the staff.

John took care of the boats and helped people if they needed it. He had a story that gave me more insight into Farnham Yardley:

> Once, old Grampa Yardel was on the river fishing in his guide boat. He must have hit a stump or something because the next thing I knew, he tipped right over. He was wet up to his butt, his fly rod floating in the water and he was trying to see where it was. Then he looked up and saw me looking at him. "Go back up and mind your own business," he said. "Go on back up to your job at the club. I'm all right."

And another story that gives me more information about Mr. Wayne:

Towards end of my second summer there in 1940, nobody saw Mr. Wayne for two days. I asked Cookie what was going on and he said "Well, ol' Pinhead Wayne tried to attack Katherine, our head waitress, in the parking lot and her husband came down and beat the hell out of him. He's in the hospital with serious bruises near his head. Serves him right."

I know Mr. Wayne didn't like me much. It wasn't much later when I guess I stood up to him and he fired me for insubordination, gave me my final pay and had someone drive me to Tupper Lake. Well, I called my daddy and he said "Call LG!" So I called Mr. Treadway who said to come visit him in Massachusetts and tell him what happened. "And don't say anything 'til you talk to me." I got on the train and went there and LG fired Mr. Wayne and brought in a new manager for the rest of the season. That was fine with me.[17]

I'm almost afraid to call John in April 2008. I haven't heard from him in a while. Will he still answer? The phone picks up. His voice sounds frailer, but still coherent. "I'm almost blind," he says. "I am limited, but not verbally." Well, maybe he's blind, but he certainly sees clearly in his mind.

He tells me that while Mr. Wayne was manager, Treadway made improvements to several cottages and built a new dock on the river. Then, after Mr. Wayne departed, the staff heaved sighs of relief and welcomed a new manager who looked forward to welcoming guests in the summer of 1941 by sending postcards as far away as Cleveland, Ohio. *It's a lovely season now at Bartlett Carry Club. Summertime will be even lovelier. Mail us your reservation. You're coming, aren't you?*[18]

I talk with John for the last time in 2010.

"Bartlett Carry was a turning point in my life," he tells me. "I am lonesome for those old days. They were such beautiful times for a young person who had just gotten out of the hospital. I dream of Norway Island on Round Lake; I loved to camp on that little flat rock. I'll introduce you as Fran Yardel, the lady who is forever wild. You follow through. The ball is yours. Bye bye. Peace, peace."

In his obituary later in 2010, the heading reads "John Sennott, 91, 'Tiny' of Bartlett Carry."

V

In the fall of 1977, eight months before all work on the Lake House stops precipitously, Jay installs new windows and begins to add exterior siding. I make another visit to Mrs. Macro. I may have finished work on the nine lodges, but I have one more house, ours, to sew curtains for.

The Lewis family returns for a second winter in Douglass. They bring Barbara's parents who christen winter occupancy of Ampersand. When we trudge up the snowy hill to visit our temporary neighbors, the alluring aroma of freshly baked cookies wafts on the wintry air.

Our January 1978 letter to guests goes out as usual, saying "It has been a very busy fall at Bartlett Carry. Among other things, we have installed electric heat in the bathrooms in all the lodges. We hope that this will provide added incentive to our guests to greet the new day at Bartlett Carry."

We include our maple syrup, now sporting a professional looking label: sepia tone paper, brown typeface—*Adirondack Maple Syrup from the Sugar House at Round Lake, Fran and Jay Yardley, props. One half gallon.*

Life rolls forward. What did we have for breakfast? Was the winter cold? What important things did we discuss? Scrapbook pictures don't reveal these things, but they do remind me that we gutted the interior of the Lake House, dug ditches, laid water pipes; we cut the only three black cherry trees on the property for our living room paneling; and we harvested 150 cedar posts to enclose the pasture by the River House for Bud and Silver.

May 1978 arrives. We have nine houses to open, two thousand more Christmas tree seedlings to plant and the others to tend to, and a cement pad for a garage to lay at the new house. And we have to drill for water at the Lake House. We have a full lake of water at our front door, but we can't trust that it's safe to drink.

All winter on my daily walk, I have noticed one particular young beech tree about half-way down our road. It has seemed for months as if it will never come to life again. Today, on the tips of its branches, dozens of tiny buds peak out, a promise of things to come. Not long after—why did I not see the progression?—a hint of green appears, and it seems the next day a leaf bursts out. This new spring leaf, just at my eye level, invites me to touch it. Ah, the newness, soft as my dog's ear. Almost silky. I crush a hemlock twig between my fingers to release the earthy, sap-green aroma, not as aromatic as balsam, definitely green hemlock. This tiny hemlock branch whispers old secrets, if only I could hear.

On June 17, 1978, headlines announce a huge fire at the Saranac Inn, an enormous historic structure, nine miles north on Upper Saranac Lake. When first built in 1864, ten years after Bartlett's, it was called the Prospect House and had fifteen bedrooms. Over the course of a century, it expanded into a grand hotel serving over 250 guests at a time. In 1962, it closed its doors on empty rooms, peeling paint and hollow voices echoing down long corridors. For sixteen years, no one came forward to renovate it. This one day, in the process of being torn down, it erupts in gigantic flames and burns to the ground.

One morning in late June, I notice a lump the size of a golf ball on Jay's neck.

"What's that?" I ask.

"Oh," he says, "I'm going to have it looked at when we're not this busy."

My stomach lurches. After Jay takes off for work, I get on the phone.

The receptionist offers me a 7:30 p.m. appointment the next evening, the only one available, with Dr. Fritz Decker, our friend and neighbor. Never one to interfere with our evening family time, I don't even pause.

"We'll take it." I say.

Jay comes home, a stark white bandage on his tan neck. "Fritz did a biopsy. It'll be back in a few days."

The phone rings on Sunday morning.

"Hi, it's Fritz. Can I come over?"

It's Hodgkin's Disease. Jay will need surgery, the sooner the better. We decide Johns Hopkins is the best place to go. No matter what needs doing, I will go to Baltimore with Jay for the surgery. We'll figure the rest out as we go.

Rhythm—I latch onto traces of it in the midst of the ensuing whirlwind. For once, I don't mind that we have only a few reservations for the beginning of July—returning families, so they'll know what to do. The kids have finished school. My mom comes for a few days. Then Tori Jenkins, babysitter extraordinaire, takes over while Jay and I go to Baltimore.

My grandfather graduated from Johns Hopkins in 1903. The hospital has expanded a lot since then so it takes me a while to discover the original section with the floors he would have once walked. It's a good distraction. I pace those same floors while the docs operate on Jay. They confirm Hodgkin's Disease, Stage 4A. Sounds like a military ranking. Not good. They prescribe a regime of chemotherapy, possibly to be followed by radiation.

It will take Jay a while to recover enough to come home. Then he'll travel over two hours to Burlington, Vermont, for chemo. I must go home now. Home to our kids; home to the Club, by now in full swing with guests; home to four thousand Christmas trees to fertilize and mow, two thousand more seedlings still to plant; and home to a house arrested in the middle of construction in late June, but now, thanks to a cadre of workers, bustling with activity. What else? Who knows? I just know I have to leave Jay, and I don't want to.

The small commuter plane circles once over the mountains and the airport in Lake Clear, only thirty minutes from home. Part of me really looks forward to hugging my daughters, to smelling that North Country smell. Part of me wishes we will never land. I want to stay in the clouds, suspended in this no-man's-land between the reality of what I just left and coming home to full responsibility and some skewed sense of being in control. The racing airplane engine echoes my speeding heart.

The pilot passes through a gateway of pointy spruce trees and soft feathery hemlock to make a smooth landing. With my first scent of Adirondack air, I no longer have doubts. I wonder, was this the place I once felt no connection to? Now I am so connected I can't stay away.

I careen back into my life, grateful for what I have to do, no time to think. I bless Chuck, who keeps an eye on the Club, and Tori, who tends our kids when I can't. She becomes a regular, positive presence in their lives.

One day, I seek the simplicity and solitude of the Christmas trees after checking progress on the Lake House, where workers dig ditches, nail on siding, and drill for water. We had rain recently. This early morning, blue sky and sun promise warmth by midmorning; a perfect day to spread fertilizer. I measure one, two, three, four scoops into the bag, strap it around my waist. This will easily get me down one row of twenty-five trees and back up the next. Then I'll have only thirty-eight rows to go in this plot before moving on to the next thousand trees. Doing the math comforts me. It's precise, and there's always a correct answer.

Spraying Christmas trees, late 1970s.

I grab a handful of granules from my bag, fling it at the base of the first small tree, pace six feet to the next tree, dig my hand into the bag, fling the fertilizer, step to the next. Early morning dew shimmers on one spider's web after another, laced amongst the fresh green growth. Tree number eight, nine, ten. Step, scoop, fling, step, scoop, fling. Can Jay come home soon? Can we keep the Club operating smoothly this summer? So much to do. At least I have good help this year—hopefully.

Twenty, twenty-one, twenty-two. Yup, I still have more than half the bag of fertilizer left, this'll work out okay. At the end of the row, I pause to look south toward the Seward Range. A robin trills in a high pine at the edge of the planting. I take a moment to stretch. That pine looks really healthy. Maybe we should have planted pine instead of balsam.

I turn back, head down the second row. Twelve, thirteen, fourteen. From this direction, the dewdrops glisten from branch to tiny branch like miniature Christmas tree lights. How appropriate. Step, scoop, fling, step, scoop. Wow, this tree needs real pruning. It has a double leader. Come to think of it, quite a few of them need pruning. I don't have the time. How am I going to make this work? Will Jay be okay? Can't dwell on that. Well drillers are coming again today to look for water at the Lake House. No luck yesterday and they drilled three hundred feet. How can that be with the house so close to the lake? Step, scoop—I stop dead. A deer stands at the edge of the field, right by the huge boulder the kids love to climb. She raises her head and for a moment, a brief second really, her wide velvety eyes lock on mine. Then she whirls and with a flick of her white tail disappears.

To welcome Jay home from Baltimore, we tape a ten-foot-long colorful homemade WELCOME HOME DAD sign in the living room so he will see it when he first comes in the door. His eyes look bewildered, but he makes an effort to seem okay. This pretty much sums up the next few weeks. No memory of how the days actually went. I want to say it all went smoothly, the Club practically ran itself, the cleaning ladies took over, and Chuck took care of the rest; the Lake House construction progressed, the Christmas trees grew strong and healthy, and we found well water. I want to say this, but I don't really remember how it all went down. I try to keep track by writing doctor and chemo appointments, kid play dates, arrival and departure of guests all on a large desk-size blotter calendar. In ink.

The Club hums with activity. I greet guests old and new. The Tiranas return and bring a family of friends. The Donalds arrive with two rambunctious boys who take to the wilderness and don't put on shoes for two weeks.

The Bennett family returns for their fifth year. On July 22, 1978, Annie Bennett marries Phil Petronis in Au Sable Forks, and they come to Bartlett Carry for their honeymoon. Annie stands on the back porch of Pine Lodge and tosses her bridal wreath over a thin pine sapling. The wreath lands mid-trunk and stays there for several years.

VI

Back in the summer of 1941, Annie's bridal-wreath sapling had not yet burst through the soil, but happy occasions similar to the Bennett and Petronis honeymoon very likely occurred at the Bartlett Carry Treadway Inn as well.

Events in December 1941 changed everything. Early Sunday morning, December 7, over 350 Japanese war planes droned over the U.S. Naval Base in Pearl Harbor, Hawaii, and attacked Americans on their own soil.

The nation and the world came to a standstill. President Roosevelt declared war on Japan.

Those not on the battlefield stepped up to do their part: volunteering for the Red Cross, planting Victory gardens, painting light bulbs black for dark-outs, and watching for low-flying planes. I wasn't born until 1944, but my dear friend, Pooh Ritchie, reflected on her teen years when she lived in Philadelphia. "There was such a shortage of gasoline, I bicycled everywhere or used my little pony cart. It's hard to explain, but in the midst of all the hardship, there was a feeling we were all pulling together towards a common cause. There was a different feeling, different attitude, a sense of camaraderie. We had our gardens, and we wrapped gauze and cotton bandages for our soldiers."[19]

Few had time, money, or means to travel north to the Adirondacks for a vacation. After six years of operation, the Treadway Inn did not renew its Bartlett Carry contract in 1942. All fell quiet at the Club that year, bungalows empty except for the Merritt, Douglass, and Yardley families. The mail boat, the only motor boat allowed on the lake, created possibly the only wake on the water other than that made by landing loons.

The war did not stop Harriet and Farnham from making their annual pilgrimage from Llewellyn Park, New Jersey, to the Adirondacks. Again, they seemed relatively untouched by the mayhem around them as they traveled with their retinue including a chauffeur named Gervaise (a perfect chauffeur name) and personal maids. The local staff greeted them as they arrived: caretakers Lena and Harry Cummings, handyman Walter Drew, a cook, and always Elmer Dockum. In 1942, Albert Saunders moved to the house by the river to be caretaker for the Club. Farnham and Harriet paid all wages. Jenkins Manufacturing must have been doing remarkably well.

In the midst of the disaster of war, a protective cocoon seemed wrapped around this family. They had many visitors. Old black-and-white photos show Farnham playing tennis in his golfing trousers, presiding over backgammon and bridge games, smoking his pipe. Katharine Merritt, the grown daughter of Schuyler and now a children's doctor, traveled the mile from the Club to spend an overnight at camp.

Farnham entered a proud note in the family guestbook in August 1941. "Alfred Jenkins Yardley, Jr., born October 18, 1940. First visit to the family camp at the age of nine months." They juggled his initials and called him

A family picnic, 1941: Harriet Yardley, Schuyler Merritt, Babs Lynch, Farnham Yardley, Al Yardley.

Jay. He was a bright ray of hope during a dark time. Little did they know then that Jay, in his twenties, would return to this place and be the one to keep not only the family camp, but also the Bartlett Carry Club alive.

The family seemed to make it through the war relatively unscathed by death or financial difficulty. However, they did not escape illness. Jay's mom, Kim, told me about it one day.

"It was June 1943. Jay was only two and a half. I will never forget this—I was walking by the sea, and suddenly, I just collapsed."

The diagnosis: cancer of the spine. At the age of thirty, with two young children, she entered the hospital for an undetermined length of time.

Al, most likely trying to retain a semblance of normality, brought the children to camp with a nurse in tow. He was in his early thirties. Why didn't he fight in the war? Perhaps because of his commitment to Jenkins Manufacturing, part of the war effort; perhaps because after Kim collapsed, he was the only functioning parent.

Kim had many stories about that time.

"The doctors told me I would probably die. When I didn't, they said you'll never walk again. I had the most amazing doctor. The day I met him, he walked into my room, examined me, and said, 'The next time I see you, I expect you to look better,' and walked out. That was the day I first asked for a comb and my lipstick. He gave me some unusual muscle-strengthening exercises."

After months in the hospital, they told her she might walk, but never without aid. They underestimated her. She may have mourned the fact she would never again play tennis, but she didn't let anyone tell her what she could or couldn't do. It took years. She not only walked without assistance, she learned to fly an airplane. This woman of gargantuan spirit and fortitude lived almost eighty-three years, until April 1997.

While Kim waged her battle, hope for an end to World War II sprang alive when Nazi Germany surrendered on May 9, 1945. After the United States deployed nuclear bombs over Nagasaki and Hiroshima in August, Japan surrendered to the Allies and the Pacific War ended.

At the end of the war, soldiers returned with visible physical wounds and not so visible psychological ones. In this new peacetime world, a resurgence of jobs and a vigorous economy lifted spirits. Millions moved out of cities to the suburbs to seek a better life. The Depression had loosened its steely grip.

On July 5, 1946, Al Yardley took advantage of the new commercial air service from New York to the Lake Clear airport, thirty minutes from the family camp. The flight took one hour and twenty-five minutes, a far cry from ten hours by car. In August, four years after her collapse, Kim felt well enough to fly up and join Al and her children for a short visit. The thrill of skimming above the earth in this small plane may have inspired her to later become a pilot.

Farnham, now seventy-eight years old, and Harriet, seventy, bore full responsibility for the Club. They still operated as Bartlett Carry Realty Co. (BCRCo). No more Douglasses with deep pockets. Due to the hardships of war, no more Treadway Inn with a vast network of potential customers. What could they do? In this precarious postwar time, despite a growing economy, they had little hope of selling the property. They needed to find new managers and try to generate income. In February, 1946, they signed an agreement with Mrs. Dorothea P. Doring and her sister, Miss Lillian J.

Purdy. Perhaps Mrs. Doring was a war widow in need of whatever income she could find.

The contract allowed the two women "to operate and manage for hotel and resort purposes from May 14, 1946 to September 30, 1946, the land, club house and cottages, all furniture, fixtures and equipment, boathouses, boats, automobiles and other personal property."[20] They took over everything except Yardley, Douglass, and Merritt cottages and the caretaker house on the river. The BCRCo agreed to pay taxes and insurance, dam maintenance, and salary for a caretaker. Mrs. Doring and Miss Purdy held responsibility for everything else. Net operating earnings would be divided equally. The two women would bear any loss. In June 1946, they flung open the doors of the Main Lodge and bungalows and welcomed their first guests. Once again, someone recognized the potential of the Club. The abiding question lingered: would it work?

6

Balancing

I

In 1978, if I had known strong, hardworking women like Mrs. Doring and Miss Purdy, I would have hired them in a heartbeat. I never knew if I'd get everything done: complete changeover of guests every two weeks; monthly two-hour chemo trips to Burlington; a nine- and a five-year-old to engage, delight, and educate; horses to feed, water, and exercise; fast-growing Christmas tree seedlings to fertilize, prune, and mow; and our unfinished house on Middle Saranac Lake.

All this with a constant knot in my gut. The hectic schedule might possibly have kept me from feeling too much. Meanwhile, our vacationing guests at the Club blissfully hiked mountains, paddled canoes, picked blueberries, and basked in afternoon beach sun. I longed for that normality. I wanted our lives to be as they had been before June 28.

I hadn't realized how simple our lives were when we first came even though we had taken on a huge challenge. So much to plan, demolish, renovate at the beginning; so much to keep track of in the middle; and when we were fully open, I was exhausted giving prospective guests a tour of the Club and saying *here's Douglass and here's Ampersand and here's Pine and the Main Lodge and Fir and Hemlock and Birch and here's Maple and Cedar and Merritt and here's the beach and here's this boathouse and . . .* About half way through, I had to fight an irresistible urge to lie down in the pine needles, heave a huge sigh, and close my eyes.

I felt overwhelmed during those days, no doubt about it, but there was a simplicity about them, a steady progression. We had a plan and it unfolded, albeit slowly, day by day, but always in a positive direction.

Now, with the new reality of Jay's illness, we have no plan we can depend on, only the minimal comfort of writing in my calendar his treatments and appointments over the next six months, and at the end, patting the calendar and saying *There! Six months and we're done! It will all be over then.*

Over the course of each month's treatment, Jay has two weeks of feeling terrible from injections and pills, and then two weeks to recover before the next onslaught. I begin to look at it as a roller-coaster ride. From the few times I've ridden on a roller coaster, I know it's important to hang on tight. Screaming is okay, thrashing from one curve to the next, just hang on tight.

Vignettes:

September 1978. Both our girls are now in school, and I have full days free. While part of me delights in this, I'm not sure I want this much space to think.

On a splendid, colorful Adirondack day, we climb into the 1930 Packard Jay's dad gave him and head for an antique-car meet about two hours away. We are amazed that we get all the way there and back with only a little engine tinkering. Jay's face looks brighter than it has all summer.

Chuck begins to dig postholes around the field by the barn. Finally, the promise of a fence for the animals.

Thanks to help from a myriad of workers, the Lake House on Middle Saranac nears completion. We use gravel from our pit to level the half-mile road.

In the distance, log trucks rumble as they pick up the weekly tree harvest from our land.

One by one, we have visitors: David, of course, because he is Jay's best friend; Jay's parents; his sister, Pammie. My parents even come for

Thanksgiving—a rare visit by Dad. He usually stays home when Mom visits and calls every day to ask when she'll be coming back. This flurry of visitors in such a short span doesn't fit the norm. In the air hovers a sense of the unknown. Do they think this is the last time they'll see Jay? I think they're surprised to see how well he is functioning.

In December, the Lewis clan returns for Christmas break. We wonder if the weather will cooperate. Just before they arrive, we have a storm where snow seems more to grow out of the ground than to descend from above. I want to lay my head in this magical snow. I want to allow every fiber of my being to relax into the soft mound, allow each miraculous, infinite snowflake to alight on my hair and parka, to cushion my tiredness and freshen my ripe-red cheeks. We celebrate the last of Jay's chemo treatments and ski and skate our way into 1979. I'm not sorry to say goodbye to this year.

How could we have such a life-changing event, yet maintain this veneer of normality? Perhaps the commotion of our lives buried the underlying unease. Did we make maple syrup the next spring? Our January 1979 letter refers to it and mentions nothing of the black cloud on our horizon.

It was a very mild fall at Bartlett Carry. With so many glorious days outdoors, it was hard to believe winter would be coming. Nevertheless, as we look out the window now, Gwyn and Shana are skiing across the field and the lakes are ready for skating.

When we see the ground again, it will be time to tap the trees and to spend long days in the Sugar House at Round Lake. We hope you will enjoy our maple syrup. Try it on pancakes, french toast or ice cream. We like to put some in the bottom of the pan when we fry our eggs.

Again, we are beginning to receive inquiries about the Bartlett Carry Club, so if you are planning to return next summer, please let us know by the first of February.

All of the Yardleys send best wishes to you for a Happy New Year.

The fall may have been mild. Not so the winter. On February 15, 1979, Saranac Lake reports 42 degrees below zero, coldest spot in the country. One evening, Jay laughs as he's reading the local paper.

"Listen to this," he says. " 'Once it gets past 35 below, there's not that much difference.' That's the truth!" The cold snap, with temps dipping to at least thirty below every night, lasts six days, worthy of mention in the *New York Times*. The reporter, undoubtedly writing in a warm office, says the cold is good news for construction of the annual Saranac Lake Winter Carnival ice palace which has "clear, blue-green blocks of ice cut from the lake."[1]

Jay feels well enough during the girls' spring vacation to help dig more post holes, By May, we have the fence up. We have found a new home for Bud, but I lead Silver, the pony, to the two-acre field and unhook the rope. He lowers his head, kicks his heels in the air, and is off with a snort. Oh, to be that free! Sun glistens off his white back as he bends to the new spring grass. The barn menagerie now consists of Silver and the barn cats, Butterball and Ferzy Cat. We plan to add two goats soon.

At the Lake House on Middle Saranac Lake, we have sanded and finished floors and installed bright-yellow kitchen counters and green cupboards. Jay builds a wall behind the house with enormous, grey stones to hold back a hill of sand. I perch on a two-story-tall ladder to paint brick-red trim on twenty-three exterior windows. I learn by trial and error how to cut with a paint brush and get so used to the ladder that one day, while working on a second-story window, I almost step back to see how my paint job looks. I catch myself just in time.

Late that spring, Jay goes to Baltimore for a checkup. He calls to report: "Dr. Abeloff says I need six weeks of radiation at Johns Hopkins."

"Oh god." I say before I can stop myself. "Six weeks? You'll be gone for six weeks?" I try to sound calm.

"No. Five days of radiation, then two off. I'll come back and forth. I can take our car down and fly home on weekends. You'll be okay with the truck, right?"

"Right!" I say quickly to cause him the least worry. And now that I can drive a stick shift, I will be okay with our red truck, even without power steering. Jay finds a good deal for flying back and forth and a place in Baltimore to live fairly cheaply during the week. I take garbage to the dump in the truck, cart home thirty or forty bales of hay, ferry kids around, and pick up two goats, Holly and Cinnamon, to join Silver in the barn. I talk to Jay on the phone every night.

Holly the goat.

Somehow, reservations fill the mailbox, letters of confirmation go out, and the '79 season at the Bartlett Carry Club takes off as if nothing has changed. I hate not having Jay, not having the security and strength of his presence no matter how ill he feels. I play full-time single parent five days a week, and guests come to me with problems. We tell those we know well about Jay, but for the most part, we leave the others in peace. Years later, they reminisce . . .

> *I'll always remember the beauty and the water like black glass . . . the deep peacefulness and sense of stability, order, and safety—like time was standing still—while sitting on the little beach and looking across the lake.*[2]

> *What happy memories come flooding back of our times. Thank you and Jay for creating a little piece of heaven on earth and allowing us to share in it.*[3]

In 1947, the "little piece of heaven" at the family camp on Round Lake saw a big change. For the first time since A. B. Jenkins had established the camp in 1903, Elmer Dockum would not be there. On the afternoon of January 24, 1947, he helped saw sixteen logs with a drag saw. In the evening, he played cards. After retiring to bed, he sustained a coronary thrombosis and died.[4] Farnham Yardley wrote in the Waubenoo guestbook: "With sorrow, record is made of the passing on of Elmer Asbury Dockum on Jan 24, 1947 in his 83rd year. Dockum was a guide for Mr. Jenkins at the Saranac Club beginning about 1890. He was in charge of the laying out of Camp Waubenoo and took satisfaction in the thought that he served four generations."[5]

Elmer had always been the steady one, dependable, knowledgeable, calm. No more. No longer would he design and build the next sleeping cabin or a house for the children's children. No longer would he take little Pammie and Jay on fishing expeditions. When guests went looking for that special added touch for their clothespins, Elmer would not be there to lend them a hammer, wire scissors, and some tin. When Harriet turned instinctively to ask a question about the hot water or when Farnham needed advice about the spruce-bark exteriors of cabins, Elmer would no longer tip his hat, tweak his mustache, and grace them with his extensive knowledge and love of this place he had nurtured and taken care of for over forty-four years.

The Masonic Lodge in Saranac Lake honored his passing. "At the Special Comm. Of Jan 27, 1947, 24 Brethren assembled to pay their last Respects to Brother Elmer Dockum, the recipient of a Grand Lodge 50 Year Service Medal. The seat cushions in the Lodge room were donated to the Lodge in his Memory, by his Sister-in-law, Mrs. Ruth McCoy."[6]

While I never knew Elmer in person, he springs to vibrant life in my imagination through family stories and sepia photos; the one of him rowing Jay's great-grandfather grounds me every time I look at it. These many years later, he remains a silent, strong support.

Much as the family must have missed Elmer, they did not stop their usual routine the next summer. Harry and Lena Cummings continued as caretakers. Farnham and Harriet arrived in their chauffeur-driven Cadillac. Their daughter-in-law, Kim, still struggled with the cancer that had struck in 1943, so while Al drove their children, she once again took advantage of the commercial air service. Farnham noted proudly in the guestbook; "Jay, age six, swimming for the first time."

Even though Jenkins Manufacturing provided a steady income to support their lifestyle, Farnham searched for ways to subsidize taxes, insurance, and maintenance. These perennial problems had also plagued Virgil Bartlett, the Saranac Club, and later would plague Jay and me. In 1946, Farnham considered logging as one solution. He must have been heartened by the New York State Hammond-Demo Forest Practice Act offering "the most comprehensive aid to private forest owners of any state or federal program so far initiated."[7] By the mid-1940s, the forest had recovered after the logging onslaught of the mid and late 1800s.

It wasn't until May, 1948 that Farnham contacted his caretaker, Harry Cummings. He wrote:

> I would like to have you get in touch with Mr. W. E. Petty [brother of Clarence Petty] who is the District Forester and located at Saranac Lake. You will see by reading the act that the purpose is to set up definite standards for the practice of forestry on privately owned woodlands in the State and for assistance from the State Conservation Department in carrying out these practices.[8]

I find no other mention of this, and no evidence exists that any logging occurred on our property in the two decades before we came. Perhaps Farnham's initiative inspired Jay in the 1970s to contact Chris, a local forester, to begin our own sustainable logging operation to offset the hefty cost of our Club renovations. By the time we arrived, our forest, denuded during Bartlett's days, abounded with towering pines, hemlock, birch, and maple. Chris drew up a multi-year sustainable forest management plan to ensure we could harvest trees regularly. We wanted to produce income and also to maintain the long-term health and diversity of the forest.

Not long after Farnham penned his letter to District Forester Petty in May 1948, Miss Purdy, now of The Seville in Florida in winter, traveled north to attempt by herself a third year of managing the Club. I have no record of what became of her sister, but perhaps after the less-than-successful '47 summer, Mrs. Doring declined to return. This year, things didn't look much better. Harriet and Farnham very likely again considered selling the Club, but the same old problem persisted—who would want or be able to buy 267 acres of land with twenty buildings and a dam?

This seemingly unsolvable problem didn't stop Farnham from enjoying their family camp sitting on 732 acres which they had no intention of selling. He rowed, swam, tried to catch a pike, and celebrated his eightieth birthday in August. He did encourage his son, Al, now thirty-seven, to take over operation of Jenkins Manufacturing as well as the care and upkeep of the family camp and the Bartlett Carry Club.

Perhaps with this huge responsibility in mind, Al approached David Young about leasing the Club property. David was president of Bankers Trust Company of New York, a historic American banking organization. For years it had operated a place south of the Catskills for their employees to spend inexpensive summer vacations. This had become so popular, the company was looking for a second location, specifically for junior managers and their families.

By the fall of 1948, Al and David had worked out an agreement, and Bankers Trust drew up an ambitious map in preparation for leasing the Club, the same map Jay and I discovered in the safe twenty years later. It showed the twelve existing "cottages," Main Lodge, Icehouse, dormitory, boathouses, roads, electric lines running from the power house on the masonry dam; ten-thousand-gallon water-storage tank that gravity fed to each building; spring-water pump house for drinking water; footbridge across the rapids; tennis court; disposal field; bridge over the river; caretaker's house, barn and garage; fire hydrant sites; swimming dock; and, my favorite on this map, a fireplace "for roasting wild duck, wild turkey, young hogs, broiling venison, fish and bear steaks." It also showed proposed sites for five new cottages.[9] Bankers Trust was raring to go.

Before finalizing the deal, Al needed to resolve a lingering issue regarding the estate of William A. Douglass. On September 24, 1948, he met with Harriet and Farnham and trustees for the Douglass estate. As pens dipped in black ink and marked legal documents, William's sons, Kingman and Benjamin, and William's son-in-law, Clyde Shorey, officially released the

Douglass interests in Bartlett Carry Realty Co. to Harriet J. Yardley. The records don't clarify if she had to buy them out, but as the only daughter of A. B. Jenkins, she was now the sole legal owner of the Club property and could move forward with a lease to Bankers Trust.

The Douglass family had been deeply woven into the fabric of the Club from Robert's first entry in the Saranac Club Minutes in January 1889 to this moment just shy of sixty years later. As ink dried on parchment, a big band should have boomed on the Main Lodge flagstone patio. Instead there were probably handshakes and solemn nods of heads. It seems anticlimactic, but this was it—the end of the Douglass family involvement with the Bartlett Carry Club.[10]

Thus Harriet Jenkins Yardley joined an unusual history of female property owners. Since the death of her father, she had owned the 732 acres on Round Lake once owned by Pauline Shaw. And she was now the sole owner of the 267 acres of the Club, once owned for a few years by Caroline Bartlett between the death of Virgil and the formation of the Saranac Club. These two pieces of property plus Ship Island on Middle Saranac Lake made up the one thousand acres Jay and I moved to in 1968.

Harriet took up the banner in 1948 and had legal authority to sign a contract with Bankers Trust. A win-win situation. She would retain ownership of the 267-acre Club property, receive a small lease fee, and have no other responsibility. Bankers Trust would pay the lease, property tax, and insurance and have carte blanche to upgrade the facilities and bring the old place back to its former glory. In return, they would have an upscale place for their junior managers and families to vacation, and they would hopefully turn a small profit. Just as when L. G. Treadway had stepped in, Harriet and Farnham must have felt huge relief.

On November 16, 1948, the Bartlett Carry Realty Co. (represented by Harriet's son, Alfred J. Yardley) signed a twenty-year lease with Bankers Trust Co. of New York (represented by David R. Young, president). The lease, which led up to the year Jay and I arrived, included an option to renew for another twenty years. Bankers Trust named their new enterprise Pyramid Camp. The pyramid was its logo, a symbol of its prosperity as one of the country's wealthiest financial institutions. The renowned top of their building at 14 Wall Street in New York City sported a seven-story stepped pyramid.

A company newsletter in late November announced the "acquisition" of the Bartlett Carry Club property. Pictures, a map, and enthusiastic, flowery language enticed managers and families to travel north the following summer.

> This is vacationland, a location unmatched in the country. The clean, crisp air will lave away the year's accumulation of automobile exhausts, crowded subways and glue factories. It will make you whole and pure again. The water, diamond-clear, beckons to the swimmer, the angler and boater. Natural trails through the cool, scented forest will call to the wandering foot and lead him off to enchantment. To speak further, to add to the perfection, would be to sound like a travel folder, but to know one fact of this new camp is to know enthusiasm, an enthusiasm you all will, one day, enjoy.[11]

The ambition of Bankers Trust matched its optimism. In their March 1949 newsletter, they reported extensive repair work, acquisition of china, silverware, beds, blankets, sheets, dining room tables, and chairs. They planned to overhaul the kitchen and purchase twenty-four new rowboats and canoes as well as a camp bus and utility truck.[12] They drew detailed floor plans of each cottage and gave them names inspired by native trees. #1 Cottage became Fir; #2, Birch; #3, Maple, and so on. The cottages had these same names when Jay and I arrived, names that skipped through my restless mind in the interminable nights of my first few months.

Bankers Trust accomplished more in one year than Jay and I did in five. Granted, they had the company money behind them, but they did bring about an impressive transformation.

In spring of 1949, Frank Hynes came on as the new Pyramid Camp manager from mid-June through mid-September. In March, Frank wrote to Mr. Burrowes, assistant vice president of Bankers Trust: "Day by day I am becoming more and more enthusiastic about the prospects for Pyramid Camp this summer. As I study the floor plans and general lay-out, it seems to me to be a perfect set-up for a summer camp. When present plans are completed, Pyramid Camp should be a pride and joy to the Bankers Club."

As I read this, I think—Wait. It already *was* a wonderful place. Did it really need all the "improvements" for it to be more wonderful? I have to admit, my realistic side knows full well the importance of flushing toilets, good running water, comfy beds, screens on the windows, all the things Jay and I "improved" when we came. We were a modern version of Bankers Trust as we put our own mark on the place and spiffed it up to meet our standards. Each incarnation of this place has seen enterprising people doing exactly this: Virgil and Caroline, the Saranac Club, Treadway Inn, Bankers Trust, and then Jay and me.

In the long view, each set of improvements has been fleeting, waiting for time to take its toll, screens to develop holes, mattresses to sag, septic tanks to overflow, until the next group comes along to fix things up again. Meanwhile the place itself not only endures, it doesn't change much. Water tumbles over rocks, trees grow tall, chipmunks look for handouts.

Frank Hynes had big plans. "An excellent chef and assistant chef have already been engaged and good wholesome meals are a certainty. We are planning picnics, old-fashioned country hay rides, barn dances, bingo nights . . . to formulate a well rounded social program which will make Pyramid Camp even more popular than the beauty of the place insures." He was no doubt pleased to learn in 1949 that the Adirondack Fish Hatchery in Lake Clear expanded its production to 1,500,000 trout. That meant more fish migrating into Upper Saranac Lake. The more fish to catch, the happier his clientele.

For the 1949 season, employees of Bankers Trust and their families would pay twenty-five dollars per week, children $12.50 to $17.00.[13] With a capacity to sleep 125 people, the newest manifestation of Bartlett's was off and running.

II

Thirty years later, in 1979, we too are off and running. In December, we come full circle as we move back to Middle Saranac Lake and the newly renovated Lake House, just below where our first home, the Guide House, once stood on the hill. A full moon shimmering above a not-yet-frozen lake welcomes us on our first night.

We may have moved to our new home, new furniture, new rugs, new curtains, but we carry with us the bundles of worry accruing in our lives. In addition to keeping track of what's left to renovate, caring for our daughters, monitoring the logging operation, sugaring, advertising for next summer's Club opening, tending 6,000 Christmas trees, and following school schedules, Jay's illness now goes on the list of things to deal with. At least for now, he is in remission. I'm so busy trying to function, I don't have time to truly register the lurking terror of uncertainty; we have no idea what the future will bring.

Baking comforts me. The aroma of warm Christmas cookies fills our new kitchen. Gwyn and Shana slather frosting everywhere. Before it dries, Jay wanders through the kitchen and picks up a green frosted star with red sprinkles. "Dad!" they protest. Munch. "Great!" he says, raising one eyebrow. "Try one!" They do.

It's time to write our annual letter. We want every lodge filled with returning and new guests next summer. Just as Robert Douglass never hinted in his Minutes of personal disruptions, we don't either:

> We are sending this Adirondack maple syrup to you with best wishes for a Happy New Year. We have had a late fall at Bartlett Carry so we have been able to clear some more land for a spring planting of balsam Christmas Trees.
>
> The "new" in the Yardleys' New Year is that we are now living on Middle Saranac Lake. It is nice to be back at the place where we lived during 1969 and 1970.
>
> We hope you will be able to be with us again this summer. Please let us know by February 1st if you would like to return as we will begin taking other reservations at that time.

Our 1980 rates range from $650 for two weeks in Cedar to $1,600 for Merritt and Douglass. We have several families who return every year and who have become good friends.

Mom comes for her annual winter visit to check out our new house. This stay is a far cry from when she slept in David's cabin our first frigid February. Now, Mom can stay right in our house so we don't have to sprint over frozen snow. Before bed, she can click off a real electric light and stay warm under one or two blankets instead of four. When I wave goodbye as she heads out the driveway, my two daughters stand close. While I am sad to see her go, this time I feel only a tinge of that old loneliness.

In February 1980, we rent winterized Ampersand and Douglass to *Sports Illustrated* magazine reporters. They are covering the XIII Olympic Winter Games in Lake Placid, only twenty-two miles away. Tickets cost a lot, and restrictions make travel difficult. We only go to a few events. David travels from South Carolina to stay for several days and stands with us in the crowd chanting *Eric! Eric! Eric!* as Eric Heiden skates to his fifth gold medal. We come home to a patch of ice we have cleared, lace up skates, hunch our shoulders, and pretend to be Olympic champions in the final sprint.

In the spring, between planting 2,000 new balsam seedlings and tending to the thousands already in the ground, I set tiny seeds in my new garden on the knoll above our house. I envision rows of corn and sunflowers, lettuce and carrots, beans and potatoes. In late summer, before dinner, I climb the hill with two girls in tow. "Hey, want to help me pick the beans?" One for the basket, two for their mouths. I don't worry about vegetables for dinner this night.

At some point, I get it in my head I want to go on an Outward Bound experience. We have heard Club guests talk of this organization that provides challenging outdoor expeditions. It's crazy, but I become fixated

Skating on Middle Saranac Lake, 1980.

with the idea. It will mean time for *me*, away from Everything. I plan it all carefully. I will enroll in their short course in October, a precious three days when the Club will be closed, the kids in school, and Jay hopefully feeling well enough to hold down the fort.

I particularly can't wait for the exercise when each student stands on a high place and falls backwards into the arms of her fellow students. Trust. That's all about trust. And the twenty-four-hour solo excursion when I will be completely on my own in the woods. That's about survival skills. If I can do this, I will know for a fact I can survive on my own.

Several months ahead, I go into training, attempting a daily three-mile run plus ten push-ups, pull-ups, and sit-ups. When I am finally able to do ten pull-ups, I know I'm ready. One day, in the simple act of maneuvering the non-power-steering red truck in a parking lot, I yank on the wheel and feel a twinge in my back. I can barely move with the pain.

"You have arthritis in your neck," the doc informs me. "I would seriously consider abandoning your Outward Bound trip."

The thought of falling backwards into unknown arms seals my decision. I don't get over the disappointment for a long time. Now, how will I ever know if I can survive on my own if required?

For almost two years, I have watched Jay travel back and forth to Baltimore, struggle with one treatment after another, grasp for one more hope for a cure. Driving alone on our dirt road one day, I slam on the brakes, grip the wheel, stare at the dark outlines of giant pine and hemlock against a grey sky. I hear the words before I realize I have spoken out loud. *He could die.* Amazing it has taken this long. This is the first time I have allowed myself to say it. *He could die.* Sometimes, alone in my garden, I sit amongst the beans and try to bargain with the Universe. I latch onto any shred of hope. Martha Reben is one such shred. When we first came, we had heard about this woman who had been ill and found solace and strength from the beauty of our own Round Lake. Now I think of her often. Maybe, I think, just maybe Jay can have her same outcome.

Martha first came to Saranac Lake in 1927. She suffered with tuberculosis and joined the hordes of others attracted to this small village in hopes of finding a cure. Over three years later, she still struggled. One day, she answered an ad in the local paper: *Wanted. Some invalid who is not improving who would like to go into the woods for the summer.*

Fred Rice, a local guide, had placed the ad. For years, he had built guide boats as his father had. In the early 1930s, his eyesight began to fail and, with the stock market crash, the guide boat business had crashed as well.[14] Very likely he discussed with his wife what he would do next. He was a big man, often prone to chuckling, but at this moment, I imagine he was quite serious. "By the jesum, Kate, I'm no spring chicken any more, but I need to make a living. I got an idea." He had his own theories about how to treat TB patients. He firmly believed if he could get them out of stuffy buildings and into fresh air, with food cooked over an open fire, nature would do the rest.

Fred received only one response to his ad—Martha. He wasn't expecting a frail, yet beautiful young woman. A guide just didn't take a woman out in the woods for a whole summer. On the other hand, how could he pass up the five months of work Martha could give him? Practicality and Martha's fervent determination won Fred and Kate over.

In the spring of 1931, he tucked a weak and coughing Martha under blankets in his outboard and navigated the fifteen miles from Lower Saranac through the river and into "our" lake. According to her first book, *The Healing Woods*, published in 1952, during that summer, Martha learned to live in a tent, to squelch her terror when a squirrel rustled in the leaves, and to eat food even covered with wood ash from an open fire. And, her favorite of all, she learned to fish. Years later, in her second book, *The Way of the Wilderness*, she wrote, "Out here, time, as we measured it, seemed to stand still, and perhaps that, more than anything else, was what men found so sustaining and so seductive."[15]

Time standing still—the same phrase used by one of our 1979 guests when describing the peace at Bartlett Carry. Did I too experience time standing still? Perhaps. I know while our lives teetered, the certainty of sturdy pines and quiet lake waters did create a foundation to hold whatever distress I might have felt on a particular day.

Martha responded well enough that she decided to remain in Saranac Lake the following winter. She wrote that for the next twenty years, each summer she and Fred Rice returned to the rejuvenating woods of Round Lake and Weller Pond.[16] Martha may have taken some poetic license and simplified and compressed her experience, but the fact remains, her years camping in the wilderness brought her some level of healing.

Martha Reben.

Fred Rice.

And so I wonder. Jay lives in this same rejuvenating wilderness. Maybe he can thrive as Martha thrived. She reported that after ten years without a medical exam of any kind, X-rays showed no sign of active TB. Maybe one day, Jay will go to Johns Hopkins for his checkup and they will say, "You are free of cancer. You can go home."

According to Martha's account, by 1949 she had camped with Fred for eighteen years in the wilderness. In this same year, Bankers Trust celebrated the successful opening of their new Pyramid Camp for managers and their families. Farnham wrote in his journal: "Much work has been done to put the property in order. This year, for the first time that I can recall, all the bungalows on the Carry are occupied." He must have been relieved to know a new, successful chapter had begun at the Club.

Farnham also gave a glimpse into life at the family camp in 1949. "Al and the children arrived by motor August 3, departed August 25. Kim flew up and down, arriving August 7, leaving Aug 22. Pam and Jay aquaplaned for the first time." Kim still had health problems and had to limit her stay at camp. Jay was nine, raring to explore the wonders of Adirondack woods and lakes. He would have preferred to have stayed for months.

Farnham made his last journal entry that year. What a loss for me in my research. I no longer have the Saranac Club Minutes, and now I will no longer have Farnham's journal entries. What will I do for a guide to imagining life back then?

One day I hear a knock on my door. I open it to three women.[17]

"Hi! We thought you might be interested in these pictures from Pyramid Camp."

Three sisters tell me they vacationed at Pyramid Camp with their family some sixty years ago. What a gift! When they leave, I hold a stack of evocative black-and-white photos of kids, adults, and familiar-looking Club buildings. My head swims with their stories.

No more need for yellowing, almost indecipherable minutes or faded journals. Now people from my generation knock on my door with stories. These photos as well as conversations with others with vivid memories of Pyramid Camp in the '50s evoke nostalgic images from my own childhood—young girls, freckled, barefoot, in sleeveless cotton shirts and plaid shorts, stubbing toes on tree roots, jumping off a dock, balancing in a tippy canoe—universal images of summer life on a lake.

Frank Hynes, portly, balding, and with a kindly look, greeted each family as they arrived after a long trip on curvy roads with squiggly siblings and pets vying for choice window spots.

Frank Hynes, manager Pyramid Camp, 1950s.

Along Route 3, on the last stretch of road between Saranac Lake and the Club, huge white rocks guided drivers. These were painted by road crews for safety on the narrow, curvy roads. Weary travelers counted to see if they were the same as last year. Then, finally, they piled out of the stale car, took in the heady scent of pine. And the rush of rapids. Always there. Never changing. The same in 1980 at our Bartlett Carry Club as in 1950 at Pyramid Camp and for years before and since.

Families planned their vacations to coordinate with friends. They worked in New York City, but lived in New Jersey, Westchester, Long Island. They didn't have a chance to socialize during the rest of the year, so they looked forward to this rare week or two living close together. Adults could gather on the flagstone patio. Kids could run barefoot next door to rustle up a game of Ping-Pong or a trip to the swim dock.

Little kids could play safely in closed-off swim areas on this dock. Older kids jumped in the lake, swam out to the raft, and took solo boat trips. After family breakfasts, everyone scattered to their various activities. Parents seemed blissfully unaware that their offspring might be wandering in the woods,

Pyramid Camp swim dock, 1950s.

climbing a tree, or hopping from one rock to another in the rapids—just a little dangerous, but as long as they showed up for meals, all was well.

Everyone ate in the Main Lodge central dining room and converged in the adjoining living room for card games, board games, jigsaw puzzles. In the evening, Mr. Hynes and his wife arranged entertainment: bingo night, talent night, movie night—maybe one night a showing of the movie, *Father of The Bride* with Spencer Tracy and Elizabeth Taylor, released in 1950. If the activities lasted until after dark, the lights sprang alive, powered by DC electricity from the dam.

Possibilities of what to do abounded: tennis on the court in the field where once stood the Sportsmen's Home, where once a horse and wagon waited to transfer guide boats; fishing with the incentive of having your fish prepared for lunch by kitchen worker Big John O'Mahoney; canoeing on Upper or Middle Saranac Lake; hiking, often up Ampersand Mountain to catch the exhilarating 360-degree view on the bare rock summit caused by Verplank Colvin's 1873 survey and subsequent fires; kick the can, hide-and-go-seek, Ping-Pong.

Climbing Ampersand Mountain, 1950s.

I wonder, in addition to all these activities, if they ever walked down the road just noticing, taking in the wild beauty as I do almost every day. I love this road that continually reconnects me to this place. I remember one morning after a rip-roaring, torrential thunderstorm, the gravelly road looked newly washed. Rivulets ran down an incline and off to the left toward the pond. In the fresh coolness with emerging sunlight slanting across the road, tall dark pines draped in mist waited like mysterious brides for the first organ note to begin their march down the aisle. I cocked my head at the melodic warble of a hermit thrush. A white-throated sparrow added her bright whistle to the mix. With the next waft of breeze came fresh, dewy, green-leaf morning air. If I could have breathed in deeply enough, it would have cleansed my soul. I wonder if Pyramid guests ever walked the road this way.

On the last night of vacation, the Pyramid Camp wait staff invited everyone to a farewell campfire where they toasted marshmallows, sang songs, danced in the rec hall.

In the spring of 1954 came an ebullient newsletter stating: "This season will mark the 5th year Pyramid Camp has been open for the benefit of Bankers Trust Co. and their families. [sic. This is most likely an error. Pyramid Camp's first season was 1949. This newsletter was written in 1954 which would make it their 6th year.] This season, an effort will be made to make it an outstanding one that will be long remembered by not only the perennials but also those making their initial visit."[18]

Despite the enthusiasm, business floundered. For six years, Bankers Trust had provided two separate summer camps for their employees. Distance made the difference. The drive from Long Island to Pyramid Camp took ten hours; to Baker Camp, just south of the Catskills, less than two. They decided to close Pyramid Camp after summer 1954, even with a continuing twenty-year lease and annual expenses of over $15,000. They contacted Clinton Ayres of Ayres Realty in Saranac Lake to find a sub-lessee and prepared a brochure.

> Wanted: A "large business firm or institution" looking for "a vacation spot for employees, for sales promotion meetings or seminar use" to accommodate 100–125 persons.[19]

When our Bartlett Carry Club was in full operation, we had three fewer houses and fewer bedrooms to allow space for kitchens and dining rooms so we could only accommodate fifty which I thought was a lot!

Their explanation: "Because of other facilities available to our employees, it has become superfluous and the institution is now in a position to make it available to someone else."

Their plan: Mr. Frank Hynes would remain as resident manager; the lease would expire October 31, 1968 with an option to renew; the annual rent (payable to Bartlett Carry Realty Co., aka Harriet Jenkins), would be $3,000. The "only other estimated costs were taxes—$4,460, insurance—$4,800, and ordinary repairs and maintenance—$3,500."

Their selling points: The buildings and original equipment were in first-class condition and well maintained. And because the Camp would be leased instead of purchased, it would not require an outlay of capital funds.

The question once again: Was there a business firm or institution willing and able to take this on?

No one responded. In 1955, after six summers of bustling activity, Pyramid Camp ceased to exist. Without income from a sub-lessee, Bankers Trust still had to pay rent, taxes, and insurance. They would have cut back on maintenance, but annual costs still amounted to well over $10,000. Any vestige of hope they might have held to reopen Pyramid Camp disappeared in October, 1961 when the Saranac Inn, at the other end of Upper Saranac Lake, went up for auction. If that huge, famous resort couldn't survive, neither could Pyramid Camp.

Frank Hynes drew up a detailed inventory of everything purchased over the past six years to determine what to transfer to the Catskills and what to leave behind. While they did not take the dishwasher, refrigerator, glass washer or potato peeler, they did take twin beds, Windsor chairs, free-standing wardrobes, square tables and baby seats, rowboats, canoes and china. Also the Ping-Pong table, a Bendix radio, and a train bell. Mr. Hynes noted they left enough for fifty people, more than they found when they came; sixty to eighty dining room chairs, ten to twenty tables, a plethora of wicker chairs, some china, but no silverware.[20]

After years of wondering what happened to the silver, I solve the mystery with the help of Mr. Hynes. He wrote: "Most of the silverware is stainless steel and purchased by the bank; 351 tea spoons, 404 dinner forks, 229 dinner knives, oyster forks, 181 butter knives." Of course. They took the silverware with them.

As far as butter knives, I think they only took 180, because the 181st, wrapped in yellowed tissue paper, was waiting in the safe for me to discover. Finally, I know what happened to the rest.

Mr. Hynes recommended all selected items be moved to Baker Camp in Spring, 1962. Jay and I arrived six years later, and I armed myself with pad and pencil to do my first inventory of those same buildings. I remember the place felt vastly deserted, as if no one had entered for many decades rather than the thirteen years between the closing of Pyramid Camp in 1955 and our arrival in 1968. What happened during that time? I find little information and begin to call it the Mystery Period.

I discover something that did happen. One day in the mid-1950s, Dick Kibben, a long-time Saranac Lake resident, and his friend Dave Merkel, later a doctor in the same village, went on a jaunt in Dick's small outboard. They decided to traverse Bartlett Carry from the river to Upper Saranac Lake so they took the motor off and lugged the almost two-hundred-pound boat up the hill, past all the buildings at the Club, and to the beach. No sign of anyone. After going back to get the motor, they headed out into Upper Saranac.

At the end of the day, they faced the daunting task of getting that heavy boat back down the hill with no Bartlett's horse-drawn wagon to carry their boat for fifty cents. They "borrowed" a trailer stashed behind one of the abandoned buildings, pulled the boat and motor back down the hill, and then dragged the trailer back. And during that whole day, they saw no one.

That pretty much sums up my conjecture about the Club during the mid-1950s. Water still tumbled over rocks as it always had, chipmunks still scampered, but the buildings, set amidst overgrown grass, saw minimal if any human activity, except for an occasional pair of adventurers out on a day's jaunt.

III

In the spring of 1980, Jay and I see a lot of human activity as we juggle reservations for the upcoming season. Envelopes stuff our mailbox almost every day. July and August fill up fast.

Meanwhile, we navigate the uncertainty of our lives like a ship in iceberg-packed waters. During times Jay doesn't feel well, I make a gargantuan effort to keep everything on an even keel and buffer his occasional cranky, impatient moods. I pretend all is okay, probably hoping if I exude this positive attitude, it will be. Recovery *is* a possibility. The docs told us Hodgkin's Disease was a "good cancer" to get if you had to have one.

Jay says one day. "I can't just be a cancer patient. And there are ways I think I can help the Oncology Center at Johns Hopkins. I'm going to talk to them."

On his next trip to Baltimore, before tests and treatment, he meets with Dr. Owens, the Director of Oncology.

"This is a great hospital." Jay tells him. "You give me excellent care, about 85% of what I need. I think I can help you give me and other patients the other 15%."

He inspires them with his vision of a residence where out-of-town patients as well as families would be able to stay instead of in a motel as he did; a place that could give them control over their environment and where they could maintain their dignity. He researches places such as Hospice in England who have addressed the same issues: simple, but crucial things such as beds oriented in a room to face the door so a patient can see who enters; light and temperature controls at a patient's fingertips.

His words carry credibility. He tells the Oncology Center: "With the utmost professional competence and love, you lead us through the corridors and stairwells of cancer care. But sometimes that is not enough. Some of us feel a loss of self-control and, with that, a loss of hope, and without hope, there is very little room for medicine." They welcome him because of his confidence and because he represents those "in the trenches."

I recognize the light in his eyes when he tells me, "We can make this happen." That light and his fervent determination remind me of when we first tackled the Bartlett Carry Club. He has a dream, and he will do anything he can to carry it through.

From this point on, he spends the majority of his time researching, designing, consulting for the Oncology Center. He also manages to help turn around a struggling branch of Jenkins Valve Company in Lachine, Quebec. He is far from "just a cancer patient."

During spring vacation, we take a family trip Out West. We rent a camper. We usually like to camp in tents rather than in a camper, but with a twelve- and an eight-year-old and a guy who may not always feel the best, we embrace the Camper Opportunity. Two blessed weeks away from our regular lives. We marvel at the impossible colors and size of the Grand Canyon, the vast unearthliness. Then on to the torrid heat of Death Valley and then to wild waves lashing the rocky shore on Route One along the California coast. The kids hunt for Easter eggs in and around the camper in ninety-degree heat.

Back home, I seek out a new creative endeavor during our off season. Now that I no longer have to sew curtains and furnish lodges, I realize how much I have missed acting. Over a decade has passed since I graduated from the University of Colorado with a major in Theater. Jay may have taken the Creative Writing course where we met, for which I am eternally grateful, but he has never had the passion I have for all things theatrical.

I act in a couple of plays at the new Pendragon Theatre in Saranac Lake. Even though I revel in the community and creativity, I realize evening rehearsals disrupt our family time. And family ranks number one.

One day, Janet Decker, a friend and neighbor, asks me how I am doing.

"Oh, Janet, I need a creative outlet, but something that doesn't conflict with family!" Janet doesn't miss a heartbeat.

"Why don't you try storytelling?"

"What's that?" I ask.

"I'll put an article in your mailbox." She does and a new door opens wide. I fall into a world of like-minded people I never knew existed. There is even an organization called the National Association for the Preservation and Perpetuation of Storytelling (NAPPS—now called the National Story-telling Network). I go to workshops, conferences, and to my kids' school where I offer to tell stories to their third-grade class (not so incidentally my younger daughter's class). I welcome the outlet, and it doesn't conflict with my family or work at the Club.

When summer arrives, cars crunch in our gravel driveway, kids and parents jump out. We delight in seeing one another after a year. *Look how big the kids have grown! How was your winter?* I give them my standard answer—*Long, cold, and snowy!* Those who know of our challenges look at me with concern. *How are you doing?* I answer as briefly as I can. These returning guests know the routine and head up to their lodges. We take new ones up and orient them. I love watching the slow absorption of this unique place relax their shoulders and soften their faces.

Jay stays home on days he doesn't feel well. My heart sinks just a bit more every time this happens. Then I perk up on the days he rises with strength to take on the world. On those days, I can take on the world, too. Now that every curtain has been sewn, every lodge stocked with pots, pans, dishes, and cushions on the wicker chairs, I take charge of making sure everything runs smoothly as I water flowers, gather dirty linen, and deliver clean. Every two weeks, we transform the place from chaos to order, ready to greet a new group of guests from beginning of the season to the end.

IV

In the 1950s, the Club did not have that same bustle of vacationers coming and going. But the rest of Upper Saranac Lake saw plenty of activity. Earlier in the century, grand hotels and estates with distinctive names such as Fish Rock, Panther Point, Moss Ledge, Wenonah, and Wawbeek had sprung up along the shores. Now, property owners suffering from the accumulating disasters of the Stock Market crash, the Depression, and World War II looked for ways to deal with the ceaseless, massive upkeep of such splendid properties. Breaking their extensive pristine lakeshore acres into smaller, marketable parcels became a viable solution. People who hitherto had never dreamt of coming to this area found they could now afford a small place of their own.

Blythmere, Robert Douglass's one-hundred-acre property adjacent to the Club, had survived several owners who kept it intact. In 1957, Emerson Wertz, a Miami, Florida, real estate man poised on the brink of this new era, purchased the property and chopped it into a thirty-two-lot subdivision called Saranac Shores. It's just as well Robert had long since departed.

Charles Vosburgh, another enterprising developer, bought the 3,500-acre Saranac Inn property at the northern end of Upper Saranac Lake in 1961 and began his plan to auction the buildings, golf course, and prime waterfront lots. This seminal moment marked the end of a certain lifestyle on Upper Saranac, a time of large waterfront summer homes and grand resorts. Bill McLaughlin, *Adirondack Daily Enterprise* reporter and friend of Mr. Vosburgh, wrote: "God made the world, but Charlie broke it up into real estate plots and is selling it off in small bundles so the man on the street can rope off a section to call his own and tell the rest of the world where to go."[21]

The Bartlett Carry Club escaped this subdivision fever. The lease with Bankers Trust would not expire until 1968 so Harriet was not at liberty to sell, even if they had found someone willing to take on an overwhelming number of buildings and a crumbling dam.

Property surrounding Middle Saranac Lake also escaped, for the most part. New York State owned most of the shoreline which, under Adirondack Park regulations, protected it from subdivision. The Yardleys had no interest in carving up their acreage.

Only one other stretch of private land existed on Middle Saranac Lake. This chunk of about fifty acres and a little over 3,000 feet of shoreline lay on the northwestern shore. A few years after A. B. Jenkins bought his land from Pauline Shaw in 1903, Daniel P. Kingsford purchased this piece from a Mr. Curtis. Mr. Kingsford built his camp in 1907, but his only son, Irving, never found the same connection or love for the place that captivated so many others. After his father died, Irving put the land up for sale in 1953.

Harry Duso, an astute businessman who operated a marina on Lower Saranac Lake, recognized the Kingsford property as a good investment opportunity despite no access to roads, electricity, or phone. He divided the property into twenty parcels of one to two acres, eleven of them shorefront. He ended up with seven original buyers, a number of whom continued coming for generations. They have been welcome summer neighbors.

Barb and Paul Skerritt, teachers from the Albany area, came for years to the small cabin they bought from Harry Duso about 1958.

The Hensel family bought 3.7 acres with 500 feet of shoreline in 1953. Ralph told me about his dad. "He built this place. I know every nail." To this day, the camp still has no electricity and no generator, only kerosene lamps, gas stove, and fridge, but the structure is rock solid.

Like the Hensels, Bob and Dorothy Claesgens also came to Middle Saranac Lake in 1953. Their son, John, has memories going back over fifty years. Having no electricity presented only a minor problem. John tells me about their refrigerator. "It was seventy-five years old. Ran on propane. We used it for forty-eight years. One time, we called a service person. He came out, fifteen miles up from Lower Saranac by boat. He pulled out the burner, whacked it with a hammer to take off the rust, and put it back in. All fixed! He charged us thirty dollars because what he really wanted to do was come back to fish!"[22]

I ask John what made this place special for him.

"I think about it all the time . . . I look back to my uncle showing me all these living things, how you come through, everything is living symbiotically, everything is so peaceful, it is like right. Every kid should have a chance to do that and he would never go off the deep end hurting other people."

In 1958, Barb and Bill Schultz bought two parcels—about three and a half acres, with 305 feet of shoreline at $10 per running foot. Bill said, "We started out sleeping on pine needles. We put up a tent platform and then a little shack for a gas refrigerator and an outhouse." His son, Bill, Jr., told me, "That fifty-dollar outhouse is still standing. Now we have a composting toilet and a tank, up in the tree, gravity-feeding hot water so the girls can take a shower."[23]

These families took vacations at the same time. They looked forward to seeing each other, just like Pyramid Camp and Bartlett Carry Club guests. John Claesgens remembers, "There were talent shows, slide shows. Dr. DeGray was a camera buff, took a picture of a chipmunk holding a parasol! He knew all the flora and fauna and had 45,000 pictures." Bill Schultz tells me, "We had picnics. Hensel's daughter played the trumpet, I played the banjo. We had good times."

The Yardley family, less than a mile away across the water, didn't share those particular good times. They tended to live an insular life at their camp. After 1949, Farnham was too ill to make the trip. He must have been sad to not be in this place where he could relax, where fish he caught in the morning appeared on his dinner plate, where he could make observations in the Waubenoo guestbook for posterity. Harriet most likely stayed home with Farnham. He died in December of 1956.

Farewell, Farnham. Thank you for your intriguing handwritten notes, and your sense of history. Your effort to pass the story down through the generations has kept your spirit alive even today.

Four years before his father died, Al had assumed most of the responsibility for the family camp. After Farnham's death, Al and Kim took full charge. Although they spent several weeks each summer, they were apparently unaware of the festive activities just across the lake. Jay and Pammie brought teenage friends and created their own entertainment.

To get a clearer sense of that time, I ask Jay's sister what she remembers. Pammie tells me, "We were really cut off from civilization. We were in our own bubble. We did play family card games . . . hearts was the favorite, and Daddy was always a winner."

Jay's pal, David, remembers: "It really did feel like another world. Jay and I had our own little cabins. We swam in the cold lake . . . lay around the dock . . . went out in the canoe . . . took hikes . . . went through the locks to Lower Saranac and maybe even all the way to town."

Pammie again: "We made forts in the woods . . . picnicked by the river, sat on a big rock and watched the water swirl by, skipped stones . . . On rainy days, I curled up on my bed in my cabin and read a book and threw logs in my Franklin stove to combat the chill. Once a summer we climbed Ampersand carrying sandwiches and other treats . . . banana and peanut-butter sandwiches were my favorites."

They both remember special evenings when they dressed up and went by boat to the Saranac Inn to see a movie. Pammie said, "I think there was dinner there and *people!*" David remembers women in furs sitting in chairs overlooking the lake.

The family had little to do with activities at the Bartlett Carry Club up the river. David remembers only an occasional tennis game. "The Club was simply not a part of our lives." A generation earlier, Jay's dad, Al, had found compatriots at the Club, perhaps because he was an only child and had no friends visiting him at Camp. Jay and Pammie had each other and sometimes friends as companions for adventures. Like the Camping Trip.

One day, Jay, David, and Pammie planned an overnight camping trip to Ship Island, a ten-minute paddle from the camp dock. As they gathered their gear together, they helped themselves to a bottle of vodka from the liquor cabinet and tucked it in a knapsack. About 5 p.m. that evening, the "Commodore" (David's name for Jay's dad) cruised out in the motor boat to see how the campers were faring. "By that time," David told me, "we were totally ripped" and already in the tent for the night. "We're fine!" they called out. Luckily, the Commodore was satisfied and did not land for inspection.

David said, "My time in the Adirondacks during those years was an easy, relaxing, thoroughly enjoyable occasion. I loved Mr. and Mrs. Yardley. They had a wonderful style and panache. And Jay was my best pal. Period."

Jay had David for an occasional week, but he also spent a lot of time by himself. When fourteen, he paddled solo the entire ninety-mile route from Old Forge to Saranac Lake. Ninety miles alone in a boat. I know that stretch, the route of the three-day Adirondack Canoe Classic. I know the moments of peace—tawny, velvet deer bent over water at river's edge, prehistoric heron landing gracefully just ahead. The moments of challenge—wind whipping up, a mile portage to slog over. And the moments of stark isolation—no sign of anyone for mile after watery mile. At least, as I raced alone, I had other boats passing me (always passing me), officials and pit crews waving, handing out water and snacks (*Go! Go!*), cheering as I stumbled along one of the carries. Jay had no one. Maybe this appealed to his loner nature. He could use this as an escape from family demands, and perhaps it was here that he most connected with this land, these waters and woods, this place he never got out of his system.

Kim did not consider camp her favorite place. Once Pammie had gone to college, Kim and Al came up less frequently. I discover only a few snapshots from the late 1950s:

- Sixteen-year-old Jay playing tennis on the Club tennis court, grass growing between the lines. He wears tennis whites— completely out of character for the man I married.

- Clothespins made by visiting guests: one was 1958—Boris Karloff. *Boris Karloff?* He was a good friend of Jay's parents. He titled his clothespin "Self Portrait"—black string around the clothespin head and white stripes and red dots—possibly, and appropriately for the characters he played, a skeleton. He had died before I came along, but his wife, "Aunt Evie," was a kind and lovely soul.

- And a snapshot of Jay skiing, age nineteen: 1959, this one taken in Alta, Utah. He was on his way out, escaping the upper-class childhood where he never felt he belonged. He had graduated from the New England prep school he endured for five years, hitchhiked across the country, and joined the Alta ski patrol.

Jay on ski patrol in Alta, Utah.

That was only the beginning. Then the Marine Corps (*Winners never quit—Quitters never win!*), Viet Nam, Poland and Spain, the University of Colorado. In September, 1965, he enrolled in Creative Writing 304; and I walked into the same class.

After Jay set out on his own, Kim found even less reason to return to camp. Al came in the fall to hunt and maybe to reconnect with the life he had known as a kid. Much like the Club, during most of this time the family camp lay sleepy, idle, as if waiting for someone to stir it awake.

The only other occurrence I know of during that Mystery Period from 1955 to 1968 concerned Will Rogers Hospital. In 1964, the year Jay moved to Colorado, Bankers Trust finally found a sub-lessee for the Club. Will Rogers had been built in Saranac Lake in the late 1920s as the National Vaudeville Artists' Lodge for vaudevillians and vaudeville managers with tuberculosis. In 1936, the name was changed to Will Rogers Memorial Hospital in memory of that esteemed entertainer. Employees and retirees of the entertainment industry and family members over age fourteen were welcome. Veronica Lake, Jack Norton, and Vincent Sardi, Sr. of Sardi's Restaurant in New York City joined many others seeking renewed health in private rooms and on sleeping porches.

This lasted until the discovery of streptomycin in 1944 as the first effective medical treatment for tuberculosis, and of isoniazid in 1952. This meant far fewer TB patients, and it forced the hospital to shift its focus to research on pulmonary cardio-vascular diseases.[24] In 1959, Will Rogers initiated a summer institute for students to learn about the mechanics and philosophy of research in order to determine which branch of medicine they wanted to enter.

These medical students, mostly in their sixth to eighth year, came from schools across the country as well as from England, and they needed lodging. Will Rogers solved the problem by subleasing the Bartlett Carry Club in 1964. Students and families slept in the Club bungalows, ate in the central dining room, and enjoyed outdoor sports from tennis and canoeing to more leisurely shuffleboard. At the same time, Bankers Trust was able to recoup at least some of its loss.

Four years later, in 1968, several stars aligned, and four things happened: the Bankers Trust twenty-year lease expired; Harriet Jenkins Yardley died, freeing up her estate; Jay assumed ownership of the property; and we moved to the Adirondacks to revive the Sleeping Beauty. The Mystery Period officially ended, and the story of the history of this place beginning in 1854 finally caught up with my story beginning in 1968.

V

Thirteen years later in summer 1981, Jay and I have reawakened the Club from its Mystery Period, and we are almost full. Chuck Phillips had to quit last fall due to ill health, so we have hired Clarence Peets, better known as Pete, to take his place. It hasn't taken him long to settle into the rhythm of jobs needed to keep our families well taken care of. He takes pride in his work and becomes indispensable.

Fran and Sally Ward come for their first visit with their two girls. They marvel at the Milky Way, on moonless nights brighter at the Club than anywhere else, and they share my strong sense of those from the past whose spirits linger here. We don't know this at the time, but they will figure in the longevity of the Club for years to come.

One day, another new family makes a memorable entrance. As they arrive at our house, thunder rumbles in the blackening sky. Jay has just taken a family to their lodge, so it's my turn for the meet and greet. They emerge from their car to stretch, and their eyes widen as they follow tall tree trunks up practically to the sky.

"Hi! You must be the Coulters." Ed and Lorraine introduced themselves and their kids, Patrick age five and Christine age twelve.

"I'll take you up to your lodge." Eddie works in New York City as a policeman. This is the first vacation he has taken in years. In the Club parking lot, just as we start taking bags from the car, the sky opens up as if some giant parted the clouds and dumped water—*whoosh!*—on the world below, mostly on Bartlett Carry. None of the Coulters has a raincoat. They're drenched within seconds. Then, out of the misty rain appears Jay, in his raincoat and favorite Western hat, raindrops cascading off the wide brim. He strides up to the Coulters, grins as he greets them, and hands each of them a large garbage bag. Instant Bartlett Carry Club raincoats. We have to tie Patrick's so he doesn't trip on it. The kids scamper ahead through puddles, we all carry what we can, and finally get them to their cozy abode for the next two weeks.

This grows into a favorite family story, and they return regularly. Just as with every other family, they succumb to the relaxed pace: up later than usual, maybe freshly baked muffins for breakfast, a walk to the Main Lodge to see who else is there or to stick a load of wash in the machine, settle on the sunny patio with a cup of coffee, and eventually head down to the beach for the important job of occupying an Adirondack chair. Patrick and Christine connect with kids their ages, find rocks to climb, and games to play. Eddie says one day, "I'm a New York City cop, and here I'm friends with doctors, lawyers, who knows who else?" When he tells me this, I know he has joined the Bartlett Carry Club family.

Bartlett Carry Club beach, early 1980s.

One day in August, we have weather similar to the day the Coulters first arrived. The wind howls, the sky darkens. Guests gather in twos and threes near the Main Lodge, look up with worried faces. Jay, blessedly feeling okay this day, Pete, and Carl Hathaway, our friend and long-time caretaker for a large camp up the road, tie ropes to the trunk of a colossal white pine, fasten the other ends to several neighboring trees. Gazes fixate halfway up the trunk.

When Jay first saw that this tree was beginning to split, he had called Pete, even though it was his day off, and Carl for help. Carl said, "I'll bring Tom too!" Tom Phillips is Carl's son-in-law and also part of the Adirondack caretaker tradition.

Tom scales a ladder, a ¾" rope coiled at his waist. He heads twenty feet up where the tree, already divided into two large trunks, has started to split. Wild wind whips the thick top branches. With each howl, the crack in the main trunk widens, and frowns on faces below deepen. If one of those split trunks breaks off just wrong, it will take out the side

Carl Hathaway, early 1980s.

of Hemlock Lodge. And who can really tell just how tall that tree is and just how far it will reach when it does fall? It could take out two lodges. Time is of the essence. The wind grows louder, and pelting rain stings every upturned cheek.

From below, we see the whole tree swaying, Tom holding on for dear life. He says later, "Those two trunks were like a big mouth opening and closing right in front of me. I had to pull those two pieces together to stabilize the tree before we could cut it down." After what seems to Tom like a year, he has the rope around the two trunks and has descended safely. Wet hair plasters every face. No one goes inside. The time has come to execute the felling of this giant. Carl, with decades of logging experience, stands eighty-four feet off from the base of the tree, pipe in mouth, ax in hand, and says "Well, the top's gonna land about here."

The chain saws scream; Carl on one side of the tree, Tom on the other, Pete on the bulldozer ready to help. As if choreographed, everyone watching begins to back up. It takes a while. The chainsaws get stuck, they quit, they need more gas. The tree sways in ever howling wind, but it does not give up quickly. Finally, in seeming slow motion, it begins to fall. A moment of eerie silence, the chain saws quiet. They have done their job. The wind even seems to stop. No one speaks. All eyes focus on the magnificence of this tree. And then the crash, cushioned by a pillow of the tree's own giant outer pine-needled branches, deafening just the same. Every foot feels the reverberation of the death throes. The top of the tree rests twenty feet from where Carl said it would, and it does not damage one building in its fall.

No one speaks. Tears shine in many eyes. We haven't noticed that it stopped raining. Finally, George, a scientist and the one staying in the lodge most threatened by the tree, breaks the trance. "Well! Let's go see how old this giant was!" Kids reach the trunk base first. Everyone follows. The pungent scent of fresh pine shavings fills the air. George uses the moment to explain about tree rings and how we can tell a good growing year from a poor one. It takes a while to count, especially with little fingers helping and a lot of volunteers to keep track of how far they have counted thus far. Finally, George proclaims, "126 years! Let's see, that means this tree began growing in . . . 1854."

1854: the year Virgil Bartlett ventured into the wilderness from Saranac Lake and settled in what became known as Bartlett Carry. In the same year Virgil first stepped onto the shore of the Saranac River, this tree sent its first shoot up through a layer of composting leaves and into the sunlit hill just above that same river. Now, 126 years later, we look up at the space left in the sky, holding our breath, speechless in wonder at the tree's grandeur.

7

Finding True North

I

During Jay's illness, did I hold my breath? Sometimes when I get to the scariest part of a novel, I realize I hold my breath because the story terrifies me. I flip the pages, skim, think—*Slow down, take it all in*. I can't. I have to flip, skim, push ahead to see what will happen next, all the while holding my breath.

In our real lives, pages flip, and we have no idea of the outcome. I *am* the story along with Jay, so I hold my breath, at least metaphorically, in this purgatory of not knowing. If I dared to take even one honest, life-giving breath, I might inhale the possibility he could die. I want to stand stock-still so I can hear whatever lurks in the closet, under the bed, behind the tree, in the dark woods, so it can't sneak up on me. I want to be ready for anything. I somehow hold my breath and still function on many levels, but no matter how successfully I keep watch, I can't stop the flipping pages.

In the spring of 1984, the docs tell Jay they can do nothing more for him and send him home. A sense of finality spreads over our lives. We can only try to prepare, although we don't have a clue how. We wander in a new landscape with no map. I latch onto anything tangible, any small thing I can control. Water the flower boxes. Yes. I know how to do that. Sweep the Main Lodge. Get dinner on the table. Move from one moment to the next. Don't think about the future.

One afternoon, Jay says, "We have to talk. We have to make some plans." I look away from him, speechless. Can I do this? Jay has always been the pragmatic one. I pull myself together, grab a yellow pad to take notes, and we talk about everything: the kids, property, the dam, taxes, insurance, the antique cars, employees, logging, sand and gravel, more taxes, more insurance, much more about the kids, the dump truck, bulldozers, boats, the Club business, Christmas trees, real-estate investments, maple sugaring, the land. How will I manage it all alone? I put my notes in a red three-ring binder and organize it with colorful tabs. Maybe if I do this, things will somehow make sense.

We talk a lot about the Bartlett Carry Club. We agree our work over the past sixteen years—the renovation, marketing, and managing—challenged us mightily, and we succeeded. Now we need to pass the Club on. It has functioned more or less since the day Virgil and Caroline Bartlett welcomed their first guests 130 years ago, and we don't want to see it end.

To help us, we hire Tom Phillips to take on the job as caretaker for our property and our family. He lives and breathes these woods. He feels more at home on a deer perch high in a tree than at a formal dining-room table, but he can make either work. He has the confidence to find a solution to any problem, and if he can't, he knows who to ask. He moves into the River House with his wife and daughter, and we depend on him.

We want to sell the lodges to people who will love and care for this place as much as those of us who came before: Virgil and Caroline with the aroma of brown bread wafting in the cool air; Robert Dun Douglass and his brothers as they rallied after fires, Depression, and world wars; A. B. Jenkins when he bought 732 acres from Pauline Shaw and built a camp on the shore of Round Lake; and all the others who have paddled these waters, rambled with joy through the woods, and discovered the wonders of this earthy, watery heaven.

Our tenure as managers will end after this summer of 1984. Somehow the Club buzzes along as usual. Guests, many returning, tumble out of dusty cars, give us a hug, head for the lake. Jay mostly stays home. I make as much of a presence at the Club as I can. Sunny afternoons at the beach with laughing children and relaxing adults seem unreal and mesmerizing. Part of me wants never to leave Jay, and part of me wants never to come home to the reality that my whole life as I have known it is ending.

I still manage to find time for daily walks down the road, time to recharge and reconnect with familiar trees, moss, ferns, and birds. It seems every year a hermit thrush sings from the exact same place as the year before. I know these melodic birds will leave in early to mid-August. This particular year, that means more to me than ever. Each day, as I reach the top of the hill and break out from dark shadows into sunshine, one hermit thrush welcomes me—full open-throated warbling, gurgling song—from the highest pine. Then others sing, some near, some far off. They trill back and forth. One day, it takes until well past that crest of hill for me to notice. Silence. No hermit thrush. That silence hangs on my shoulders through my whole walk.

In the fall, after the last car pulls out of the Club driveway, my cleaning ladies and I go to work and leave every lodge spanking clean, shipshape for the winter. I put the last sheets on the linen-room shelf, shut and lock the last door. Jay and I put finishing touches on the "Offering Plan," a document for prospective buyers. It includes both Jay's and my ideas about how to preserve what we have created. Jay's best friend, David, helps design a brochure, this time offering lodges not for rent, but for sale.

Only now, as I look back and write, am I aware as never before of the parallels between us and those who came before. For our various reasons, at some point, we all came to think we couldn't do it anymore. We all exclaimed some version of *We need to make a brochure and sell the place!* Jay's and my brochure has the same rustic elegance of our first advertisement: textured light-brown paper, sepia photograph of a wicker chair, blazing fire, pine trees, and a lake.

We have the same qualms we had in the early 1970s when we first advertised for the summer season. Will anyone want to commit to buying one of our lodges? We dash for the phone when it rings. The Bennetts want Douglass, the lodge they love the most! Their support and friendship over ten years has buoyed us, now more than ever. The Wards want Hemlock, the lodge threatened three years ago by the giant pine tree. And the Maxwells, guests for the past nine years, want Merritt, "their" lodge. All good friends we are delighted to have on board.

Over the fall, as Jay's energy wanes, two more lodges go to former guests who have become friends, and new people express an interest in the remaining four. We have found people who want to invest in and safeguard the continuity of our original vision. Jay lasts long enough to know this place we have worked so hard to create will endure.

On Thanksgiving night, with the same sense of sureness I always loved about him, Jay tells me he is ready to die, ready to "go home." The time has come. In a matter of hours, in one second, he is gone. No chance to turn back, to escape. In that last second, searing anger shakes my being. A jolt through my whole body. Then, just silence.

A death takes on its own rhythm. David Rawle has been with us all week and is invaluable as my support and the main Do-er. He lets people know, arranges for a service. Jay was specific about this occasion. He told me he didn't want a funeral, just a simple wake at the funeral home with few people, mostly family, and to be held as soon as possible.

Whirlwind. Our families somehow make arrangements and arrive from Buffalo, Connecticut, Florida by the next evening. David arranges for dinner to be catered at our house, and in the cold, darkening afternoon, everyone appears on our doorstep, almost as if for a party. David has turned on every light in the house which we have rarely done. This evening, surreal light floods the house so no dark corners can harbor unknown terrors.

Jay had talked to David about the service: "Rawleburg, I'd like you to read our wedding ceremony. Because it's what I believe. Do you think you can handle it?" David told him "I don't know. But I'll try."

Whirlwind. The next day at the funeral, David stands up. "Jay was always prepared to deal with the highs and lows of life, and he believed they went together. He believed that pleasure and pain went together and he believed in pushing back the walls of experience. As intense as Jay's love was, it was the very best kind of love. Because it didn't compromise his individuality. And it never asked others to compromise theirs."

Then David reads Kahlil Gibran from our wedding ceremony . . .

You were born together, and together you shall be
   forevermore.
You shall be together when white wings of death scatter your
   days . . .
But let there be spaces in your togetherness,
And let the wind of the heavens dance between you.
Love one another, but make not a bond of love:
Let it rather be a moving sea between the shores of your souls.[1]

I can't look directly at anyone and stay pulled together. This melding of our wedding and Jay's death is even more surreal than the glaring lights the evening before. The funeral director presents me with a folded American flag to honor Jay's service in the Marine Corps.

Jay had made a specific request to have our dear friends, Karen and Fred Baker, play three pieces: "Perhaps Love" and "The Rose," songs Gwyn had filled the house with as she practiced for a piano recital; and "Take the A Train," Jay's all-time favorite tune. The notes from Karen's nimble fingers on the keyboard and Fred's rich saxophone resonate in my heart's core as I clutch the flag in my lap.

I drive the girls home with the rhythm of "Take the A Train" swirling in my mind. Suddenly, I have a vivid image of Jay's spirit dancing joyously alongside and then ahead of our car. Everyone comes back to put Jay's ashes in the ground. We follow a shoveled green path through a light layer of new-fallen, powdered-sugar snow to the place Jay chose on the hilltop by the lake. The path leads right over the spot Jay's great-grandfather built his cabin in 1903. It feels almost beside the point to bring Jay's ashes here. His dancing spirit arrived long before us, and he will now reside by the lake where he can dangle his feet in the water. I know he will also be on top of Ampersand Mountain with the wind blowing his black hair, a smile on his face, as he looks down at Middle Saranac Lake and Bartlett Carry and the wide expanse of Adirondack mountains etched into his being.

II

Jay was my partner, my guy. He showed me the world, literally, and then poof he was gone. I expected him to sit in the other rocking chair on the

Jay on top of Ampersand, 1972.

porch when we reached a certain age. Somewhere inside, I suppose I know I will go on, though at this moment I can't conceive of a future without him. Every fragment of my life blasts into the air. I lurch, off balance. No bright center, no Jay to revolve around. Only my daughters, now eleven and fifteen, ground me in reality. Tension and fear permeate our house like dark smoke, infiltrating everything unspoken, unheard, but sensed, felt, ingrained in the fiber of all our beings. My girls give me a reason to get up in the morning. Without them, I might curl in a ball and not budge.

I operate on automatic. Each day and in the dark of night, I take crash courses in

1. Lack of Self Confidence

2. Loneliness

3. Panic

I get an A in all of them. I float, untethered. Where is home for me now? I know only this place, but I don't know it like this, without Jay, without the man I followed, the one I committed my life to, the one with the vision, with the history, the bond to this place. Why stay? I love it here, but I don't love the remoteness of the first winter without Jay on the silent, frozen lake.

At dusk on Christmas Day, I walk down to the lake and watch two coyotes cavort across the ice in frigid purple air. Not long after, I begin to assess my new situation. I am forty years old. I still blessedly have my two girls. I also have responsibility for 1,000 acres of land, a Christmas tree farm, logging and sand-and-gravel operations, and a multitude of buildings, boats, and equipment. Because of Jay's extraordinary forethought and planning, at least I don't have full responsibility for the Bartlett Carry Club. The lodges will all be sold and no longer my concern. If Jay hadn't had the vision to set this up, and the stamina and courage and determination, and yes vision again—I would have been landed with more than I probably could have dealt with. I wonder, now that he is gone, if I will be able to follow through. Very possibly, the place would not have survived this far without his foresight. It still overwhelms me to think of what he did in his last months, weeks, days.

As it is, I still entertain the idea of leaving. One early February morning, I walk down our dirt road and ponder my next steps. If we move somewhere else, maybe it won't hurt as much. There. That sounds like an idea. But what about this place? Could I possibly leave?

A full moon, floating down in a gradually lightening sky, breathes out puffy clouds. I stop to bask in its light between a giant pine and hemlock, lift my cold nose to the silver chill, and soak up the essence of an unspoken message from lightyears away. As smoky vapor billows over the moon face, I suddenly know: I will never give up this place. Even though I feel balanced on the edge of a tree branch, at least I know now my tree is here. I may be teetering, but I am not going to leave. Over the past sixteen years this has become my home—the tiny Guide House on the hill, the River House, the Lake House, A. B.'s grave far back in the woods. That's not all: light glinting off a lake—stormy one day, placid and blue another—Christmas tree seedlings in the snow, and my tree friends along the road. And more: haunting whispers of A. B. Jenkins and Elmer Dockum, chickadees on my shoulder, picking beans in the garden with my girls. I may not know exactly what lies ahead, but how could I even think of giving up this place that has cradled my life?

It isn't until now, years later, that I recognize I have joined the line of women dedicated to my small corner of the Adirondacks. I especially appreciate the parallel with Caroline Bartlett who carried on for a few years after her husband died before moving to Glens Falls to live with her niece. She was a fifty-six-year-old widow in 1884, so isolated here—no roads, no neighbors, not even a phone. If only she could appear just for a moment, I would ask: *Caroline, how did you manage? How did you feel about being the one everyone looked to for answers, the one to make all the decisions, without your partner by your side?*

After my moonlit walk, I know I will stay, but now come the hard questions. Who is this new Fran, Widow, Mother, who will not move away? What will I do now?

I will remain committed to the land and to my home and life on Middle Saranac Lake, but the Club, the first focus of Jay's and my work, will figure less and less in my life. I careen from one "To Do" list to the next: make sure the kids get up and to school; cook meals; make appointments for haircuts, teeth; the stuff of living. I act as consultant and manager for the new owners of the Club, but the days of non-stop work from May 1 to September 30 are over. During the long, lonely day, I sit at my desk, face legal documents and ledgers, insurance policies, tax forms—all the things that used to be Jay's bailiwick. I would rather sit outside in a snow bank waiting for my daughters to come home from school.

For as long as Jay could, he continued his consulting work with the Johns Hopkins Oncology Center to realize his dream of an outpatient residence. He did not live long enough to see the spark he lit turn into a flame. The Oncology Center initiates a "Partnership Program" to enable patients and families to play a more active role in their own care; they present two symposia in Jay's name with notable physicians and respected scholars from across the United States; and in 1986, inspired by Jay's vision, they build the Joanne Rockwell Memorial House, a home-away-from-home for patients traveling to Baltimore for cancer treatment. Jay would not have wanted his name on a building. He only wanted patients to get the care and respect they deserved.

For a while, I try valiantly to carry on our Christmas tree operation. Before Jay died, he and I had decided, once our trees were of marketable size, to mail them directly to customers. Direct mailing trees is a new concept so I take a workshop to learn how to box a newly harvested tree in a six-foot-long, wax-lined box and have it on a customer's doorstep less than a week later. Sounds like a good plan. I do find some buyers, especially loyal past Bartlett Carry Club guests, but the business never really takes off. The problem is my trees aren't full, fluffy, cozy Christmas trees to hang tons of ornaments on. They are mostly tall and skinny, like me.

Not being willing to take full responsibility for my less-than-perfect trees, I blame it on the tree strain, and decide I will now take on the cultivation of The Best Adirondack Christmas Tree Ever. I approach the project scientifically, targeting ten different seedling sources that have succeeded in terrain and climate similar to ours. I buy one hundred from each source. I plan a grid in a field we haven't yet used, plant the 1,000 trees strategically, and then I wait.

It takes me a couple of years after all this work to come to my senses. One day at lunch with my friend, Pooh, I say, "Okay! Once the seedlings are big enough to develop their own cones, I'll determine which strain looks the healthiest, harvest those cones, dry them, collect the seeds, plant them, wait 'til they are two-year seedlings, replant those, and then grow The Best Adirondack Christmas Tree Ever!" At this point in my monologue, I catch the look on Pooh's face, and I stop. It hits me. It will take twenty years for the trees to develop cones, another couple of years to start the seedlings, then another seven-to-ten years to grow a marketable tree.

"Wait a minute!" I say to Pooh. "I will be at least in my seventies before that happens. *And* I will have to use insecticide and herbicide." *And* it is a lonely job. Suddenly, I know what I should have realized with the tall, skinny trees—I am just not a farmer. The whole Christmas tree venture made sense when Jay and I could do it together. Suddenly I don't want to do it anymore.

Even as a wave of relief washes over me, thousands of trees we've planted still stand in the field, and since I no longer have the energy or gumption to continue, what will I do with them? Tom Phillips comes to the rescue. He is a Mason. "Why don't you donate them to the Masons? They can sell them and you can get a write-off for your donation." Brilliant idea.

Tom Phillips, ca. 2015.

Tom Phillips becomes an invaluable part of our lives, not only with his perfect solution to my Christmas tree dilemma. He is the glue that keeps the property together. Much like Elmer Dockum years before, he knows everything about the infrastructure. He maintains property lines, keeps an eye on the far reaches of the thousand acres I still have only an inkling of, plows the road, and harvests firewood for our furnace. He reports coyote sightings, eagle nests, and recent bear visits. With any problem, we turn to him first.

Because I can depend on him, I find the courage to look for work beyond the property. To fight my feelings of isolation, I become a part-time substitute teacher. I like to be involved where my kids are involved. Within a year this morphs into becoming an 8th Grade French teacher. I also test out a new career in storytelling and take jobs in schools scattered around the Adirondacks. Mostly I do the work alone. I leave home at 6:30 a.m., travel on back roads to tell folk and traditional tales on a "cafetorium" school stage to three hundred kids, ages six to ten.

Fran telling stories in Hamburg, NY, 1988.

I have a brief, lively connection with them, but mostly, I am by myself. I begin to seek out tales of the Adirondack wilderness and the people who claimed it both before Virgil and Caroline and after: an Iroquois legend of the Great Bear in the night sky, the tale of a Bottomless Pond, stories of a porcupine named Needles, and Buster, the fastest hunting dog in the North Country.

I revisit the story of Martha Reben overcoming tuberculosis in the Adirondack wilderness. Tales of her love of fishing in the rain, the aroma of campfires, and the clear sunset air tie me more deeply to these woods I, too, love. Her healing comforts me, even though my naïve hope that Jay could also be healed has evaporated like smoke from Martha's campfire. My story about her piques the interest of our local Hospice. I never had the benefit of this group since it was organized in our community a year after Jay died. Once I know of Hospice's compassionate work, I realize how much I missed. I'm asked to tell my Martha story at Hospice annual meetings in New York, Ohio, Massachusetts, and the National Association for Home Care.

My storytelling veers down a new healing path, focused as much on listening as telling. With my dear friend and excellent musician, Peggy Lynn, I co-found Creative Healing Connections, Inc. to offer arts-and-healing retreats for women with cancer and chronic illness, and for women veterans. We use music, story, and dream workshops to create a safe space for them to tell their important stories and to hold the stories of others.

Martha Reben and the healing Adirondack woods constantly inspire me. As women gather in the vibrant oranges and reds of autumn, we form a community as nurturing to me as it is to them. This will continue for more than sixteen years.

My daughters continue to grow, so much in fact that soon I realize I look directly into their eyes, not down at them. As the single mom of two teenagers, I find myself in another foreign landscape with no map, no concept of how to negotiate unexpected curves almost daily; no partner with whom to talk about my bewilderment, hopes, anger, compassion, and fear. A new kind of lonely. I don't have a clue how, but one day (where has the time gone?) we wander on tree-shaded college campuses, and meet with admissions directors. My girls prepare to take off into the world.

Staff of Creative Healing Connections Retreat, September 2008.

Six years pass, sometimes zip by, sometimes slog through the mud. Then one day, a vagabond actor—vagabond because he had been living in his home on wheels for four years as he traveled the country performing two one-man shows about Ben Franklin and Shakespeare—drives into town and into my life. His big, white van says nothing on the outside, doesn't even hint at the cozy interior. He has a kitchen complete with sink and microwave and artwork taped on the cupboards. My favorite is a bookshelf stocked with a dictionary, thesaurus, *Travels with Charley*, *Blue Highways*, and, of course, a multitude of volumes on Franklin and Shakespeare.

Burdette Parks has come to Saranac Lake to direct a play at Pendragon Theatre. I had returned to acting during the past few years. This summer, I had decided to take off. Is it the Universe that intervenes? In the middle of Burdette's rehearsals, one cast member has to bow out. The artistic director asks me to pinch hit. Intensive rehearsals with Burdette. Late-night discussions about character and plot. Our eyes meet in an inquisitive way that

Burdette's van.

evolves to intense interest. What a way to get to know someone. Clearly, we share more than a mutual love of theater.

One day that summer when I'm not home, he picks armfuls of yellow wild flowers and fills every vase and container he can find in my house, including the garden water buckets. When I return, a sunny explosion of black-eyed-Susans, goldenrod, sun flowers, and lemon lilies fills every room. What is the likelihood of my finding someone as enamored of the Adirondacks as I am? A fellow thespian, lover of the outdoors, willing to live eleven miles from anywhere, someone who respects my history on this land, including my life with Jay and our girls. Burdette has no kids, but understands how deeply I love mine. He is curious, intelligent, full of humor and joy in life, and comfortable with himself. And he can hold space for me and my negotiations with grief.

A year later, on a misty August 10, 1991, we exchange vows sur-rounded by friends and family in a hundred-year-old, log-cabin church

Burdette and Fran, 1992, photography by Alice Vera.

near the shore of Upper Saranac Lake. Sun comes out during the service. Stained-glass blues, reds, and yellows splash onto the polished church floor. As the bell chimes and we stride down the aisle hand-in-hand, a bat flies over our heads and out the arched door. We consider it a good omen.

At this moment, I stop perching, ever-ready to fly, on the delicate tree branch and settle back into this place I have always loved. No longer teetering, no longer lonely, no longer seeking what I need around some next corner. I realize I have survived the deluge of silence, inventing answers for things I knew nothing about; survived dealing with life on my own with no one to lean on or ask to change a lightbulb or share cooking a meal. It took me years after Jay died to learn to say "I" rather than "we." Now I relearn "we." Burdette understands I have trouble being away for more than a few weeks. Who will feed the birds in winter? Who will shovel the path and keep the house warm? In spring, I want to plant the garden; in summer, I have to weed it and mow the lawn. And how can I miss the glorious fall colors? We do take marvelous trips to the far corners of the globe, but at any time of year, for the most part I prefer to be here, walking the road I've walked for almost five decades, watching wind play on water, paying taxes, embracing the solitude.

One day a truck pulls into our driveway. Jack Rifenburg of Rifenburg Construction has taken on the job of another major rebuilding of Route 3 between Saranac Lake and Tupper Lake—"our" road, the one we use almost daily.

"We need a place to stage our rock-blasting operation for the boulders on that road. You have a clear field that would work. Can we make a deal?"

The field he refers to is none other than the once-upon-a-time golf course/Christmas tree farm. Now that Mr. Merritt no longer wields a golf club and the trees have gone to the Masons, the field is clear. We make the deal, and Jack goes to work. Months later, he has cleaned up the field and moved on, and we have a brand new road and unexpected money in the bank. I know the perfect use for it. We have been worried about our ancient three-story barn, the one here when Jay and I arrived, here since the 1890s, the only building we kept that Jay never fully renovated. Now, one hundred years later in the 1990s, we discover one side is about two feet lower than the other, and it needs a new roof. What better way to spend our serendipitous money?

The money earned by our field pays for the renovation of one of our most treasured buildings. Jay had at one point reconfigured the inside of the barn for our horses and goats, but now, for the first time since we arrived, our wonderful old barn has a new roof and will stand for a long time to come. Once again the land has helped us preserve this place and restore one more venerable building.

I still feel overwhelmed by the responsibility of 1,000 acres of land. This Jay foresaw clearly. During our talks his last summer about what to do if I wanted to sell some of the property, he said "Get in touch with the Nature Conservancy. This is valuable land." Even though I have now explored it numerous times, often with our forester, Chris, and learned new facts and new respect with each foray, I know I am ready to let a large part of it go. In the late 1990s, I talk with the Conservancy and with New York State. After several years of difficult, prolonged negotiations, New York State purchases over seven hundred acres of my land and designates it "Forever Wild," protected from development forever under a law enacted by the 1894 Constitutional Convention.

My land? Only years later, after I begin research for this book, do I fully understand that this land does not belong to me. It is an exquisite gem, and I am merely its caretaker. I honor those who came before me: Native Americans who never had an official deed, Virgil Bartlett, Pauline Shaw, A. B. Jenkins, Harriet, Jay, and more. And now it will be here for another adventurous traveler to paddle up, get out, smell the balsam, sit on a warm rock, and watch the loons. It will always be here, and only Nature will change its look, its way of being. On the day in 2001 when I sign the contract with New York State, part of my restless soul, quivering with unease since Jay's death, comes to rest. I have a distinct sense that behind me, Jay and his ancestors stand tall, nodding approval.

The dam persists, another piece of unfinished business; the dam that plagued us from Day One, the dam New York State refused to take over, the dam controlling the water level and thus property values on the thirty-seven-mile shoreline of Upper Saranac Lake. It presents an undeniable liability. I can't take on the expense of repair by myself, and I have never wanted the responsibility.

Fortunately, the Upper Saranac Lake Foundation realizes the obvious—the over 400 shorefront properties on the lake depend on the health of this

Bartlett dam being repaired, 1993; Merritt in background.

dam. They agree to take ownership and, most importantly, to raise funds to keep it in good condition. Another piece of my soul takes a deep breath.

IV

It seems only a flash of time before both Gwyn and Shana graduate from college, another flash, and they marry, another, and I have two glorious grandchildren. They come to visit, to ramble, explore, discover. Each time I follow them into the woods to build a fort or sled down a snowy hill or roast marshmallows on the point where once stood their great-great-great-grandfather's cabin, each time, it seems more roots thrust down, more reason to stay.

One mid-December afternoon, I walk in the woods with Evan, six years old.

"Nonnie!" he says suddenly. "Want me to teach you how to sword fight?"

"Yes!"

Evan chooses the perfect sword for me, a fairly thin stick about three feet long. He then chooses a thicker, four-foot stick for himself.

"Stand like this," he says, as he strikes the perfect sword fighter's pose. I do the best I can. He nods.

"Okay, now we cross swords."

We do.

"And say 'en garde!' and then 'fight!'"

After that, we continue our walk as he explains more about the intricacies of sword play. It has just rained, and the woods emanate an intensity of earth colors. Columns of black tree trunks line both sides of our path. Tiny green princess pines (*Lycopodium obscurum* or clubmoss, a distant relative of ferns) carpet the ground.

"Okay, here's how you do a thrust and parry. I'll do it first. You watch and then you can try." We stop for Lesson #2 in the midst of the loamy brown of the woods.

"Look, Evan. There's two ways we could go—over the hill to see where Daddy Jay's great-grandfather is buried or straight down to the river. Which way?" Evan doesn't hesitate. He takes off toward the grave, then waits for a quick *en garde* and a thrust and parry or two. A shaft of gold sunlight splinters the ever-greened darkness.

At the bottom of the hill stands the huge boulder grave of A. B. Jenkins. I stop and watch Evan. For the first time on our walk, he stands still, his whole attention on the brass plaque in front of him. He has just started to read and studies the words: "About this boulder . . . Sweet Mother Earth . . . Let your green mantle cover him . . . give him rest."

Perhaps the challenge of sounding out words stops him. Or perhaps some palpable energy rivets him, some sense of his mustached, bespectacled ancestor reaching across time, through the solid, granite stillness of the woods. Jay's family may have settled here originally, but our family, my family, here in the form of this little boy, now makes visceral connection with the place.

Then, one day, a few months later, I open the dark-red, leather-bound book with gold embossed letters: *Saranac Club Minutes*. As I plow through Robert Douglass's fairly indecipherable handwriting from the late 1800s, I just want to know about the history. I have no idea what adventures lie

Evan at A. B. Jenkins's grave, 2010.

ahead as I stumble on entries about the difficulties of traveling here and the innumerable problems with the dam. *Oh!* I think. *I know about trouble traveling here. I definitely know about the challenges of that dam.* I read about Robert and his compatriots persevering despite major fires and lack of funds; about Caroline losing her husband exactly one hundred years before I lost mine; about Pauline, a woman in the late 1800s also committed to this same land I gave myself to with Jay; all strands of connection across decades, even centuries. These strands say we aren't so different—you in the 1800s, we in the early twenty-first century. All of us have committed ourselves to making this place succeed; we have loved it and found solace in it as our home.

My sense of those from the past is almost palpable. It goes beyond my research about the people and buildings that were here, beyond plain facts. I sense movement just beyond what I can see, smell, or touch, a sense of aliveness, of people devoted to being here. Beyond my ken, they waft unseen, a fine line between us, fine as spider's silk, but opaque as ice on the lake and impenetrable. I can neither see nor hear them, but am completely aware.

I feel it right here in my office. A. B. Jenkins practically jumps out of his sepia picture on the wall. I wish he would! And the faded picture of Bartlett's in the 1800s feels as real to me as the color picture of Hemlock Lodge's living room in the 1980s. Each building and person exists for me, not just as a one-dimensional experience from photos and history books, but in the same 3-D way that my knees have experienced every hardwood floor in all ten of our lodges. My challenge is to recapture this for others. I want to provide an evocative glimpse into the past—to part the curtains for just a moment, to *feel* what it was like back then, to understand what a specific group of humans did here. Virgil sneezed. I am sure of it. He probably had a big old handkerchief he pulled out of his pants pocket and blew his nose into. Robert Douglass had to go to the bathroom like anyone else. That's why they were concerned about drainage into the swamp behind the Sportsmen's Home.

As I gain knowledge and respect for those who came before and how they interacted with the land, how they mustered the determination to stay, I come to understand my role in the story, that I am one of them, and that this story is much bigger than just mine. They give my experience solidity, validity, and me a new sense of belonging.

As I begin to write, it gradually grows on me how important these people and their experiences are to me and my being here now. My understanding of them starts slowly, builds gradually, and gives me a much greater historical context, connecting me to all of them and ever more strongly to this place. How could I ever feel alone here again?

One day, several years into my research, I take members of Adirondack Architectural Heritage on a tour of the Bartlett Carry Club. I feel a bit like a walking text book. No, not textbook, more like a library, alive with thousands of references. As I tell the stories, people of the past come back to life: the guides and guests from the Bartlett days and from the Saranac Club, Elsie Wolff waiting on tables at the Treadway Inn in the 1930s, John Sennott taking care of the boats in the 1940s, and children from every time, running around, happy to be let loose again. In my mind, every past guest Jay and I welcomed also shows up on this day. And every workman or woman who picked up a hammer, scaled a roof, washed a window, pointed a chimney, waxed a floor—they are all here—along with those who, in the face of a gigantic fire or a world war or not enough money, got back up, dusted off, rolled up sleeves, and made it happen all over again. And again and again.

I draw the attention of my tour group to the sound of the rapids with us the whole morning, no matter where we are. The rushing sound permeates this place and always has. It binds those who came even before Virgil all the way to those here now 160 years later as I tell the story. I know this story. It oozes out of my pores. It begs to be given light and air and a place to breathe. It wants to swirl in the ears of those who come, to work its magical way through their minds and hearts and bodies until they too don't know where the facts end and the truth starts, and they don't care because it's such a great story.

One early morning, walking the new-fallen snowy road with my dog, Merlin, that palpable sense I have of those who have been here before happens in a new way. We follow mysterious fresh tracks in the snow along our whole half-mile trip—almost dainty canine tracks, about half the size of Merlin's. I wonder—is this four foxes or is it one fox who crisscrossed back and forth? I sense the presence of this invisible, pointy-nosed, black-tailed fox, alert, ready for anything, and happy to accompany us. She gives me a sense of connection with the wildness surrounding me, but from which I am often insulated as I curl up in my cozy home with an evening fire blazing, and walls and windows to protect me from the howling wind. After this walk, I will not forget that outside in the dark, maybe just outside, a small fox hunkers down against the cold.

V

I have one last story to tell. Late summer, 1984. Jay sat on our porch, looking out over Middle Saranac Lake. A hermit thrush warbled in the distance, perhaps the same one as last year. I watched a breeze playing on his thinning hair and could almost feel the late-afternoon sun warming his back. He had struggled with cancer for over six years. He squinted his eyes.

"This is the same view it was forty years ago."

View of Middle Saranac Lake.

I could believe it. The wild evergreens and range of Adirondack Mountains on the other side of the blue lake seemed like they would always be there, never change. He bent over the compass resting on the wide railing, turned it this way and that.

"Ha! Magnetic north. Good. Now I have to factor in the local declination value." He consulted a chart, and then marked with a pencil the direction of true north. That's what he was after.

"Can you hand me the dragonfly?" I picked up the tarnished four-inch-long brass door knocker, the one we salvaged from the door of Jay's great-grandfather's cabin before tearing it down twelve years earlier. Jay positioned and repositioned it until it was facing true north, about to take off and fly into forever. He secured it strongly with two screws and sat back. He had completed his job.

Almost thirty years later, I want to give our grandchildren a sense of the vivid history of this place. I hope at least a tiny bit of what I feel can be instilled in them. They represent the sixth generation of one family to dip paddles in these waters, listen to the call of a loon, scramble onto a rock and proclaim themselves rulers of that towering height. I hope that they will fall in love with a tiny island or a tree by the lake, that the musty smell of loamy earth will fill their nostrils, and that leaves will tangle in their hair before they come back to tell of their adventures in the woods.

What better way to dive into the story of this place than through the dragonfly? But where is it? I'm sure I saved it when we replaced the railing. When was that? Four years ago! It's lost. I scramble around the house looking everywhere. That night, as my head hits the pillow, I pop up, cross the room, and there on the bookshelf with all my other "important" stuff, I see the dragonfly. I have been walking by it for four years.

I buy a simple compass. When Evan, age six, and Hannah, age two, come to visit, I bring them out on the porch and show them the dragonfly. "When your grandfather, Daddy Jay, and I first came here, we found this on the door of the cabin your great-great-great-grandfather slept in. Then, many years later, Daddy Jay decided he wanted to put it on this railing."

Evan says "But Nonnie, it's not on the railing. You're holding it." He is very practical.

"Yes, you're right." I say. "That's why we're here. We're going to put it back just like it was. He wanted it facing true north."

"What's true north mean?"

"Well, it's the direction to the North Pole, but I think for Daddy Jay, it meant more than that. He knew whenever he was lost, if he could find true north, he could figure out where he was and he could find his way home. He wanted this dragonfly pointing true north in case we get lost or confused. So we'll always know where home is. For Daddy Jay, the dragonfly marked true home, and so it does for me too."

I show them the compass. "We can use this to figure out how to put it." They stand, transfixed. "First let's find the direction of Whiteface Mountain right out there." They lean over me, much as I had leaned over Jay when he first positioned the dragonfly. Little fingers move the compass this way and that. The red needle settles. "Look at that!" I say. "That E means east, so that's the direction of Whiteface Mountain. Okay, and the N is magnetic north. Now we'll figure true north, just like Daddy Jay did."

Once we finish the calculations, we position the dragonfly to take off into the great beyond. I think of all the things I want to say to them about their Daddy Jay, about their Yardley and Jenkins family ancestors who first came here. I want to tell them about Virgil and Caroline, about this land, I want them to make their own clothespins. But within a minute, Evan has run off to climb a tree down by his favorite rock, and Hannah runs after him. That's okay. The dragonfly won't get lost again. It sits on the railing, as yet unfastened, but not taking off. The next time I can get their attention, we will recheck the orientation. I may tell them another story, maybe one about their great-great-great-grandfather, how he first built a cabin in 1903 on the same point where we now have campfires and toast marshmallows. I will have the screws ready. This time we will fasten the dragonfly to the railing and check to be sure it is securely in place.

The dragonfly, pointing true north, will always tell us we are home.

The End

Acknowledgments

I am indebted to so many old and new friends for their memories, information, encouragement, and love of this place in the Adirondacks.

A huge thank you to those who facilitated my research: from the Adirondack Museum—Jerry Pepper, past Librarian; Hallie Bond, past Curator; and Angie Snye; Harold Best for a photo of Bartlett's saw mill; Kathleen Canzano, secretary St. Luke's Church, Saranac Lake for information on its history; Mike Carr, Nature Conservancy past director for information about Pauline Shaw and Follensby Pond; Rivka Cilley for conversations about Round Lake history; Ted Comstock for Adirondack history information and research leads; Dick and Cindy Coursen for a 1909 map of Upper Saranac Lake; the late Ron Delair for his records of possible builders/designers of Bartlett Carry Club buildings; the Douglass Family, particularly Jamie, Hoby, and Bruce Douglass; Jack Drury for how to explain an arch for sugaring; the late Ray Fadden and his son, John Kahionhes Fadden of the Six Nations Indian Museum; Joe Hackett for leading me to Melissa Otis and Native American information; Sharron Hewston—Town Historian, Au Sable Forks for leading me to Virgil Bartlett's grave; Leslie Hoffman for information about Will Rogers history; Nancy Howard for old postcards; Jethro M. Hurt, III, archivist, Bethesda-by-the-Sea, Palm Beach, Florida for information on Robert D. Douglass; Ray and Dickie Jenkins, the late Arthur and Airlie Lennon, and the James Wood family for the 1864 James Wood journal; Chris Leifeit for information about Princess Pines and musings about how the woods used to be; Susan Lenoe for connection with Lillian Margolis and information about Pauline Shaw; Guy Middleton, Upper Saranac Lake Manager, for statistics about Upper Saranac Lake; Debi

Murray, Curator, Historical Society of Palm Beach County for Robert D. Douglass information; Minney Robb for letter from Harrington Mills of the Upper Saranac Lake Association; Skip (Leslie) Smith, great-great grandson of Tom and Kate (Calista) Healy; Ruth and Craig Smith for loan of Birch Island History and Lore book; Sally Svenson for information on architecture and obscure writings about Bartlett's; Phil Terrie for support and in-depth analysis of the formation of the Adirondack Park; Betsy Tisdale for Martha Reben information; Bryon Varin, Franklin County Treasurer, and everyone in the office including Gail and Darlene for help with microfiche records of property owners going back to 1873; Alice Wand for permission to use her photograph; Marc Wanner for great historical photos, his management of Historic Saranac Lake Wiki, and general good-natured interest in my project; and Historic Saranac Lake Wiki for countless visits to corroborate, investigate, and discover.

Also thanks to Bonnie Brewer, Angie Fontana, John Gagnon and Judi McIntosh at Compass Printing for generous and prompt help, Mark Coleman for transcription advice, and transcribers Cheryl Ploof and Melanie Strack.

Beyond research and technical help, this book found its voice through the help of many with personal memories of the Bartlett Carry Club including Louise Bennett, Anne Bodnar, Vicki Boies, the Fallon family, Lisa Johnson, Alex Holtzman, Annie and Phil Petronis, the late Barbara Starfield, Laurie Thomashow, Turhan Tirana, and Sally Ward; and memories of Bankers Trust/Pyramid Camp days—Vicki Dawson, Susan Gossen, three sisters of the G. Ronald Ince family, Nancy Keet, Sue Lione, Bruce McClanahan; and evocative memories of Middle Saranac Lake—John Claesgens, Laurie Gorgas, Ralph and Mary Hensel, Bill Schultz and his parents, Barbara and the late Bill Schultz; and Pam Paul with her memories of childhood summers at the Yardley family camp. Thanks also go to Doug Bombard for memories of delivering mail by boat on Upper Saranac Lake; the late Charlotte Bombard DeSormo for personal memories of Martha Reben; Duncan Cameron for connecting me with Ev Shorey; the late Frank Casier for his memories over ninety years; Tony Holzman for inspiration and historical details gleaned from his books, for making Bartlett Carry Club archives available, and for his memories of the Bartlett Carry Club; Dick Kibben for his story about a 1950s trip through Bartlett Carry with Dave Merkel; Natalie Leduc for her vivid memories of great-uncle Fred Rice and

Martha Reben and for stories about her mom, the late Charlotte Bombard DeSormo; Clarence Peets for firsthand knowledge of the Bartlett Carry Club and his many years as caretaker; the late Clarence Petty for stories spanning over 100 years in the Adirondacks and his son, Ed Petty, for his extensive historical knowledge; the late John Sennott ("Tiny" of Bartlett Carry) for unforgettable phone calls and his stories of working at Bartlett Carry in the 1940s; the late Ev Shorey for detailed personal memories of a time just beyond my reach; Curt Stiles for his memories growing up in the Adirondack summers; and Dave Wolff for facilitating an enlightening conversation with his parents.

I could not have finished this book without invaluable support from my friends: Joel Baehr for moral support; current members of the Bartlett Carry Club; Karen Baker, one of the wisest people I know; Wanda Burch for inspiration and good marketing ideas; Jim and Chris Crane; Karen Davidson, fellow writer and explorer; Pat Davidson and Kathy Lobo for Bartlett Carry Club archives and personal memories, general support and great food; the late Janet Decker—always interested, always available; Henry Darlington, Jr. for copious information about his grandfather, Robert Dun Douglass; the late Maitland DeSormo for photos and information about Martha Reben; Steven Englehart for support through many years of Bartlett Carry Club tours and his love of Dr. Romeyn; Karen Glass for writing support; Carl Hathaway for fifty years of friendship and memories; Jane Maxwell for truly honoring the tradition and history of Bartlett Carry; Anita Montgomery; Chris Shaw; George Strawbridge III because he asked about my book; Nathalie Thill, director of Adirondack Center for Writing for general encouragement; Caper Tissot, fellow writer; Dot Valhouli; Caroline Welsh for loans of books from her and the late Peter Welsh's extensive library, her interest in my work, and her encyclopedic knowledge of all things Adirondack; Mary Watson for information on the Douglass family and the Robert D. Douglass house on Upper Saranac Lake and hours shared as we pieced together the history of the Douglass family; and the late Phil and the late Elsie Wolff for interviews and memories.

It took an enormous leap of faith to entrust my manuscript to my first readers. They handled it like the young infant it was and told me what I needed to hear: everything they loved and what they thought needed fixing. So much gratitude to Mary Hotaling, my very first reader, who also fed me delicious, obscure facts throughout this project; Lenny Golay and Ray Sherman for paying attention to every word, to the rhythm of the story, and making sure it all worked, for general good wisdom about books, publishing advice, and unfailing support; Ellen Rocco for incisive editorial comments; Karen Kittenger Rumsey for support, thoughtful comments, and being my friend for almost 70 years; Mary Sanders Shartle, fellow writer, supporter, encourager, and introduction to SUNY Press; and Jay O'Callahan for flights of imagination.

This book would not have been published without the initial enthusiasm and support of Amanda Lanne-Camilli, Acquisitions Editor and her assistant, Chelsea Miller; as well as the expert help of Diane Ganeles, Senior Production Editor; and Anne Valentine, Executive Promotions Manager. To them I owe my utmost respect and gratitude.

Finally, I want to thank Gail Brill for her unique artistry in creating three exquisite maps to transport the reader to the world of Bartlett Carry; Lynne Burns and Marni Gillard for wise coaching and believing in this project; Doug Lipman for listening the best out of me, for wisdom and marketing support; Lani Peterson for nudging me out of the nest of research and into the wide spaces of writing, and for her excellent listening and feedback throughout the creation of this book; Ed Kanze for his passion about Bartlett Carry, cheerleading from start to finish, good natured, wise support, and creating a video with Josh Clement featuring the Bartlett Carry Club ("Fifty Beds, Two Lakes and an Otter"—https://www.youtube.com/watch?v=4JDcQr3iTHk); Tom Phillips for his spiritual connection to this place, his insight, and his inspirational support; David Rawle for devoted memories of Jay and their Adirondack escapades; the late Charlie Ritchie for invaluable memories, information, and unfailing interest and encouragement; my dearest friend, the late Pooh Ritchie—without her unconditional support, I may have never left off research and begun writing; and Michelle Tucker, Adirondack Room, Saranac Lake Free Library, always ready and eager to help, no matter how obscure the question.

My most special gratitude goes to Carol Burnes for her insatiable curiosity and open-ended questions leading me to new images, greater understandings, and deeper writing; Gwyn Conway and Shana Carlson, essential always to my life; and Burdette Parks, my partner, my constant support, gracious, generous, and insightful from beginning to end.

Notes

Chapter 1

1. Kahlil Gibran, "The Prophet: On Love" (London, 1926).

2. Ibid., "On Marriage."

3. "History of Jay, New York," *The History of Essex County*, ed. H. P. Smith (Syracuse, NY: D. Mason & Co., 1885). Accessed July 7, 2017, http://history.rays-place.com/ny/jay-ny.htm

4. Henry W. Raymond, *The Story of Saranac: A Chapter in Adirondack History* (New York: The Grafton Press, 1909), 52.

5. Frank Leslie, *New Family Magazine*, November 13–20, 1858, 338.

6. S. R. Stoddard, *The Adirondacks: Illustrated.* (Albany, NY: Weed, Parsons & Co., Printers, 1874), 86.

7. James Wood, *Adirondacks—A Personal Journal, 1865*, unpublished, 27. Personal archive.

8. Leslie, *New Family Magazine*, 338.

9. Alfred L. Donaldson, *Scrapbook 8*, Adirondack Research Room, Saranac Lake Free Library, Saranac Lake, NY, 1.

10. Alfred L. Donaldson, *A History of the Adirondacks Vol. I.* (New York: Century Co., 1921). Reprint. (Harrison, NY: Harbor Hill Books, 1977), 307.

11. Hallie E. Bond, *Boats and Boatbuilding in the Adirondacks* (Syracuse, NY: The Adirondack Museum/Syracuse Press, 1995), 79/80.

12. Henry Van Dyke, *Little Rivers, A Book of Essays in Profitable Idleness*; (New York: Charles Scribner's Sons, 1895), 63.

13. Estella E. Martin, *A Few Jottings about Virgil Bartlett*, 1915. From Donaldson Collection of Letters Adirondack Room, Saranac Lake Free Library.

14. Stoddard, *The Adirondacks: Illustrated*, 1874, 86.

15. Martin, *A Few Jottings*.

16. Leslie, *New Family Magazine*, 338.

17. Martin, *A Few Jottings*.

18. Donaldson, *A History of the Adirondacks Vol. I*, 312.

19. Martin, *A Few Jottings*.

Chapter 2

1. Van Dyke, *Little Rivers*, 63, 64.
2. *Plattsburgh N.Y. Republican*, February 2, 1889, as quoted in Bryant F. Tolles, Jr., *Resort Hotels of the Adirondacks* (Lebanon, NH: University Press of New England, 2003), 108.
3. John J. Duquette, "'Lake of the Clustered Star' was home to hotel with enigmatic name—Ampersand," *Adirondack Daily Enterprise*, June 3, 1989.
4. Robert Dun Douglass, *Minutes of the Saranac Club 1889–1913, Vol. I*, unpublished journal, 17. Personal archive.
5. Seneca Ray Stoddard, *The Adirondacks: Illustrated; 20th Edition* (Glens Falls, NY: published by the author, 1890), 101.
6. Douglass, *Minutes of the Saranac Club, Vol. I*, 38.
7. Ibid., 39.
8. Franklin County Office, Malone, New York, Book 84, 554.
9. Donaldson, *A History of the Adirondacks Vol. I*, 336.
10. State of New York, *Annual Report of the Forest Commission for the Year 1893* (Albany, NY: James B. Lyon, Printers, 1894), 185–87.
11. Including to:

- construct a suitable water closet building and place therein:
    eight porcelain Hopper water closets and two urinals for the Club and guests
    four porcelain and cast iron Hopper closets for the help and guides
- install
    a 450-gallon tank, and a six-inch cast-iron sewer pipe with connection therefrom to closets, laundry and kitchen
    a slop sink in kitchen, laundry and closet
    a grease trap for kitchen; a sink for dish washing in kitchen—Hot and Cold water faucets and connections, suitable traps
    Two porcelain basins and marble slab for office
    4 in. drain pipe therefrom to river and pipes for suitable water supply
    a 9 ft. French Range with two grates and 3 ovens, water back stack pipes, faucets, shelves for warming dishes
    a 63-gal. galvanized iron boiler.

12. Douglass, *Minutes of the Saranac Club, Vol. I*, 58.
13. Ibid., 82.
14. Anthony DePalma, *New York Times*, "In Adirondacks, An Old Lion Still Bares His Fangs; Nearing 100, Park Advocate Remains Bane of Developers," March 14, 2005.
15. Burdette Parks, "In Their Own Words; An Interview with Clarence Petty," *Upper Saranac Lake Association Centennial Year Look 1901–2001, Vol. V* (New York: Upper Saranac Lake Association, 2001), 88.
16. Douglass, *Minutes of the Saranac Club, Vol. I*, 97.

17. George Marshall, "Adirondacks to Alaska: A Biographical Sketch of Robert Marshall," *Ad-i-Ron-Dac XV(3)*, 1951, 44.

18. State of New York, *Annual Report*, 185–87.

19. Mary P. Windsor, *Reading the Shape of Nature, Comparative Zoology at the Agassiz Museum* (Chicago and London: University of Chicago Press, 1991), 135.

20. W. H. H. Murray, *New York Times*, 1872, as quoted in Frank Graham, Jr., *The Adirondack Park; A Political History* (New York: Alfred A. Knopf, 1978), 66.

21. Frank Graham, Jr., *The Adirondack Park; A Political History* (New York: Alfred A. Knopf, 1978), 70.

22. Verplanck Colvin, "Ascent of Mount Seward and Its Barometrical Measurement," *New York State Senate Documents*, 1871, No. 68 (republished in the 24th Annual report of the New York State Museum, 178–80), as quoted in Graham, *The Adirondack Park*, 70–71.

23. Philip G. Terrie, *Forever Wild; Environmental Aesthetics and The Adirondack Forest Preserve* (Philadelphia: Temple University Press, 1985), 96–97.

24. Mar. 15, 1893—(from survey of lands by E. M. Merrill Civil Engineer Mar/Apr 1893) Smith M. Weed and others to Pauline A. Shaw—$21,000 including:

1. 267 acres [on Middle Saranac Lake; separate from the Saranac Club 267 acreage]—Included in this deed: "reserving the right to use South Creek so called and the banks thereof for the purpose of floating or driving logs down the same. And the right to boom logs temporarily at the mouth of said South Creek. And also a right of way across said land as near said creek as practicable to draw logs, timber and wood."

2. 464 acres north of the river and west of Middle Saranac Lake—part of this description includes ". . . to a point in said Bay due south from a tall dead pine stub. . . ."

3. Islands on Middle Saranac Lake in SE quadrant of "said township." [Ship Island and a couple of small rocks]

25. Article VII, Section 7, of New York State Constitution, approved November 1894, going into effect January 1, 1895.

26. *Adirondack*, Nov. 27, 1896, as quoted by Howard Riley, *Adirondack Daily Enterprise*, Nov. 27, 2010.

27. Van Dyke, *Little Rivers*, 64.

28. John Paul Newport, "The Lost Courses of the Adirondacks," *Wall Street Journal*, 2008.

29. Peter J. Martin, *Adirondack Golf Courses . . . Past and Present* (Lake Placid, NY: Adirondack Golf, 1987), 11/12.

30. Donaldson, *A History of the Adks Vol. 1*, 316.

31. Mary Hotaling, "W. L. Coulter, Adirondack Architect" (Thesis, University of Vermont, October 1995), 106.

32. Mary B. Hotaling, *A Rare Romance in Medicine; The Life and Legacy of Edward Livingston Trudeau* (Saranac Lake, NY: Historic Saranac Lake, 2016), 29, 30.

33. Ibid., 80.

34. Ibid., 80.

35. Jean S. Mason, "Two Women Chronicle the White Plague: A 'Herstory' of America's Magic Mountain," *The Journal of American Culture*, June, 2014, 37:2, 149–61.

Chapter 3

1. W. H. H. Murray, *The Adirondack Tales, Vol 1* (Springfield, MA: Springfield Printing and Binding Company, 1897). Inscribed to Margaret Yardley by Murray, December 25, 1899. Personal archive.

2. William H. H. Murray, *Adventures in the Wilderness or Camp-Life in the Adirondacks* (Boston, MA: De Wolfe, Fiske & Co., 1869), 10.

3. Ibid., 11, 12.

4. *New York Times*, "Camp Life at Saranac Inn," Saranac Inn, July 25, 1903.

5. Douglass, *Minutes of the Saranac Club, Vol. I*, 124.

6. Ibid., 138.

7. Ibid., 169.

8. Ibid., 214.

9. *Tupper Lake Herald*, no specific date. Personal archive.

10. Robert Dun Douglass, *Minutes of the Saranac Club 1889–1913, Vol. II*, unpublished journal, 226. Personal archive.

Chapter 4

1. Malone, NY, Franklin County, Liber 148. 83. Sept. 24, 1913. Corey sold 267 acres to BC Realty Co. (deed mentions "the State Dam, called Norton's Dam"). Personal archive. Also contains deed for the dam from Henry B. Corey and M. A. Corey to Bartlett Carry Realty Co., Liber 148, 83.

2. Secretary Harrington Mills, letter to Upper Saranac Lake membership, July 14, 1923. Personal archive.

3. Bartlett Inn brochure, 1915. Personal archive.

4. Donaldson, *A History of the Adks Vol. 1*, 316.

5. Charles Lathrop, *War Gardens Victorious* (Philadelphia: J. B. Lippincott, 1919), 15.

6. Robert Bogdan, *Exposing the Wilderness: Early-Twentieth-Century Adirondack Postcard Photographers* (Syracuse, NY: Syracuse University Press, 1999), 12.

7. S. R. Stoddard, *Picturesque Trip Through the Adirondacks in an Automobile* (Glens Falls, NY: Published by the author, 1915) as quoted in Jeffrey L. Horrell, *Seneca Ray Stoddard: Transforming the Adirondack Wilderness in Text and Image* (Syracuse NY: Syracuse University Press, 1999), 48.

8. Bogdan, *Exposing the Wilderness*, 13.

9. Clarence Petty, as recorded by author at Bartlett Carry Club, August, 2007. Used with permission of his son, Ed Petty.

10. State of New York Conservation Commission, *Eleventh Annual Report 1921* (Albany, NY: J. B. Lyon Company, Printers, 1922), 1.

11. Peter C. Welsh, *Jacks, Jobbers and Kings—Logging the Adirondacks 1850–1950* (Utica, NY: North Country Books, Inc., 1995), 134 ff.

12. *Chateaugay Record and Franklin County Democrat, July 1, 1921* (Chateaugay, NY: Chateaugay Record Print. and Pub. Co., 1921). 4. Accessed June 28, 2017, http://nyshistoricnewspapers.org/lccn/sn87070301/1921-07-01/ed-1/.

13. State of New York, *Eleventh Annual Report 1921*, 105.

14. Robert Cooney, *A Comprehensive History of the Northern Part of the Province of New Brunswick* (Halifax, 1832), as quoted in Donald MacKay, *The Lumberjacks* (Toronto: McGraw-Hill Ryerson Ltd., 1978), 266.

15. Inspired by description by Donald MacKay, *The Lumberjacks*, 266.

16. State of New York Conservation Commission, *Twelfth Annual Report 1922* (Albany, NY: J. B. Lyon Company, Printers, 1922), 168.

17. Robert Frost, "The Need of Being Versed In Country Things," *Harper's Magazine*, December, 1920.

18. Secretary Harrington Mills, letter to Upper Saranac Lake membership. Personal archive.

19. Bartlett Carry Club brochure, 1924. Personal archive.

20. Ev Shorey, in discussion with the author, March 8, 2011.

21. William Douglass, representing the BCRCo. to "Hon. Schuyler Merritt," Sept. 19, 1925. Personal archive.

22. Helen Tyler, "This 'N' That," *Adirondack Daily Enterprise*, Nov. 7, 1966.

23. Farnham Yardley, *Waubenoo Guestbook*, journal entry, 1923. Personal archive.

Chapter 5

1. "Reid Signals End for Tent Platforms," *Adirondack Daily Enterprise*, Saranac Lake, May 14, 1975.

2. Bill McLaughlin, "Battle Looms Over Controversial Tent Platform Issue," *Adirondack Daily Enterprise*, Saranac Lake, September 10, 1971.

3. F. Scott Fitzgerald, "Echoes of the Jazz Age," *Scribner's Magazine Vol. XC, No. 5*, November, 1931.

4. Daniel Stern, *One Hundred and One Queries* (Chicago: The American Artisan). Personal archive.

5. The Club was referred to as either the Bartlett Carry Club or the Bartlett Inn beginning in 1913 when BCRCo created "Bartlett Inn."

6. R. D. Douglass, letter to Farnham Yardley, September 17, 1934. Used with permission of his grandson, Henry Darlington. Personal archive.

7. Ancestry.com, Rootsweb. Accessed July 7, 2017, http://wc.rootsweb.ancestry.com/cgi-bin/igm.cgi?op=GET&db=treadway&id=I22537.

8. Charles M. Hart, Vice President, L. G. Treadway Service Corporation, *Survey of Bartlett Carry Club, Upper Saranac, New York*, January 17, 1936. Personal archive.

9. Ibid.

10. Ibid.

11. Name changed to protect identity.

12. Elsie Wolff, interviewed by author, August 15, 2009.

13. Phil Wolff, interviewed by author, August 15, 2009.

14. Frank Casier, in discussion with the author, Nov. 29, 2011.

15. Louis J. Simmons, *Mostly Spruce and Hemlock* (Tupper Lake, NY: Vail-Ballou Press, Inc., 1976), 333.

16. Carl Hathaway, in discussion with the author, May 26, 2008.

17. John Sennott, in discussion with the author, various conversations 2005–2010.

18. Treadway Inn post card, 1941. Personal archive.

19. Pooh Ritchie, in discussion with the author, Nov. 2012.

20. Original agreement between BCRCo, Inc. and Mrs. Dorothea P. Doring and Miss Lillian J. Purdy, Feb. 23, 1946. Signed by Farnham Yardley, President and Alvin D Reiff, Secretary of BCRCo. and Doring and Purdy. Personal archive.

Chapter 6

1. John Kifner, "Saranac Lake Thermometers Crying Below," *New York Times, A1*, February 16, 1979.

2. Lisa Johnson, letter to author, January 27, 2010. Personal archive.

3. The Fallon family, letter to author, August, 2012. Personal archive.

4. *Tupper Lake Free Press and Herald* (Tupper Lake, NY: Colonial Press, Thursday, Jan 30, 1947), 3.

5. Farnham Yardley, *Waubenoo Guestbook*, journal entry, 1947. Personal archive.

6. Dennis W. Stevens, pamphlet, "The History of Whiteface Mountain Lodge No. 789, Free and Accepted Masons, Saranac Lake, New York, Sept 1884 to May 1992," 42.

7. William G. Howard, "New York's Forest Practice Act," *Journal of Forestry, Volume 45, Number 6* (New York: Society of American Foresters, June 1, 1947), 405–07.

8. Farnham Yardley, letter to Harry Cummings, Caretaker, May 13, 1948. Personal archive.

9. Bankers Trust Co., "Proposed Vacation Camp," Sept. 30, 1948. Personal archive.

10. Release of Douglass Interests to Harriet Jenkins Yardley, Sept. 24, 1948, original document. Personal archive. Parties named: Bartlett Carry Corporation interests: Farnham Yardley, A. J. Yardley, Alvin D. Reiff, Harriet Jenkins Yardley. Douglass interests: A. Kingman Douglass, Benjamin P. Douglass, Clyde E. Shorey as trustees under will of William A. Douglass of trusts for benefit of Benjamin P. Douglas, Lillian M. Douglass, and Elizabeth D. Shorey.

11. Egon W. Loffel, "The Pyramid," periodical for employees of Bankers Trust Co., November 1948. Personal archive.

12. Frank Hynes, "Pyramid Camp—An Interim Report," *Bankers Trust Newsletter*, March 1949. Personal archive.

13. *Bankers Trust Newsletter*, April 1949. Personal archive.

14. "Fred M, Rice Boat Builder dies at Age 90," *Adirondack Daily Enterprise*, April 14, 1966.

15. Martha Reben, *The Way of the Wilderness* (London: Hammond, Hammond & Company, 1956), 168.

16. Martha Reben, *The Healing Woods* (New York: Thomas Y. Crowell Company, 1952), 249.

17. These women wish to remain anonymous.

18. A.L. Rice, *Bankers Trust Newsletter*, Spring, 1954. Personal archive.

19. Bankers Trust Co., letter to Mr. Clinton Ayres, Ayres Realty, July 28, 1954. Personal archive.

20. Frank Hynes, memorandum to Mr. H. C. Burrows, V.P. Personnel Relations, Oct. 6, 1961. Personal archive.

21. Bill McLaughlin, "The Master's Touch," *Adirondack Daily Enterprise*, July 2, 1964.

22. John Claesgens, in discussion with the author, July 26, 2011.

23. Bill Schultz, in discussion with the author, July 26, 2011.

24. Thomas M. Daniel, "The History of Tuberculosis," *Respiratory Medicine, Vol. 100, Issue 11*, November 2006, 1862–1870, accessed July 7, 2017 at www.sciencedirect.com/science/article/pii/S095461110600401X.

Chapter 7

1. Gibran, "On Marriage."

Illustrations

Maps

Figures

Selected Bibliography

The Adirondack Reader. Edited and with introduction by Paul Jamieson. Glens Falls, NY: The Adirondack Mountain Club, Inc., 1982.

Angus, Christopher. *Reflections from Canoe Country; Paddling the Waters of the Adirondacks and and Canada (New York State Series).* Syracuse, NY: Syracuse University Press, 1997.

Angus, Christopher. *The Extraordinary Adirondack Journey of Clarence Petty.* Syracuse, NY: Syracuse University Press, 2002.

Apps, Jerry. *Old Farm, A History.* Wisconsin: Wisconsin Historical Society Press, 2008.

"A Sense of Place," *To the Best Of Our Knowledge* Radio Show: Program 09-05-24-A. Wisconsin Public Radio, 5/24/09 and 4/04/2010.

Barnett, Lincoln. *The Ancient Adirondacks—The American Wilderness.* Alexandria, VA: Time-Life Books, 1973.

Benson, John P. "My Boyhood Memories." Unpublished typescript: New York, 1983.

Bogdan, Robert. *Exposing the Wilderness: Early-Twentieth-Century Adirondack Postcard Photographers.* Syracuse, NY: Syracuse University Press, 1999.

Bond, Hallie E. *Boats and Boatbuilding in the Adirondacks.* Syracuse, NY: The Adirondack Museum/Syracuse Press, 1995.

Bob Marshall in the Adirondacks; Writings of a Pioneering Peak-Bagger, Pond-Hopper and Wilderness Preservationist. Edited by Phil Brown. Saranac Lake: Lost Pond Press, 2006.

Brumley, Charles. *Guides of the Adirondacks; a History.* Utica, NY: North Country Books, Inc., 1994.

Chapin, Mott. "Martha Reben—Weller Pond, 1933; as recalled in 1969." Unpublished. Personal archive.

Chateaugay Record and Franklin County Democrat. Chateaugay, NY: Chateaugay Record Print. and Pub. Co., July 1, 1921. Accessed June 28, 2017 at http://nyshistoricnewspapers.org/lccn/sn87070301/1921-07-01/ed-1/.

Daniel, Thomas M. *Wade Hampton Frost, Pioneer Epidemiologist, 1880–1938; Up To The Mountain.* Rochester, NY: University of Rochester Press, 2004.

Daniel, Thomas M. *Captain of Death: The Story of Tuberculosis*. Rochester Studies in Medical History, BOYE6, 1999.

DePalma, Anthony. "In Adirondacks, An Old Lion Still Bares His Fangs; Nearing 100, Park Advocate Remains Bane of Developers," *New York Times*, March 14, 2005.

DeSormo, Maitland C. *The Heydays of the Adirondacks*. Saranac Lake, NY: Adirondack Yesteryears, Inc., 1974.

DeSormo, Maitland C. *Summers on the Saranacs*. Saranac Lake, NY: Adirondack Yesteryears, Inc., 1980.

"Devotees of Tent Life." *New York Times*. August 12, 1906.

Donaldson, Alfred L. *A History of the Adirondacks Volumes I and II*. New York: Century Co., 1921. Reprint, Harrison, NY: Harbor Hill Books, 1977.

Donaldson, Alfred L. *Scrapbook 8*, Annotated News, July 23, 1914; "When The "Water Lily" Ran Up To Bartlett's Carry, Etc." Adirondack Research Room, Saranac Lake Free Library.

Douglass, Robert Dun. *Minutes of the Saranac Club, Volumes I and II*. 1889–1913. Unpublished journals. Personal archive.

Duquette, John J. "The rise and fall of the Saranac Club at Bartlett's Carry." *Adirondack Daily Enterprise*, August 29, 1992.

Duquette, John J. "Indian Carry at Corey's was Major Junction." *Adirondack Daily Enterprise*, August 8, 1987.

Duquette, John J. "'Lake of the Clustered Star' was home to hotel with enigmatic name—Ampersand." *Adirondack Daily Enterprise*, June 3, 1989.

Duquette, John J. "The Famous Adirondack Guides' Association; Heyday of the guides." *Adirondack Daily Enterprise*, June 18, 1987.

Duquette, John J. "When Great Camps Divide—more people, more pollution." *Adirondack Daily Enterprise*, September 22, 1990.

Duquette, John J. "Invalid Found Strength in Forest's Peace." *Adirondack Daily Enterprise*, February 24, 1990.

Early, Eleanor. *Adirondack Tales*. Boston: Little, Brown and Company, 1939.

Fox, William F. *History of the Lumber Industry in the State of New York*. Washington, DC: Government Printing Office, 1902.

Fox, William F., Supt. State Forests. "Forest Fires in 1889," *Fourth Annual Report of the Commissioner of Fisheries, Game and Forests of the State of NY*. New York and Albany: Wynkoop Hallenbeck Crawford Co., Printers, 1899.

Frost, Robert. "The Need of Being Versed In Country Things." *Harper's Magazine*, December, 1920.

Gast, Richard (Franklin County Cornell Cooperative Extension). "Brook Trout Fishing in the Adirondacks," *Adirondack Daily Enterprise*, April 3, 2013.

Gerster, Arpad Geyza. *Notes Collected in the Adirondacks 1895 & 1896*. Reprint, New York: The Adirondack Museum, 2005.

Gerster, Arpad Geyza. *Notes Collected in the Adirondacks 1897 & 1898*. Reprint, New York: The Adirondack Museum, 2010.

Gibran, Kahlil. "The Prophet." London, 1926.

Graham, Frank, Jr. *The Adirondack Park; A Political History.* New York: Alfred A. Knopf, 1978.

Grun, Bernard, based upon Werner Stein's *Kulturfahrplan. The Timetables of History; The New Third Revised Edition.* New York: Simon & Schuster Inc., 1946/1991.

Hart, Charles M., Vice President, L.G. Treadway Service Corporation. *Survey of Bartlett Carry Club, Upper Saranac, New York.* January 17, 1936. Personal archive.

Headley, Joel T. *The Adirondack, Or Life in the Woods.* New York, 1849.

Higgins, Lisetta Neukam Higgins. "Schuyler Merritt," *The Stamford Historian, Volume I, Number 1.* March 1954.

History of Clinton & Franklin Cos. NY. Plattsburgh, NY, 1880. Reprint, Philadelphia: J.W. Lewis, 1978.

"History of Jay, New York," *The History of Essex County.* Edited by H. P. Smith. Syracuse, NY: D. Mason & Co., 1885.

Hooker, Mildred Phelps Stokes. *Camp Chronicles.* Blue Mountain Lake, NY: Adirondack Museum, 1964.

Hoppin, G.M. "The Adirondac [*sic*] Lakes," *Broadway Magazine.* London: Series 2, Vol. 2, 263–269, March, 1869.

Hotaling, Mary B. *A Rare Romance in Medicine; The Life and Legacy of Edward Livingston Trudeau.* Saranac Lake, NY: Historic Saranac Lake, 2016.

Hotaling, Mary. "Framing a Legacy; How a century-old architectural firm defined the regional style," *Adirondack Life,* March/April, 1997.

Hotaling, Mary. "W. L. Coulter, Adirondack Architect." Thesis, University of Vermont, October 1995.

Hotaling, Mary B. "Bartok's Creative Last Summer in Saranac Lake in 1945," *Adirondack Daily Enterprise.* February 2, 1996.

Howard, William G. "New York's Forest Practice Act," *Journal of Forestry, Volume 45, Number 6.* New York: Society of American Foresters, June 1 1947. Accessed July 8, 2017 at www.ingentaconnect.com/content/saf/jof/1947/00000045/00000006/art00005#expand/-collapse.

Kaiser, Harvey H. *Great Camps of the Adirondacks.* Boston MA: David R. Godine, Publisher, Inc., 1982.

Keller, Jane Eblen. *Adirondack Wilderness; A Story of Man and Nature.* New York: The University of the State of NY, The State Education Department, 1980.

Kifner, John. "Saranac Lake Thermometers Crying Below," *New York Times,* A1. February 16, 1979.

Kudish, Michael. *Railroads of the Adirondacks; A History.* New York: Purple Mountain Press, 1996.

Lathrop, Charles Lathrop. *War Gardens Victorious.* Philadelphia: J. B. Lippincott, 1919.

Leslie, Frank. *New Family Magazine, November 13–20, 1858.* Adirondack Museum Library, Blue Mountain Lake, NY.

Loffell, Egon W. "The Pyramid," periodical for employees of Bankers Trust Co. Personal archive. November 1948.

MacKay, Donald. *The Lumberjacks.* Toronto: McGraw-Hill Ryerson Ltd., 1978.

Marbury, Mary Orvis. "Favorite Flies and Their Histories." Accessed July 8, 2017 at http://wc.rootsweb.ancestry.com/cgi-bin/igm.cgi?op=GET&db=kings-highway &id=I608&style=TABLE.

Marshall, George. "Adirondacks to Alaska: A Biographical Sketch of Robert Marshall," *Ad-i-Ron-Dac* XV(3), 1951.

Martin, Estella E. "A Few Jottings about Virgil Bartlett," *Donaldson Papers,* unpublished typescript. New York: Adirondack Room, Saranac Lake Free Library, 1915.

Martin, J. Peter. *Adirondack Golf Courses . . . Past and Present.* Lake Placid, NY: Adirondack Golf, 1987.

Mason, Jean S. "Two Women Chronicle the White Plague: A 'Herstory' of America's Magic Mountain." *The Journal of American Culture,* June, 2014, 37:2.

MacKay, Donald. *The Lumberjacks.* Toronto: McGraw-Hill Ryerson Ltd., 1978.

McLaughlin, Bill. "The Master's Touch," *Adirondack Daily Enterprise,* July 2, 1964.

McLaughlin, Bill. "Battle Looms Over Controversial Tent Platform Issue," *Adirondack Daily Enterprise,* September 10, 1971.

McMartin, Barbara. *The Privately Owned Adirondacks.* Canada Lake, NY: Lake View Press, 2004.

Merrill, Richard C. *Log Marks on the Hudson.* Utica, NY: Nicholas K. Burns Publishing, 2007.

Murray, Hon. Amelia M. *Letters from the United States, Cuba and Canada.* New York: G.P. Putnam & Company, 1856.

Murray, W. H. H. *The Adirondack Tales, Vol. 1.* Springfield, Mass: Springfield Printing and Binding Company, 1897. Inscribed to Margaret Yardley by Murray, December 25, 1899.

Murray, William H. H. *Adventures in the Wilderness or, Camp-Life in the Adirondacks.* Massachusetts: DeWolfe, Fiske & Co., 1869.

Murray, William H. H. *Adventures in the Wilderness,1869.* Reprint, edited by William K. Verner. Syracuse, NY: Syracuse University Press, The Adirondack Museum, 1970.

Newport, John Paul. "The Lost Courses of the Adirondacks," *Wall Street Journal.* July 26, 2008.

Hartmann, Capt. Paul T., NYS Forest Rangers (ret). *New York State Forest Rangers; Pictorial History; Part 2—1912–1927.* Accessed July 8, 2017 at http://nysforest rangers.com.

"Camp Life at Saranac Inn," special to *New York Times,* Saranac Inn, New York, July 25, 1903.

Norris, James D. *R.G. Dun & Co. 1841–1900—The Development of Credit-Reporting in the Nineteenth Century.* Westport, CT and London, England: Greenwood Press, 1978.

Parks, Burdette. "In Their Own Words; An Interview with Clarence Petty," *Upper Saranac Lake Association Centennial YearLook 1901–2001, Vol. V.* New York: Upper Saranac Lake Association, 2001.

Patterson, Gordon. *The Mosquito Crusades; A History of the American Anti-Mosquito Movement from the Reed Commission to the First Earth Day.* Library of Congress Catalogue. Piscataway, NJ: Rutgers University Press, 2009.

Ray, Richard H. *Saranac 1937–1940—a Memoir*. California: Goodco Press, 1993.

Raymond, Henry W. *The Story of Saranac, A Chapter in Adirondack History*. New York: Grafton Press, 1909.

Reben, Martha. *The Healing Woods*. New York: Thomas Y. Crowell Company, 1952.

Reben, Martha. *The Way of the Wilderness*. London: Hammond, Hammond & Company, 1954.

Reben, Martha. *A Sharing of Joy*. New York: Harcourt, Brace & World, Inc., 1963.

Rich, Louise Dickinson. *We Took To The Woods*. East Peoria, IL: Versa Press Inc., 1942.

Roseberry, Charles R. "Martha Reben; Wilderness Lady," *Adirondack Life Magazine*. New York: Summer, 1975.

Roster of Forest Fire Protective Force. State of New York Conservation Commission Divisions of Lands and Forests. May 10, 1923. Accessed at Saranac Lake Free Library, Saranac Lake, NY.

Sanders, Scott Russell. *Wilderness Plots*. Wooster, OH: The Wooster Book Company, 2007, 1983.

Sanders, Scott Russell. Report, North Country Public Radio, St. Lawrence University, Canton, NY, October 10, 2009.

Schneider, Paul. *The Adirondacks: A History of America's First Wilderness*. New York: Henry Holt and Company, 1997.

Seaver, Frederick J. *Historical Sketches of Franklin County and Its Several Towns*. Malone, NY: Albany: J.B. Lyon Co., Printers, 1918.

Simmons, Louis J. *Mostly Spruce and Hemlock*. Tupper Lake, NY: Vail-Ballou Press, Inc., 1976.

Sleicher, Charles Albert. *The Adirondacks: American Playground*. New York: Exposition Press, Inc., 1960.

Sorden, L.G. & Jacque Vallier. *Lumberjack Lingo, A Dictionary of the Logging Era*. North Word, Inc. Library of Congress Catalog Card No. 86-63259, 1986.

State of New York. *Adirondack Park State Land Master Plan*. Ray Brook, New York: Adirondack Park Agency, 1987.

State of New York. *Annual Report of the Forest Commission for the Year 1893*. Albany: James B. Lyon, 1894.

State of New York Conservation Commission. *Eleventh Annual Report 1921*. Albany: J.B. Lyon Company, Printers, 1922.

State of New York Conservation Commission. *Twelfth Annual Report 1922*. Albany, J.B. Lyon Company, Printers, 1923.

Stevens, Dennis W. *The History of Whiteface Mountain Lodge No. 789, Free and Accepted Masons*. Saranac Lake, NY: Sept 1884 to May 1992.

St. Lawrence County, NY Branch of the American Association of University Women. "Martha Reben; Adirondack Writer." *Woman of Courage*. November 13, 2002.

Stoddard, Seneca Ray. *Old Times in the Adirondacks; A Narrative of a Trip in to the Wilderness in 1873*. Edited by Maitland C. DeSormo. Burlington, VT: George Little Press, Inc., 1971.

Stoddard, S. R. *The Adirondacks: Illustrated*. Albany, NY: Weed, Parsons & Co., 1874.

Stoddard, Seneca Ray. *The Adirondacks: Illustrated* 9th Edition. Glens Falls, NY: published by the author, 1881.

Stoddard, Seneca Ray. *The Adirondacks: Illustrated* 19th Edition. Glens Falls, NY: published by the author, 1889.

Stoddard, Seneca Ray. *The Adirondacks: Illustrated* 20th Edition. Glens Falls, NY: published by the author, 1890.

Stoddard, Seneca Ray. *The Adirondacks: Illustrated 33rd Edition*. Glens Falls, NY: published by the author, 1903.

Street, Alfred B. *Woods and Waters: or The Saranacs and Racquet*. Hurd and Houghton, 1860. Reprint, Harrison, NY: Harbor Hill Books, 1976.

Sturges, Barbara, League Member. "The History of the League of American Bicyclists," *Outing and the Wheelmen, An Illustrated Monthly Magazine of Recreation, Vol. V.* Boston: The Wheelmen Company, October 1884–March, 1885.

"Suicide of Dr. Romeyn." *New York Times*, January 1902.

Surprenant, Neil. *Brandon; Boomtown to Nature Preserve*. Paul Smiths, New York: St. Regis Press, 1982.

Taylor, Robert. *Saranac: America's Magic Mountain*. Boston: Houghton Mifflin Company, 1986.

Terrie, Philip G. *Forever Wild; Environmental Aesthetics and The Adirondack Forest Preserve*. Philadelphia: Temple University Press, 1985.

Terrie, Philip G. *Contested Terrain, A New History of Nature and People in the Adirondacks*. Syracuse: The Adirondack Museum, Syracuse University Press, 1997.

Terrie, Philip G. "Romantic Travelers in the Adirondack Wilderness." Assisted by a grant from the Bowling Green State University Faculty Research Committee. 1983. Accessed July 8, 2017 at https://journals.ku.edu/index.php/amerstud/article/viewFile/2585/2544.

Tisdale, Betsy. "Martha Reben, Adirondack Writer," R291 ms, unpublished typescript, originally given as a talk. New York: Adirondack Room, Saranac Lake Free Library, 2002.

Tolles, Bryant F., Jr. *Resort Hotels of the Adirondacks, The Architecture of a Summer Paradise 1850–1950*. New Hampshire: University Press of New England, 2003.

Treadway, L.G., History of. Accessed July 8, 2017at http://wc.rootsweb.ancestry.com/cgi-bin/igm.cgi?op=GET&db=treadway&id=I22537.

Tyler, Helen. "This 'N' That," *Adirondack Daily Enterprise*, October 27, 1966 and November 7, 1966.

Upper Saranac Lake Association YearLook, Vols. 1–5. Edited by Burdette Parks. Tupper Lake, NY: Upper Saranac Lake Association, 1997–2000.

US Geological Survey Map. *Franklin County—St Regis Quadrangle, 1902–1903*. Final drawing by Frank V. Clark, Brooklyn NY, Nov 30, 1930.

Van Dyke, Henry. *Little Rivers, A Book of Essays in Profitable Idleness*. New York: Charles Scribner's Sons, 1895.

Wallace, Edwin R. *Descriptive Guide to the Adirondacks and Handbook of Travel*. Syracuse, NY: The American News Company, 1875 and Forest Publishing House, 1899.

Wardner, Charles A. *Sunset on Adirondack Trails, A Sequel to Footprints on Adirondack Trails—The Memoirs of James Manchester Wardner 1831–1904.* Jay, NY: Graphics North, 2010.

Warren, John. "Nature's Wrath: The Big Blowdown of 1950," *The Adirondack Almanack—Adirondack Explorer's Online News Journal,* November 15, 2010.

Welsh, Peter C. *Jacks, Jobbers and Kings—Logging the Adirondacks 1850–1950.* Utica NY: North Country Books, Inc., 1995.

Welty, Eudora. *Some Notes on River Country.* 1944. Reprint, Mississippi: University Press of Mississippi, 2003.

White, William Chapman. *Adirondack Country.* New York: William Chapman White, 1954. Reprint, New York: Alfred A. Knopf, 1967.

Windsor, Mary P. *Reading the Shape of Nature, Comparative Zoology at the Agassiz Museum.* Chicago and London: The University of Chicago Press, 1991.

Wood, James. *Adirondacks—A Personal Journal.* Unpublished typescript, 1865.

About the Author

Fran Yardley is a writer, actor, and nationally known storyteller and workshop leader. With her late husband, she renovated and managed the Bartlett Carry Club for sixteen years. In 1999 she cofounded Creative Healing Connections, a nonprofit organization offering retreats for women veterans and women with cancer and chronic illness. Originally from Buffalo, she is rooted into the shores of Middle Saranac Lake, where she lives with her actor/photographer husband, Burdette Parks, and her dog, Merlin. Photo courtesy of Burdette Parks.

Index

References to illustrations appear in italic type.

Abbe, Julia, 185
Adirondack Architectural Heritage, 278
Adirondack Canoe Classic, 251
Adirondack Cottage Sanitarium. *See* Trudeau Sanatorium
Adirondack Daily Enterprise, 248
Adirondack Fish Hatchery, 233
Adirondack forest, threat to, 83–85
Adirondack "Great Camps," 105, 112
"Adirondack" Murray, 83
Adirondack Park, 85, 248, 284
Adirondacks family camp: arrival in 1968, 10–13; dormant time of, 123; after Farnham's death, 250; Jay's plans for moving to, 8–9; and renovation plans, 136–38, *137*; and sleeping cabins (ca. 1960), *12. See also* Bartlett Carry Club, tour of 1968
Adirondacks: Illustrated, The (Stoddard), 32
Adirondack Tales (Murray), 111

Adventures in the Wilderness (Murray), 83–84
advertising opening in 1971–72, 129–131, *130*, *131*
Agassiz, Louis, 82
Alford, Charles, 54, 55, 57–58, 88
Allen, Heidi, 60
Ampersand Hotel, 54
Ampersand Lodge: ready for occupancy (1977), 199; and *Sports Illustrated* renters (1980), 235; unready to rent (1975–76), 161, 190; winterization of, 158, 187; winter occupancy of (1977–78), 214
Ampersand Mountain, 24, 66, 183, 194, 241–*42*, 263
Andrea and David (friends), 98
Armistice declared, 157
Association of Residents of Upper Saranac Lake, 142
Au Sable Forks, 51, 218, 283
AuSable Horse Nail Company, 42
Ayres, Clinton J., 64, 201, 243